Ukweli

Searching for Healing Truth

South Carolina Writers and Poets

Explore American Racism

**Edited by Horace Mungin
and Herb Frazier**

With the Art of H.R. Olfus, Jr.

Published by
Evening Post Books
Charleston, South Carolina
www.EveningPostBooks.com

Editors: Michael J. Nolan/Elizabeth Hollerith
Design: Gill Guerry
Artwork: H.R. Olfus, Jr.

First printing 2022
Printed in the United States of America

ISBN: 978-1-929647-69-9

A note from the artist

As an artist, my main philosophy is to be as true to my feelings in that moment as possible. The conscious and subconscious minds are interlaced, and they work together during my creative process. I add and subtract elements as the piece develops and transforms into the creation it wants to be. After deciding on the media, approach, and size of a piece I visualize, in my mind, the piece completed.

The inspiration for the art that's used for the cover of this book was from thoughts about conflicts and resolutions. Prior to getting a call from writer Horace Mungin, I had just finished a series of works reflective of current social events. This series was primarily visual improvisations, using symbols and shapes as well as colors to create a visual narrative. The image that was selected for this book spoke to the writers and poets whose works are featured here. I'm overjoyed that the Creator made this communal artistic presentation possible. And I give thanks.

H.R. Olfus, Jr.
Artist

Contents

Acknowledgments

Before Horace Mungin joined the ancestors in 2021, we often spoke of the generous and talented writers and poets and the artist who agreed to contribute essays, poems and art to this book. We were awed by how quickly this racially-diverse team embraced the project. They explored the Black experience in America from different perspectives, examining sensitive social topics through objective analysis and poetry and personal stories that aligned with the major themes. This allowed us to pair the collected essays with the poems to give readers a double dose of truth.

I'd like to extend to all the contributors a heartfelt thank you for your time, talent and tireless efforts to produce exceptionally written essays and poems, including compositions that revealed family secrets. We took this journey together during trying times in America when the pandemic separated us and police violence gripped our aching hearts.

Horace and I also were thrilled when Steve Hoffius and Aïda Rogers volunteered to provide an extra set of editing eyes to the manuscript before we turned it over to Evening Post Books. Their collective knowledge of history and literary skills improved what we submitted.

I would also like to extend a sincere thank you to Michael Nolan, executive editor, and Elizabeth Hollerith, managing editor, at Evening Post Books. This book emerged unexpectedly from a five-part lecture-poetry series conceived by Horace and staged at McLeod Plantation on James Island. Michael sat front and center for each event under towering oaks near a row of former slave cabins — a provocative setting for a discussion on race. He understood early on Horace's vision to bring truth to a dialogue with white America to foster racial understanding and healing as a means to push against slavery's stubborn legacy.

Herb Frazier

Horace's family offers this acknowledgment of the people who shaped Horace Lee Mungin, the poet, activist and thinker.

To the ancestors who led me to arms with my collection of words
Margaret Mungin who was my guiding light
My wife Gussie my everything
My sons Vaughn Kevin Malcolm
My siblings Ted Helen Barbara
My Daughter-in-law Adriane
My grandchildren Miles,Taylor, Nazareth, Faatimah, Haru, Natalie, Amunet
Amsterdam Ave. and Black forum family and countless others

Dedication

Before he went to join the ancestors, Horace Mungin dedicated this book to: "That America in which We shall have overcome."

Herb Frazier dedicates this book to Jim Campbell, Jack McCray, L.R. Byrd and Horace Mungin, and the next generation; grandchildren, Lauryn, Nicholas, Kinsley, and Connor Thomas; Nathaniel Hamilton; and Roman Lee Frazier.

Foreword

Looking at Charleston
through African Eyes

Simon Lewis

In Nigerian-born Chris Abani's 2014 novel *The Secret History of Las Vegas*, his South African character Dr. Sunil Singh thinks to himself, "Vegas is really an African city. ... What other imagination would build such a grandiose tomb to itself? And just like in every major city across Africa, from Cairo to his hometown of Johannesburg, the palatial exteriors of the city architecture barely screened the seething poverty, the homelessness, and the despair that spread in townships and shanty towns as far as the eye could see. But just as there, here in Vegas the glamour beguiled and blinded all but those truly intent on seeing, and in this way the tinsel of it mocked the obsessive hope of those who flocked there."[1] By the same token, Charleston may be an African city whose glamour beguiles and blinds the tourists who flock here from all over the country and all over the world. But Charleston is an African city in a much more literal sense, too.

When I first moved to Charleston in 1996, I initially thought of it as an unusually European place; with its human-scale architecture and a historic downtown laid out on streets not much changed since the eighteenth century. I felt much more at home in Charleston than I had in any other place in the

---

[1] Chris Abani, *The Secret History of Las Vegas* (New York: Penguin, 2014), 30.

U.S. When I learned that some of the streets were paved with cobblestones from my former home county of Dorset in the southwest of England, my sense of familiarity was even stronger. However, it wasn't long before I started to realize that my uncanny sense of familiarity may have been due to childhood memories of Cape Town, a city founded just eighteen years before Charleston. Settled by the Dutch in 1652, who proceeded to enslave and kill off the indigenous population before importing enslaved Africans and Indonesians, and then taken over by the British as a consequence of the global upheavals of the Napoleonic wars, Cape Town—it gradually dawned on me—had a great deal in common with Charleston as the mother city that had overflowed its original fortifications. Cape Town, like Charleston, developed a sense of its own relative cosmopolitan-ness in an otherwise culturally-starved colonial backwater.

But while a comparable history of settler colonialism links South Carolina and South Africa, there's an even stronger tie between South Carolina and West Africa. For most of its 350-year existence, Charleston had a Black majority, and the vast majority of contemporary Charleston's Black population can trace their ancestry back to West Africa, particularly Senegambia's Rice Coast. The kinship has always been evident in cultural and linguistic features, from styles of worship and music to the famous Lowcountry coiled basketry traditions. Verbal similarities between South Carolina Gullah and Sierra Leonean Krio (the key pronoun "you" is "hunnuh" in Gullah, "una" in Krio) indicate the tightness of the linguistic connection, while many of the Africanisms in Gullah identified in Lorenzo Dow Turner's study of the language show the cultural connections; "tabby," the distinctive Lowcountry oystershell concrete may derive from the Kikongo word "tabi," while "benne" and "okra"– key ingredients of Lowcountry cuisine—derive from Mende and Igbo, respectively.[2]

Over the last thirty years or so, numerous efforts have been made to reconnect severed kinship ties. In 1989, the College of Charleston's Sierra Leonean/Liberian history professor, the late Alpha Bah, together with Gullah community leader Emory Campbell led a trip to Sierra Leone that was filmed by South Carolina

---

[2] Dubbed the "Father of Gullah Studies," Dr. Lorenzo Dow Turner was a leading African American linguistics professor whose seminal work *Africanisms in the Gullah Dialect* (Chicago: Chicago University Press, 1949) was based on decades' worth of research in the Carolina Lowcountry.

Educational Television network (SCETV) as *Family Across the Sea*. Subsequent films such as SCETV's *The Language You Cry In* and North Charleston, South Carolina, schoolteacher Thomalind Polite's *Priscilla's Homecoming* have similarly highlighted these broken connections. The historical sleuthing underpinning these efforts has been spearheaded by scholars and writers such as Joseph Opala and Edward Ball. Opala's work has drawn particular attention to Bunce Island, the slave enclosure in the Sierra Leone River that would have been the last patch of African soil that most Africans trans-shipped directly to Charleston would have trodden.[3]

At this end of that horrendous trans-Atlantic crossing, every year since 1998 Osei Terry Chandler has coordinated a local special ceremony commemorating the survivors and victims of the Middle Passage at Sullivan's Island, near the site where enslaved Africans were quarantined in so-called "pest-houses" before being sold into the domestic American slave market. Numerous other such ceremonies have been held elsewhere and markers erected. In 2007, the Toni Morrison Society placed its first "Bench by the Road" near the site of the "pest-houses" to remedy Nobel laureate Morrison's complaint that there was no place to visit where one could simply contemplate the history of slavery. In 2009, *DNA Sierra Leonean* actor Isaiah Washington was guest of honor at a ceremony of remembrance at Ashley Ferry Landing, site of an eighteenth-century slave sale, the advertisement for which explains that its "choice cargo" had just arrived from the Windward and Rice Coast on board the ship *Bunce Island*. In 2013 the African Literature Association (ALA) held a ceremony at Brittlebank Park on the Ashley River to commemorate the dead of the Middle Passage that included libations, songs, and readings in Yoruba, Mende, English, French, Portuguese, and Zulu.[4]

---

[3] Edward Ball's National Book Award-winning *Slaves in the Family* traced not only his own ancestry—one of the wealthiest plantation-owning families in colonial South Carolina—but also the lineage of some of the people his family had held as slaves, including Thomalind Martin Polite, the seventh-generation granddaughter of Priscilla, a young girl shipped to Charleston from Bunce Island in 1756. Some of Opala's research on Bunce Island can be seen at http://www.bunceisland3d.org/reconstructed.html (Accessed July 30, 2021). For anyone interested in researching the slave trade in general, the slavevoyages.org website originally created by Professor David Eltis et al. at Emory University is indispensable.

[4] For the interview in which Morrison first referred to the need for at least a "bench

The landscape of these ceremonies, on the banks of Charleston's broad, snaking estuarial rivers, is uncannily similar to the landscape around the sites the slave ships departed from the Senegal, Gambia, and Sierra Leone rivers. And Charleston's built environment still bears a resemblance to colonial West African cities. Alhaji Papa Susso, the ALA's long-time griot, who hails from The Gambia, commented on this similarity as I drove him into town down Rutledge Avenue for the ALA's 2013 conference.

The Beninois filmmaker Idrissou Mora-Kpai was so taken by the city's Africanness that he set out to show it on film. Not at all "beguiled and blinded" by Charleston's glamour but "truly intent on seeing" what underlies it, Mora-Kpai's *America Street* is a film about Charleston with no white faces or directive voiceover in it. Focusing on the quiet dedication of corner store owner and community activist Joe Watson, the film starkly contrasts the nonsense of so-called "reality" shows like *Southern Charm* and the stereotypical representation of "the South" as a space essentially defined by a certain kind of whiteness within which Black people move as secondary characters (*Gone with the Wind*), to provide exotic sentiment and spectacle (*Porgy and Bess*), or as a foil for White activism (*The Water Is Wide*).

Mora-Kpai was making *America Street* in 2015, though, when the gap between the glamour and the underlying poverty of Charleston (that gap Abani sees as characteristically "African") made itself painfully apparent. Even while *Condé Nast Traveler* was promoting Charleston (along with Cape Town) as one of the top tourist destinations in the world, Charleston in 2015 became synonymous with racist violence: the April killing of an unarmed Walter Scott, shot multiple times in the back by a North Charleston policeman, who had stopped him for a faulty taillight, was followed on June 15 by the even more egregious and unfathomable violence of the mass murder of nine members of Emanuel AME Church in Charleston. *America Street*, designed to show the resilience of Charleston's African-American community, became an elegy, not just to a community under pressure from gentrification and social, political, and economic marginalization, but to the spectacular violence of White terrorism rooted in the unaddressed history of racial slavery and its bitter legacy.

In the immediate aftermath of that savage and terrifying assault, it almost looked for a moment as if the Emanuel murders might have a catalyzing effect that would move Charlestonians (and South Carolinians) to face the truth of the city's racial history and move toward reconciliation. Through concerted effort by individuals and organizations (blessings upon them all), the response to murders of the Emanuel Nine was not further violence: rather, the prolonged spacing out of nine funerals, culminating in the extraordinary nearly day-long ceremony for the church's slain pastor, the Reverend Clementa Pinckney, gave the public space to grieve and mourn along with the victims' families and friends. And while the history books will record—and TV documentaries replay over and over again— the sublime moment came when President Barack Obama sang "Amazing Grace." I will remember the beautiful, heartfelt conclusion through a piece my colleague Julia Eichelberger penned a week or so after the killings: "It's starting to seem possible," she wrote, "that we could begin to accord our grief its proper weight. Grief could spur us to make things better, to undertake the much more confusing, much more uncertain work of justice and fairness, of a social infrastructure worthy of the name 'community.'"[5]

The moment, however, passed. In state court, the murder trial of former North Charleston policeman Michael Slager, who killed Walter Scott, resulted in a hung jury. But Dylann Roof, though convicted, became a sort of scapegoat and alibi; Roof's death sentence for the Emanuel murders brought a certain kind of closure by duly punishing an individual for an act of extreme racism, but at the institutional level little happened. There was an important symbolic gesture when South Carolina Governor Nikki Haley presided over the removal of the Confederate battle flag from the grounds of the state capitol in Columbia, but the legislature took no steps toward the kinds of structural reforms necessary to dismantle institutional racism. Governor Haley, and subsequently Governor Henry McMaster, continued to preside over a state

---

[5] The text of President Obama's speech is available in full at https://obamawhite-house.archives.gov/the-press-office/2015/06/26/remarks-president-eulogy-honorable-reverend-clementa-pinckney. For Eichelberger's comments, see the blog-post at https://glebestreethacks.org/2015/06/24/in-the-moment-grief-and-change/.

with massive racial disparities in economic opportunity, education, health care, housing, and so on, and both stubbornly refused—with pride in their stubbornness—to accept expansion of Medicaid.[6]

In Charleston, too, significant symbolic moves have not been matched by structural initiatives. Former Mayor Joseph Riley's massive fundraising effort to establish the International African American Museum appears to finally have come to fruition, but local community activists and residents are justified in complaining that little has been done to revitalize, or at least stabilize, the predominately African-American community on Charleston's East Side near the museum. Similarly, the City Council's apology for slavery in 2018 (which was approved by a disappointingly close vote) has yet to be followed up by significant changes in policy or allocation of economic and material resources.

So, South Carolina, unlike South Africa, still has not had its Truth and Reconciliation Commission (TRC). The current right-wing obsession with the supposed divisiveness of Critical Race Theory is entirely inimical to anything that resembles a search for truth. As far as reconciliation is concerned, state authorities seem to be much happier to continue to lay the burden on African Americans to "forgive and forget." Archbishop Desmond Tutu's memoir of his time chairing the South African TRC argues that forgiveness is indeed essential— his book's title is *No Future Without Forgiveness*—but he also rued the fact that he had earlier supported former apartheid South African President F.W. de Klerk's co-nomination with Nelson Mandela for the Nobel Prize.[7] That kind of absence of accountability for those whose deliberate actions had made them the beneficiaries of apartheid, the failure to follow through on the TRC report's recommendations for material and economic initiatives, and the lack of structural change are all factors that explain why, twenty-five years on, South Africans regard the TRC, which is still generally held up worldwide as an exemplary process, as a failure.

Nonetheless, I think we can still learn a good deal from South Africa's transition from apartheid racism to a non-racial democracy. Ethical philosopher Samantha Vice created quite a stir in South Africa in 2010 when she

---

[6] Former North Charleston police officer Michael Slager was later sentenced in federal court to twenty years in prison after he pleaded guilty to violating Walter Scott's civil rights.

[7] Desmond Tutu, *No Future without Forgiveness* (New York: Doubleday, 1999), 51.

published an essay arguing that in order to "rehabilitate" their selves in a fully ethical way, White people in South Africa needed to do so in "humility and in (a certain kind of) silence."[8] They needed, in short, to do more listening than talking. Establishing a truth-telling mechanism like the TRC in South Carolina might give White people an opportunity to follow the spirit of Vice's prescription here.

In addition to such a truth-telling mechanism, however, we need to commit ourselves to following through on recommendations such a commission might produce. In recent years, the Charleston Area Justice Ministry (CAJM) has provided a model for just such a set of processes, researching social problems, narrativeizing, personalizing, and humanizing those problems, and then making recommendations about how to fix those problems. But CAJM still represents only a portion of our full community, has resources so limited it can only focus on one priority issue at a time, and has no authority independently to implement its recommendations. The push is to get all elected authorities committed to the vision of social justice CAJM embraces.

Finally, there is one last key thing we can take from the TRC—a consistent application of the principle of *ubuntu*, the (South) African understanding that a person is a person because of other people. For the truth-telling principles of *ukweli* to happen, we must start from the recognition that I become truly human only when I accept that my personhood depends on acknowledging your personhood: I am—not because I think—but because you are.

---

[8] Samantha Vice, "How Do I Live in This Strange Place?" *Journal of Social Philosophy* 41 (3):323-342 (2010), 324.

Introduction

The Genesis of Ukweli:
A Search for a Healing Truth

Horace Mungin

During the summer of 2016, I wrote a series of poems to inform White people of that part of American history—the African American presence—they routinely ignore. After I had assembled a good number of poems, I made it known I wanted a venue to give a reading of this collection I called "Black History for White People Only."

I chose a bold title to attract attention. Those edgy poems revealed unpleasant historical facts, and they landed with an air of hostility on twenty-first century readers. But they spoke truth to power. I acquired this blunt trait over a half-century in New York City as a non-academic social justice literary activist and participant in the Black Arts Movement.

Early in my social justice participation, I wanted to demonstrate that the contributions of ordinary people could help advance the cause—leadership could come from the bottom up.

Without the credentialed accruements of academia, I founded *Black Forum* Magazine during the mid-way era of the Black Arts Movement, and it lasted five years after the Movement had petered out in 1975. Black Forum is now in a permanent exhibit on the Black Arts Movement at the National Museum for African American History and Culture in Washington, D.C. Though I retired to Ridgeville, South Carolina, in 1989, I had a rigorous lived experience that allowed me to contribute to the social justice struggle.

I eventually found McLeod Plantation on James Island, South Carolina, and Shawn Halifax, the cultural history interpretation coordinator at the Charleston County Park and Recreation Commission. Shawn was immediately interested in the concept. I shared my belief that most White people are unaware of the restraints placed on African Americans. It was my contention that if only they knew the truth, enough of them would favor a greater degree of social justice reform. I believe that a sizable percentage of Whites are confident in their individual abilities to understand they would still fare well in a more equitable society. Despite my awareness of past history, I held to the hope there were large enough pockets of honorable White people who, once confronted with the facts of systemic inequalities, would relinquish any resistance to leveling the playing field.

After a few meetings, Shawn informed me his superiors agreed with my concept, but thought the title too abrasive. Think of the irony. "Black History for White People Only" was too abrasive a title for an event at what was once a slave plantation. The plantation was owned and operated by the McLeod family of James Island, South Carolina, since 1851, and once housed seventy-four enslaved people in twenty-three cabins. McLeod Plantation was built on the riches of Sea Island cotton, and on the backs of enslaved people whose free descendants lived on the grounds into the 1990s. McLeod Plantation Historic Site is currently a thirty-seven-acre Gullah Geechee heritage center operated by the Charleston County Parks Foundation.

So I thought about the essence of my proposal and came up with the answer—truth.

My poems offered a truthful look at the history of racism in the United States, and I shouldn't let the rejection of my bold title prevent me from getting a chance to exhibit the substance of my work. I came home to search for a replacement title. The idea of truth stayed prominent in my mind. I thought to look at the Swahili language for a word or phrase to label my poems, thinking that to categorize the concept behind my poems in a language associated with their content would add an additional layer of legitimacy—as if forty million African Americans cried out in the vernacular of the ancestors "Ukweli!" In my search, I came across the Swahili word for truth. It seemed just perfect for my coarsely worded truth-telling poems, a good many of which made it into my 2020 published poetry collection *Notes from 1619.*

In further meetings, Shawn pushed me to consider a public lecture series on the essence of my poems and maybe include panel discussions with an audience. Again I went home to work on the idea. I listed several momentous moments in American history to summarize the breadth of the African American experience with heavy emphasis on nine topics White Americans ignore:

- The theory of the creation of White people during the last Ice Age
- The suffering of Africans during the Middle Passage
- The role African American women played during and after slavery
- The dehumanization of Africans and African Americans
- Using the Bible and religion to justify slavery
- The terror of Jim Crow
- The Red Summer of 1919 and the history of lynching
- The literary legacy of African American female authors
- The modern civil rights movement.

I discarded the Ice Age portion because it was too difficult to reconcile the schedule with that of the late Dr. Ade Ajani Ofunniyin, the only African American anthropologist in Charleston. I matched knowledgeable local scholars, however, with each of my other topics. I recruited Damon Fordham, Herb Frazier, Imam Hakim Abdul-Ali, Yvette R. Murray, and Dr. Karen Meadows as lecturers. With radio personality Osei Chandler as program moderator, I had a solid ensemble of well-informed people who also agreed with the Ukweli concept. I formatted the ninety-minute programs into five segments, then divided them into ten minutes for general introduction of the Ukweli approach, a five-minute introduction of that day's presenters, fifteen minutes for poetry, and twenty minutes each for lectures, panel discussions, and questions and answers.

After reconciling the schedules of the presenters with McLeod Plantation's, I created a contingency plan for unforeseen changes. Shawn also had a covered spot for us if it rained. Once those plans were finalized, Shawn continued our search for sponsors. This took some persistence, but Shawn proved equal to the task. With scheduling and funding accomplished, we set the five presentations two weeks apart on the plantation's spring 2020 calendar, starting in February. The first presentation took place under the shade of ancient moss-filled live oaks in a space once inhabited by an enslaved people. Then suddenly we were shut down when Charleston County Parks halted all operations because of the Covid-19 pandemic.

During the spring and summer of 2020, while we were in hiatus, the horrific killings of George Floyd, Breonna Taylor, and Ahmaud Arbery gave rise to massive protests for social justice and police reform. Demonstrations erupted around the United States and contained the largest aggregate of White participants ever assembled for a Black cause. There were even protests overseas. The local scholars I had assembled to give Ukweli lectures all sensed the great change created by the 2020 social justice movement. My colleagues updated their lectures to reflect those events.

We resumed in September when Charleston County Parks reopened its facilities. Once again in the shade of those towering oaks across from the slave cabins, we positioned folding chairs to account for social distancing concerns. The presentations were well attended by people of both races eager to ask questions. We were all very pleased with the outcome. Several weeks later, Middleton Place contacted me and asked if I could bring Ukweli to their property, a former plantation site on the Ashley River west of Charleston. With that news, Herb Frazier, the journalist among us, came up with the idea of memorializing the Ukweli program with a book to spread its message to a larger audience. We agreed to co-edit an anthology of South Carolina essays on the subjects covered in our Ukweli presentations at McLeod. We established a list and invited mostly South Carolina academics, educators, activists, journalists, writers, poets, documentarians, and ministers to contribute essays and poems. We suggested thirteen Black history topics, but we stressed that the authors could choose another topic as long as it informed White people about the Black experience.

I am happy to report to our readers that my colleague Herb and I have assembled an eclectic consortium of thinkers, who have greatly expanded the original content of Ukweli in depth and scope with their innovative essays. Together these writers speak with a voice so sacred that I expect this anthology to dust off South Carolina's image as a retrogressive, backwoods state. These essays shine the light of truth on slavery, lynching, and segregation. They lay bare the artificial construct of race as pseudo-science to justify slavery. One writer promotes racial conciliation in the telling of a personal discovery of an ancestor's robust slave brokerage business. The little-known lynching of a federally appointed postmaster is one of the many horrors against people of African descent. Another account provides a first-hand look into desegregation from a "first child" of school integration. The dark history of policing in America leads to a presentation on the Black Lives Matter movement. Another contributor offers a personal account of the struggle to maintain a "mysterious, kind of Southern love" in an essay about her Confederate ancestor. There is jubilance, too, in a Gullah Geechee celebration as freedom comes with Emancipation.

This eclectic cadre of South Carolina thinkers, Black and White, comes from diverse backgrounds to cover the Black topics too many White people would shun. These writers illustrate the most collective thing we all have in common—Ukweli —the search for a healing truth. This collection, crying out for racial unity in South Carolina, could serve as a template for the nation.

To enhance these stories, we have added the poetry of some of South Carolina's finest poets. We have works by three poet laureates and more than a half-dozen exceptional poets who add a lyrical reinterpretation of the essays, giving the reader yet another enriched yet sobering view of the Black experience. These poems were, in many cases, attentively tailored to their accompanying essays, so you won't be surprised at how well they're paired.

This essay/poetry pairing, as far as I know, is a new concept we pioneered at our McLeod presentations. The technique might endure beyond this second application. I thank Herb for the vision to recommend this print form of what worked so well in our verbal production of Ukweli. I also want to thank Herb for the tireless hours he put into gathering the contributors, articulating the project to them, and for working with me to configure the contents in an exhilarating format.

I want to thank Shawn for escaping much of the wearisome traits afflicting White Americans, which has allowed him to pursue his deep interest in social justice and also to treat me with such humility. I don't mind saying this, but I think that he is a model for what White America ought to aspire to become. And finally, I want to thank these wonderful South Carolina scholars, some of whom I've yet to meet, for their gracious contributions to this historic anthology of acceptance, conciliation, and healing.

Seeking Racial Truth
in an Unlikely Place

Shawn Halifax

McLeod Plantation Historic Site (MPHS) opened to the public on April 25, 2015. It's a significant day in South Carolina's history because, for the first time, a former private for-profit slave labor agricultural enterprise (plantation) would focus on the stories and experiences of the enslaved people and their descendants who lived there. Its purpose: peel away the veil of romanticized plantation myths to reveal a history that corrects the tales spun by the site's namesake family and others.

In the 1920s and 30s, the second and third generations of McLeods spent thousands of dollars redesigning the architecture and landscape of their property to create an image that glorified their parents and grandparents in an attempt to whitewash the horrible human rights abuses they committed. For the first half of the twentieth century, the McLeods of James Island were leaders in local and state chapters of the United Daughters of the Confederacy (UDC), crafting a myth of the "old South" that objectified and silenced the voices and memory of the majority of the people who lived there, Black people.[9] Charleston County Parks opened the historic site with

---

[9] In 1917, second generation McLeod sisters Rose and Wilhelmena were the corresponding secretary and historian, respectively at the UDC National Convention held in Nashville, Tennessee. In 1919 the Rutherford Committee was created to promote "lost cause" narratives in textbooks. The committee is named after Mildred Lewis Rutherford, Wilhelmina

the understanding that it would "tell the whole truth about its history," even if it's one that makes us uncomfortable or we don't want to hear.[10]

Two weeks later, on Mother's Day weekend, a man visited MPHS.[11] It seems reasonable to assume that he read the wayside exhibits. He photographed himself at the Sankofa Memorial Garden, an African American cemetery, in front of the imposing McLeod House, and in front of a former slave dwelling.[12] Six weeks later, he murdered Cynthia Hurd, Susie Jackson, Ethel Lance, DePayne Middleton Doctor, Clementa Pinckney, Tywanza Sanders, Daniel Simmons Sr., Sharonda Coleman-Singleton, and Myra Thompson at Mother Emanuel AME Church. In his writings, the man rejected corrective narratives like the one presented at MPHS with an all too familiar sentiment:

"I wish with a passion that niggers were treated terribly throughout history by Whites, that every White person had an ancestor who owned slaves, that segregation was an evil an [sic] oppressive institution, and so on. Because if it was all it true, it would make it so much easier for me to accept our current situation. But it isnt [sic] true. None of it is. We are told to accept what is happening to us because of ancestors [sic] wrongdoing, but it is all based on historical lies, exaggerations and myths."[13]

The self-proclaimed White supremacist's presence in 2015 is another unsettling chapter in the site's history; making it just as significant to the racial

McLeod's employer and mentor at the Lucy Cobb School in Athens, Georgia. In 1926 Wilhelmina was president of the Secessionville Chapter of the UDC. In 1934 she was the historian of the SC State Chapter of the UDC, and in 1942 the president of the South Carolina State Chapter of the UDC. Charleston County Park and Recreation Commission, McLeod Plantation Historic Site, McLeod Family Files, (Charleston, SC: Charleston County Park and Recreation Commission); Greg Huffman, "Twisted Sources: How Confederate propaganda ended up in the South's schoolbooks," *Facing South: The Online Magazine of the Institute for Southern Studies*, April 10, 2019, accessed June 23, 2021, https://www.facingsouth. org/2019/04/twisted-sources-how-confederate-propaganda-ended-souths-schoolbooks.
[10] Shawn Halifax, "McLeod Plantation Historic Site: Sowing Truth and Change," *Public Historian: A Journal of Public History,* 40, no.3 (August 2018): 253.
[11] Halifax, "McLeod Plantation: Sowing Truth and Change," 268.
[12] "Shocking Photos of Dylann Roof from 'Last Rhodesian' website," *New York Daily News*, accessed June 23, 2021, https://www.nydailynews.com/news/shocking-photos-dylann-storm-roof-gallery-1.2265282?pmSlide=1.2265278
[13] "Full Text of Charleston Suspect Dylann Roof's Apparent Manifesto," June 20, 2015, 1:33pm, Talking Points Memo, accessed June 23,2021, https://talkingpointsmemo. com/muckraker/dylann-roof-manifesto-full-text

terror theme of American history as the other themes of American history for which the site was already significant, including slavery, the Civil War, and Reconstruction. It reconnects, full circle, the terrorism embodied by William Wallace McLeod Jr. in the late 19th century to the vicious and racist violence the killer committed at Mother Emmanuel and his calls for a race war.[14]

Following this horrific event, MPHS committed itself to removing the well-deserved stigma attached to it by so many Americans, especially Black Americans, because of its status as one of the "plantations" which traditionally has marginalized or severely misrepresented their own history as sites of enslavement. It would strive to become a welcoming place where one could learn about and contemplate the human rights abuses that occurred there, a space where racial healing could occur.[15] Today MPHS leads the way for sites of slavery seeking to fundamentally alter the traditional roles they have filled as passive-aggressive markers of a mythical past into active agents for truth, change, and improving life in a community.

In late 2018, African American writer and poet Horace Mungin brought a new program series to MPHS centered on his poetry and titled "Ukweli: The Search for Healing Truth." Ukweli is the Swahili word for truth. But what is "truth," and whose "truth" is it, when America's own racial segregation, discrimination, and apartheid have been the normative societal principles since before 1619? The history taught in schools and at historic sites has not been the same history taught in Black households, churches, and communities. The Ukweli programs addressed that disconnect. A function of the series was to recognize that what we often call truth is really perspective based on the personal experiences of ourselves and our forebears. In other words, they are our personal truths. Understanding the different perspectives or personal truths of others is important to discovering truths that we might have been incapable of holding.

---

[14] McLeod family oral tradition recounts that William Wallace McLeod Jr. belonged to the state sanctioned Haskell Mounted Rifles, a white militia organized in part to maintain order on James Island. It also states that he belonged to a secret organization whose goal was a return to white supremacy on James Island and throughout South Carolina. The secret organization has been described as conducting night rides on the island. The secret organization's modus operandi was the same as that of the Ku Klux Klan's throughout the South in the 1870s and 1880s.

[15] Halifax, "McLeod Plantation: Sowing Truth and Change," 268-272.

Each of the five programs began with poetry written and read by Mungin that explored a topic in American history from his perspective. A Black scholar or writer then created historical context for the poem from a broader Black perspective, followed by a moderated conversation between the poet, scholar, and the audience who provided their own perspectives or personal truths in an effort to build racial knowledge, understanding, and conciliation.

The first meeting of the Ukweli series was held in late September, 2020, after a summer when the nation erupted in widespread protests following the killings of George Floyd, Breonna Taylor, Ahmaud Arbery and, over the course of America's history, countless other African Americans. Across America, the long history of racism throughout the country was acknowledged like never before. The series was introduced with an explanation of why it's important this conversation be held in the very space where so many human rights abuses occurred.

A tension exists at most sites of slavery. The tension is often over white mythologies and "lost cause" propaganda posing as "factual" history, coming face-to-face with lived and historic Black memories that have been silenced and exorcised. For generations these places have conveniently and defensively claimed, "We can't talk about the history of Black people because it's not been recorded" or, "We don't have any information about the slaves who were here." So, their history is not included, or if it is, it is at best inaccurately presented. Because of over 150 years of marginalizing and promoting negative stereotypes by sites of slavery, there is little or no trust between these institutions and gatekeepers of Black history.

Many people visiting historic sites of slavery expect the history presented to be "objective," "factual," and conform to what they "know." But what do people know when so many Americans were taught history from early and mid-twentieth-century textbooks adopted only after receiving the "blessing" of the UDC, an organization led in part by the McLeod family, and that substitutes fact with propaganda? What do people know when the history of the majority of those people who once occupied a space has been intentionally lied about, erased, even annihilated?

Americans have never held a collective conversation about slavery and racism. While the summer of 2020 caught America's attention on race in ways not seen since the civil rights era and inspired more White people to acknowledge the racial challenges we face as a country, it also created wider and deeper racial divisions. This was highlighted in the January 6, 2021 attack on the United States Capitol. To see the Confederate battle flag, symbol of treason and racial terrorism, waved for the first time inside the corridors of the Capitol, and beneath the gaze of John C. Calhoun, father of Secession and the Civil War, is deeply troubling. In less than six years the dreams for a race war by the perpetrator of the Mother Emanuel massacre moved from what was dismissed as being on the fringes of American society to front and center. The need for conciliation has rarely been more urgent in this country.

Good-faith dialogue that leads to what has been described as social truth by the Truth and Reconciliation Commission of (SATRC) is needed. Horace Mungin's Ukweli program series created an atmosphere for arriving at a "whole" truth that is inclusive, ethical, and courageous. Mungin explained the purpose of the series:

"Is not to be offensive, confrontational or revengeful, but rather to close the chasm in white people's knowledge of the neglected part of our history—that history which they avoid daily. I believe if well-meaning, good White people knew more about the history of racism, if they knew more about the origin of their advantages, they [would] be more understanding of the constraints that bind African Americans. They would be more emphatic to our plight and they would have to dust some of the luster off of their illusions of autonomous achievements."[16]

SATRC defined four types of truth in its reckoning with the abuses that occurred in South Africa. It describes social or dialogue truth as "the truth of experience that is established through interaction, discussion and debate by all sides, considering both motives and perspectives (personal truths). The process of arriving at social truths is as important as the truths themselves, because the fundamental dignity and integrity of those involved is affirmed through the dialogue process. Trust is created through this process. It is then that individuals are able to discover their own healing truths that are necessary for a healthy society."[17]

---

[16] Horace Mungin, email message to Shawn Halifax, October 30, 2018.

[17] Truth and Reconciliation Commission, *Truth and Reconciliation Commission of South*

At the final meeting of the Ukweli series, the focus was on Black female literary giants. It was introduced by pointing out the analogy between foundational and cultural literacy, and the need to develop cultural literacy in this country, especially by White Americans. Without us building cultural literacy about the history and cultures of other Americans that are not our own, it is difficult to have a productive conversation about racism. Historic sites, museums, and libraries are places where cultural literacy can be developed. Ukweli brought people together to dialogue about what our social truth is, to find agreement—or at least acknowledgement—and build trust. But Ukweli was also designed to build White people's cultural literacy. In fact, Horace initially called the series "Black History for White People," where a Black poet, five Black writers and scholars, and majority White audience listened to personal truths and held dialogue about those truths. It is a model, albeit a modest one, for former plantations to become unlikely spaces where transformative and healing truths can be revealed.

Africa Report, Vol 1 (1998) 110-117, accessed June 23, 2021 https://www.justice.gov.za/ trc/report/finalreport/Volume%201.pdf.

Slavery

Portuguese Slave Traders' Overt Notions Came Before 1619

Herb Frazier

I am annoyed with an over-emphasis on the date 1619. The excellent journalism in *The New York Times'* 1619 Project puts African American achievements, in spite of slavery's hardships, at the core of this nation's troubled narrative. It reminds us that the Emancipation Proclamation and the Thirteenth Amendment didn't cleanse America of the toxic notion that black people are subhuman. Instead of examining slavery's origin in the United States, a sad yet important marker, I want to look further back in time for that moment when slavery's net first snared our African ancestors and enslavers concocted a false justification for it.

Africans became victim to race-based slavery a century before English pirates took Angolans from a Portuguese slave ship to subsequently sell them in 1619 to colonists at Jamestown, England's first permanent North American settlement.[18] Although that transaction commenced slavery in North America, Africans were perceived as ripe for the taking in the early 1400s when Portugal's King John took Ceuta, a Muslim trading post, on the northeastern tip of Morocco. As King John pursued sea routes to gold and captives in sub-Saharan Africa, the Portuguese royal court commissioned *The Chronicles of the*

---

[18] https://www.nps.gov/jame/learn/historyculture/african-americans-at-jamestown.htm (Accessed Aug. 17, 2021).

Discovery and Conquest of Guinea in 1453 that served as the first-ever written defense of the African slave trade.[19]

The Portuguese were the first Europeans to sail along Africa's coast beyond the treacherous Cape Bojador off the Western Sahara. On the first successful attempt an expedition returned to Lagos, Portugal, on August 6, 1444, with 240 captives. As the supply of Eastern European slaves in Western Europe was being supplanted by Africans, Western Europeans were beginning to see enslaved people not as White but as Black. Before then, slaves and masters had often been of the same race in the classical world of Greeks and Romans. European slavery, during medieval times, was common between Scandinavia and the Black Sea. The modern word slave is rooted in slav, which describes the Slavic people enslaved by pre-modern Europeans.[20]

The *Chronicles of the Discovery and Conquest of Guinea* labeled some Africans as "white enough, fair to look upon, and well proportioned" while other mulattoes and still others were called "as black as Ethios, and so ugly" they appeared as if they were visitors from hell. In spite of their varying ethnicities and hues, Africans were viewed, nevertheless, as inferior people. Before Portugal opened a sea route to West Africa, Italy and Spain had been raiding the Canary Islands and buying Africans from Moroccan traders, but the Portuguese, with their sea prowess, expanded the market. The book described Portugal's slave-trading as missionary work to save the barbarians who required religious and civil salvation.[21]

The names and the exact number of the Angolans sold in 1619 are unknown.[22] One fact remains clear: that moment likely created the conditions for two and a half centuries of inhumane chattel slavery and continuing race-based discrimination in America that has infected nearly every aspect of American life. A half century after Jamestown, settlers from the tiny British island of Barbados in the far eastern Caribbean established the first permanent colony in

---

[19] Ibram X. Kendi, *Stamped from the Beginning* (New York: Bold Type Books, 2016), 23.
[20] Herb Frazier, Dr. Bernard Edward Powers, Jr., and Marjory Wentworth, *We Are Charleston: Tragedy and Trimph at Mother Emanuel* (Nashville: W Publishing Group, 2016), 37.
[21] Ibram X. Kendi, *Stamped from the Beginning* (New York: Bold Type Books, 2016), 22, 23, 24.
[22] https://hampton.gov/3580/The-1619-Landing-Report-FAQs (Accessed Aug. 17, 2021).

South Carolina near modern-day Charleston, following unsuccessful attempts in the sixteenth century by the French and Spanish. By 1708, the majority of the Carolina Colony's population was Black. Rice cultivation created a demand for West Africans, particularly those from the continent's rice-growing region, where for an estimated 3,000 years Africans had cultivated rice before Europeans arrived.[23] Approximately 12.5 million Africans were sold into slavery in the Western Hemisphere from 1501 to 1866.[24] Among them, historians estimate that more than 180,000 people arrived in Charleston. Through this unprecedented forced migration came a new culture—Gullah—a blend of African cultures from North Carolina to northern Florida.[25] My ancestors were likely in that group. It possibly explains the African and slavery references of my childhood in a segregated Charleston of the 1950s and 1960s. I didn't fully understand until I was an adult that our diet, speech, and folkways were Africanisms linked to slavery.

I grew up in the government-funded Ansonborough Housing Project bounded by streets named for enslavers—Calhoun, Washington, and Laurens.[26] Dozens of families lived in sturdy, one-story yellow-brick buildings topped with asphalt-shingled roofs, a tiny community where fireflies, clover, and mulberries are among my cherished childhood memories. A rusty chain link fence divided us from a river-side industrial site that was once the slave port of Gadsden's Wharf where the International African American Museum (IAAM) will open in the fall of 2022.[27] I and my neighbors in the projects

---

[23] https://www.pnas.org/content/99/25/16360 (Accessed Aug. 17, 2021)

[24] https://www.statista.com/statistics/1150475/number-slaves-taken-from-africa-by-region-century/ (Assessed Aug. 17, 2021)

[25] The descendants of Gullah Geechee people live in the coastal region from Wilmington, North Carolina, to St. Augustine, Florida. People of African descent who live along the coast of Georgia prefer to be called Geechee.

[26] Vice President John C. Calhoun, a South Carolinian, was a staunch defender of slavery, and he also enslaved people of African descent. A towering statue depicting his likeness loomed over Calhoun Street until it was removed June 2020. George Washington was the nation's first president. Twelve of the first eighteen U.S. presidents owned slaves at some point during their lives. Henry Laurens was president of the Continental Congress and a slave trader.

[27] https://www.postandcourier.com/news/building-a-place-of-pilgrimage-at-charlestons-international-african-american-museum/article_226a31be-347d-11e9-bfb5-8f6e468be-f5a.html

didn't know the Gadsden's Wharf history. The IAAM, however, will shed light on that and other parts of Charleston's role in the trans-Atlantic slave trade. The long-awaited museum is former Charleston Mayor Joseph P. Riley's promise to the city. Years ago, at a meeting with a small group interested in the project, Riley gazed across the shimmering harbor toward Fort Sumter to describe a museum connecting Charleston with the slave fortress on Bunce Island in Sierra Leone. His words resonated with me. As a journalist, I've reported from Bunce Island and two other West African sites where captured people were held before the Atlantic journey. I've often wondered why journalism repeatedly steered me to West Africa. A DNA test held a clue; my ancestry springs from Sierra Leone's Mende people. I was simply following my genetic compass. But this revelation wouldn't have meant much to my late father and maybe others of his generation. "I didn't lose nothin' in Africa," he once said.

Slavery changed African lives in unimaginable ways that may never be fully understood or appreciated. We do know, however, that enslaved people in the Charleston vicinity labored in torrid sub-tropical conditions. Some toiled in fields of indigo, cotton, or rice. Others served in plantation big houses. Some worked for urban shopkeepers, or as blacksmiths, or as domestic servants, or on the waterways. Still, some were free, and some of them even enslaved other Africans, either as benevolent custodians who rescued relatives from slavery, or others whose brutality matched White enslavers.[28] Nevertheless, many directly or indirectly undergirded a thriving Lowcountry rice economy. It was West Africans' rice-growing skills that made the Carolina Colony one of the wealthiest in young America.[29] Slavery and rice were linked so closely that a Black majority in coastal rice-growing areas existed before the American Revolution.

We'll never know the names of these Africans who endured hostile conditions, but history reminds us that some of them had been stolen from great empires, accomplished in science and literature. Anthropologist Melville J. Herskovits noted that even among the cultures that were non-literate, "Africa exhibits the great incidence of complex governmental structures. Not even

---

[28] Larry Koger, *Black Slaveowners: Free Black Slave Masters in South Carolina, 1790-1860* (Jefferson, North Carolina: McFarland & Company, Inc., 1985).

[29] Judith A. Carney, *Black Rice: The African Origins of Rice Cultivation in the Americas* (Cambridge, Massachusetts: Harvard University Press, 2001), 78-79.

the kingdoms of Peru and Mexico could mobilize resources and concentrate power more effectively than could some of these African monarchies, which are more to be compared with Europe of the Middle Ages."

We know some of those captured Africans who arrived in America. One of them was Kunta Kinte, memorialized in author Alex Haley's historical novel *Roots: The Saga of an American Family* that spawned a TV mini-series adaptation of his voluminous best-selling historical fiction that began airing on TV in 1977. I traveled to The Gambia where Haley claims his ancestor Kunta Kinte was stolen from before he was sold into slavery in Virginia. In The Gambia, I met Lamin Ceesay, who said he too is Kunta Kinte's descendant. Ceesay was a tour guide on the tiny, eroding Kunta Kinte Island in The River Gambia, site of the former British-owned slave fort. We strolled through a complex of crumbing ruins as he described how captives were treated. In a wide area shaded by a towering baobob grove, he spread his arms to mark where captives were graded as valid or invalid. Valids were branded on their shoulders to identify their origin on the other side of the Atlantic. Invalids were not branded nor set free. They were tossed in the swift-moving river to die.[30]

In Sierra Leone, a 13-year-old boy was captured in 1773, possibly first caught up in the domestic slave trade that led to his enslavement in Charleston. In America, the boy was known as John Kizell. He lived briefly in Charleston and worked for a King Street merchant. When the city fell to the British in 1780, Kizell joined the British military as a "Black Loyalist." With the colonists' victory, Kizell and other loyalists—Blacks and Whites—were evacuated to harsh conditions in Nova Scotia, and from there he returned to his homeland, along with other freed Africans, to establish a colony that grew into modern-day Freetown, Sierra Leone's capital. Kizell, of course, was not the only African to fight against slavery. For some, resistance came during the voyage across the Atlantic. Later in life, Kizell said he witnessed one such act of resistance when a woman on the ship that brought him to Charleston was tied on deck and flogged to death for refusing to eat.[31]

---

[30] In The Gambia as it was elsewhere on Africa's west coast, people sold into slavery were initially captured by a rival group and later sold to European slave traders. https://onlinelibrary.wiley.com/doi/pdf/10.1111/foge.12025 (Accessed Aug. 16, 2021).

[31] Kevin G. Lowther, *The African American Odyssey of John Kizell* (Columbia, S.C: The

At Ghana's Portuguese-built slave fortress of Elmina, captives stepped through a "door of no return" on their way to the slave ships. One room, marked with a skull and cross bones, is "the room of no return." The guide said people who resisted were thrown in the room and denied food and water. Those freedom fighters were left to die. A plaque at the fortress reads: "In everlasting memory of the anguish of our ancestors. May those who died rest in peace. May those who return find their roots. May humanity never again perpetrate such injustice against humanity. We, the living, vow to uphold this."

This statement can easily be applied to slave trading on Africa's east coast that predates trans-Atlantic slavery. Historian John Henrik Clarke describes the forced removal of East Africans to the Mediterranean as another "Middle Passage" perpetrated by Arab slave traders. "It is often forgotten that the Arab slave trade in East Africa and the slave trade from North Africa into Inner West Africa was protracted and ruthless," he wrote. "Sometimes the Arabs from the north who were Moslem enslaved Africans in the south, who were also Moslems, thereby violating one of the most basic customs of their faith—that no Moslem should enslave another Moslem."

Were West Africans complicit in enslaving people from rival ethnic groups? Yes. Some Africans acknowledge that fact today. Kizell was likely a victim of domestic slavery in Sierra Leone. Elsewhere on the Mother Continent, Africans sold other Africans into internal domestic slavery, and later some of those enslaved people were sold to Europeans. Slavery in Africa was not race-based as it later became with European involvement. Harvard University sociologist Orlando Patterson notes in *Slavery and Social Death* that Africans caught in the domestic slave trade remained connected to African society. They suffered, however, a "social death" when trans-Atlantic slavery severed those ties.

In The Gambia, Lamin Ceesay and I talked about the domestic African slave trade during our stroll around Kunta Kinte Island. The slave trade left victims on both sides of the Atlantic. People of African descent in the diaspora tend to blame the Africans for the human suffering slavery caused, he said. "It was you who sold our ancestors into slavery," he said, referring to comments he's heard. "They say they are the victims of the slave trade, but there were also victims left behind" in Africa.

University of South Carolina Press., 2011), 2.

African Americans and others in the diaspora accusing Africans of complicity in the slave trade creates "fertile ground" for additional research and reconciliation between the two groups who've not yet fully come to terms with slavery, said Dr. Bernard Powers, director of the Center for the Study of Slavery in Charleston at the College of Charleston. The same holds true, he explained, for African descendants of domestic African enslavers and the descendants of those they enslaved. When children were taken away to an unknown place and unknown fate, it left victims on the African continent. "Mothers and fathers were left with graves with no bodies," Ceesay explained. "In their hearts, they are victims too." The pain remains there and, of course, in America it is manifested through historical trauma in a variety of social and medical maladies. It is seen too in the self-hatred we inflict on ourselves and, of course, the racism we experience in small and large ways from White Americans, particularly through institutionalized racism and the brutal police violence on Black and Brown bodies.

When we consider the nine minutes and twenty-nine seconds that a knee — a knee — was drilled into George Floyd's neck, can we connect that murderous act to the Portuguese lack of humanity centuries ago? It all returns to bear its hateful behavior on us today. Holocaust and ethnic cleansing survivors vow to prevent repeats of those atrocities. We must embrace the same conviction to offer aggressive and meaningful reports on slavery like the 1619 Project but not be satisfied to imagine it as the complete narrative on slavery.

We must continue to speak with confidence and authority to ensure that a study of slavery connects the ever-present past with today's reality, even when reality deniers attempt to deflect the truth. In the spirit of Ukweli, it is up to us to begin a total healing from one of America's original sins—slavery—through honest, truthful, and painful conversations.

America

Horace Mungin

Let's start at the beginning — America
Has never been America
The land owners wrote some noble words on
Sheets of paper as the guide for the nations'
Behavior, but neither they nor their descendants
Have been able to reproduce the nobility of those
Sentiments expressed on paper in their legislatures
In their towns, in their cities, on their streets
In their homes, schools, churches, indeed,
Not even in their hearts

It was a mirage from the very
Beginning — maybe even a deception, a hoax
A myth and an elegantly grand dishonesty — for
What happened to the indigenous people who
Lived here and the kidnapped African people
Brought here in chains was not congruent
With the noble words on those sheets of paper

A deliriously schizophrenic nation travelled
Through the centuries glorifying the words,
Exalting the words, believing in the words, bragging
Of a nation above all other nations, originated
By the agitation of its land-owning Founding Fathers
Although the contradictions they lived, produced
Carnage to all but the landowners and their tribe
And then there did come a time when their tribe was
Led into carnage because the land owners divided into
A north/south dispute over the continuant of slavery

The Robber Barons gobbled up control of all
Wealth-producing processes and proportioned
A society of vacillating economic levels and
Social privileges contingent on tribal membership
Over whom they became the all-powerful oligarchy

The oligarchy divided the riches of the nation
Amongst a tiny one percent of the population; the banks
The railroads, the oil fields, the shipping lanes, the stock market
Then later; the automobiles, the airways, and manufacturing
And they produced a White ruling class to oversee their
Kingdom and a White managing class to select
Who eats and to whom privilege is administered
All this was done under the guise of those
Noble words written in a document known as
The Constitution of the United States of America
Bringing honor and privileges to members, but
Why the noble words remained only an aspiration
To all else is explained with sleight of hand,
Hocus pocus and unfulfilled promises of a better future

Even after the monumental failures of Reconstruction and the
Rise of the Ku Klux Klan the United States restored
Control of the South to white supremacists, the Negro was
Disenfranchised and betrayed by his country, even after
Negroes enlisted or were drafted in two world wars
To preserve the sacredness of those noble words
In the hopes of making them true for themselves
The oligarchy ordered the ruling class to warn Negroes
Against moving too fast towards Freedom — cautioning them of
Their aspirations for freedom; even after 1919's Red Summer
Of lynching they scolded Negroes for wanting too much freedom
Even after Emmett Till was murdered they bellowed — too much, too soon

About the dissent and the ruling class Whites pasted the edict down
To the managing class Whites to stifle all Black attempts to bridge the gaps

One woman's refusal to give up her seat on a bus cracked
Open the lid on a century's long bottled-up angry Black frustration
And erupted into a nationwide movement for Black freedom
The non-violent Civil Rights era came to be after the
Montgomery Bus Boycott in 1955 that elevated names like
Jo Ann Robinson, Claudette Colvin, and Mary Louise Smith
With the spilling of blood came other victories; the Civil Rights
Act, the Voting Rights Act, the Equal Employment Opportunity
Commission, America seemed to be growing a conscience
Just at the time when African Americans were awakening to the lie
And beginning to disbelieve what had been said about them by
White people, they were awakening to a history of themselves
That gave them racial pride, racial confidence, and a racial identity

A few Black men came to the notion that the problem was not of
A Black construct or of a Black import, or Black ownership
The problem, these handful discovered, was solely because they were Black
The country they lived in was constructed entirely for the security of
White people — read the Constitution — which considered them three-fifths of
A person in a compromise that proportioned more legislative seats for the
Slaveholding Southern states — three-fifths of a person from 1787 until 1865
Else they would have been slaughtered and disregarded like the native people
So the problem does not belong to the African American people

The problem persists because present-day White people don't
Want to confront the wickedness of their ancestors; nor the
Auction block, or the compromise or the chains or the whip and the lash
Or the limbs pulled apart, or the raped girl or the child sold off, or the
Young man tied all day to a tree in the sun or the wife sold down

The river or the mass lynching, or the fury of a White lynch mob
Or a hundred years of Jim Crow, or the depths of the evil from which
They spring—there is the problem; one of the White world's construct

For them to dredge up this evil would be to accept their association
To it and validate their kinship with those who invented this evil
To remember this wickedness would require them to wear the cloak
Of inhumanity and offer an apology — and to surrender a restoration to
The survivors of the evil, a burden so revolting no White person can
Endure it, so they deny the reality, they would much prefer to
Remain ignorant of it — What's really needed here James Baldwin once
Said, is: White History Week — the White man needs to understand
All of his history — needs to be pinned to it, gathered and penetrable
Otherwise here is what happens:

White Evangelicals abandoned God's morality and all
The ethics they pretend to know from the Bible to support
A decadent man whose wicked moral excesses of
Twenty-five years are well documented in print,
On audio tapes, in videos, from his own admission
White American voters in the biggest departure of
Moral judgment since slavery risked the narrow
Sliver of decency that keeps the country from sinking
Altogether to support this man whose marketing promise
Is that he will make America great again negating the
Necessity to dredge up old history — in his world, it didn't happen
He will erect a wall to create a reality so white the noble
Words of the Founding Fathers will ring true again.

"Is There No Balm in Gilead?"

Patricia Bligen Jones

Jeremiah 8:22b: "Is there no balm in Gilead?
Is there no physician there?" [32]

Racism. The word, when spoken, lands heavily in any conversation about this scourge that continues to haunt our individual and collective psyches. Even though the practice of owning human beings ended in 1865, our country continues to struggle with the remnants of slavery: generational, psychological pain, plantation capitalism, disparities in health care, housing, voting rights, and more. As a country we continue to be poor students of history, as our refusal to accept fully the connection between slavery's bitter aftertaste and our current-day woes reminds us that the issue of race will continue to be a problem in this country until this country admits that it is.

In the Book of Jeremiah, the prophet is tasked with warning the Israelites of their impending doom because of their disobedience toward God. He hopes against hope that God will withhold his wrath, but, to no avail. As he laments what is to come, he poses three simple questions. The first: "Is there no balm in Gilead?" In other words, is there no other way to spare the people of God, to turn their hearts and minds to God and not to their own devices? How is America different from the people of Judah to whom Jeremiah was tasked to prophesy? There is not much difference.

---

[32] *The Holy Bible*, Jer. 8:22b.

Our country has had many prophets speak truth to power about unjust laws, broken civil rights promises, a broken judicial system, voter suppression laws, gender bias, and broken law enforcement that continues to take the lives of taxpaying Black and Brown citizens. Those prophets, such as the Rev. Dr. Martin Luther King, Jr., Medgar Evers, Malcolm X, Fred Hampton, and the Rev. Clementa Pinckney, lost their lives for sounding the alarm about America's refusal to address — and readdress as needed — issues that keep Black and Brown people enraged and terrorized. What is the balm for America?

It is three-fold. First, we must admit that racism is a sin, emanating from the heart, presenting problems not only for Black people but for all people. Matthew 15: 18-20b tells us: "But what comes out of the mouth proceeds from the heart, and this is what defiles. For out of the heart come evil intentions, murder, adultery, fornication, theft, false witness, and slander. These are what defile a person …" [33]

I believe no one is born racist but taught racist ideology. Second, racism will never be eradicated until the majority culture grows weary of it and what it spawns: fear, distrust, violence, hate.

Third, we must abolish laws that continue to oppress and not liberate people of color. For example, in Florida, felons who have completed their sentence still are not allowed to vote, even though an earlier law restores the voting rights of convicted felons. According to The Sentencing Project, "Nearly 900,000 Floridians who have completed their sentences remain disenfranchised, despite a 2018 ballot referendum that promised to restore their voting rights. Florida thus remains the nation's disenfranchisement leader in absolute numbers, with more than 1.1 million people currently banned from voting—often because they cannot afford to pay court-ordered monetary sanctions or because the state is not obligated to tell them the amount of their sanction." [34] In keeping with former President Donald J. Trump's false claim of a rigged presidential election in November 2020, Florida's Republican Gov. Ron DeSantis signed in early May 2021 a bill imposing new limits on voting by mail and ballot drop boxes. According to a Reuters report, "The new law restricts the use of

---

[33] *The Holy Bible*, Matt. 15:18-19.

[34] Chris Uggen, Ryan Larson, Sarah Shannon, and Arleth Pulido-Nava, The Sentencing Project, "Locked Out 2020: Estimates of People Denied Voting Rights Due to a Felony Conviction" www.sentencingproject.org. October 30, 2020.

absentee ballot drop boxes to early voting period, adds new identification requirements for requesting such ballots, and requires voters to reapply for absentee ballots in each new general election cycle. Previously, Florida voters only had to apply once every two election cycles. The law also gives partisan election observers more power to raise objections and requires people offering voters assistance to stay at least 150 feet away from polling places, an increase from the previous 100-foot radius."[35] There are several other states drafting similar legislation. On May 17, 2021, South Carolina Gov. Henry McMaster, a Republican, signed into law the "Open Carry with Training Act," which allows licensed gun owners to openly carry a weapon in public. The law states, "It does not prohibit the right of a public or private employer to prohibit a person who is licensed under this law from carrying a concealable weapon, whether concealed or openly carried, upon the premises of the business or work place or while using any machinery, vehicle, or equipment owned or operated by the business."[36] However, past incidents have shown us that Black people who were licensed to carry a concealed weapon often found themselves at odds with the law whenever they encountered police.

Let me be clear, it is never easy for any of us to admit we are flawed, let alone racist, prejudiced, or biased. Yet, unless one is willing to admit they are racist, it is impossible to change the attitudes and behaviors that shape how they interact with people of different races. The need to be superior to another group of people is an indication that giving up "the ghost" of racism will not come easy, because it will require relinquishing power and privilege. No group wants to give up the power that serves their greater good, even if it diminishes others. Pulitzer Prize-winning author Isabel Wilkerson writes in her book, *Caste*, that "The vast majority of African-Americans who lived in this land in the first 246 years of what is now the United States lived under the terror of people who had absolute power over their bodies and their very breath, subject to people who faced no sanction for any atrocity they could conjure." James Baldwin puts it this way: "For the horrors of the American

---

[35] Julia Harte, "Florida Governor Signs Republican-backed Law Imposing New Voting Curbs" Reuters, www.reuters.com/worldus/florida-limits-absentee-voting-with-new-republican-backed-law-2021-05-06/.
[36] South Carolina General Assembly, "Open Carry with Training Act," www.scstatehouse.gov.

Negro's life, there has been almost no language."[37]

When this country acknowledges racism and the effect it has on this society, then, and only then, can we begin to heal. Those who harbor racist thoughts and behaviors must be willing to "unlearn" what they have been taught about humanity and race; and resign themselves to do the heavy lifting of learning about the damage racism has wrought. Hate certainly cannot undo racism, but love can surely try! Each generation is responsible for its part to chip away at racism to move humanity forward. We must have hard and uncomfortable conversations about race. This is never easy, for several reasons. Most people do not know how to start a conversation about race because they are afraid of offending or inflicting more emotional pain and frustration. When the issues of slavery and racism are broached, anger, fear, hatred, and denial rise, stalling honest and legitimate colloquy. Talking about race and injustice is not easy, yet it must be done if we are going to commit ourselves to healing the country.

After all, race is a social construct. In her article, "Race and Racial Identity Are Social Constructs,"Angela Onwuachi-Willig writes, "Race is not biological, there is no gene or cluster of genes common to all Blacks or all Whites. Were race 'real' in the genetic sense, racial classifications for individuals would remain constant across boundaries. Yet, a person who could be categorized as Black in the United States might be considered White in Brazil or colored in South Africa.[38] It is a matter of perspective."

Additionally, people must educate themselves not only about race, but about people of color. Too many judge Black people by stereotypes seen in the media, television, and the movies. We must be willing to see each other's humanity in its fullness. Often, I am puzzled by White people, who, when confronted with a race-related issue, say: "I don't know what to do." What does one do when purchasing a home or car? Do research to find the best price and quality. If White people are not willing to educate themselves about racism and its effects on communities of color, we will not move forward.

In his online series, "Uncomfortable Conversations with a Black Man," Nigerian-American Emmanuel Acho, a former NFL linebacker with the

---

[37] Isabel Wilkerson, *Caste* (New York: Random House, 2020), 47.
[38] Angela Onwuachi-Willig, "Race and Racial Identity Are a Social Construct," *The New York Times* opinion pages (Sept. 2016), www.nytimes.com.

Philadelphia Eagles, states: "White people have reached out to me, asking, 'how can I help? How can I join in? How can I stand with you?'" Acho's response is simple: "In order to stand with us, and people who look like me, you have to be educated on issues that pertain to me; and fully educated so that you can feel the full level of pain so that you can have full understanding. I fervently believe if the White person is your problem, then only the White person can be your solution."[39] Until we are willing to have uncomfortable conversations, we will remain stagnant and separated.

We must strengthen and introduce just laws that work for all people, regardless of race, creed, nationality, gender, sexuality, or disability. Laws that have "stick and stay" power, that will not need revisiting every forty years, like the Voting Rights Act of 1965, which granted African Americans the right to vote without poll taxes, reading tests, and guessing games. I am not naïve nor foolish to think laws do not need to be reevaluated over time, because there is always some entity that desires to shift the balance of power with new laws to stymie communities of color from fully experiencing the promises put forth in the founding documents of this country.

Shortly after the election of the first Black president, many people felt America had entered a "post racial" period. This misguided school of thought, however, continues to push a false narrative of equality in a country that is still "growing up" in regard to race relations. For example, South Carolina Republican Sen. Tim Scott, one of three African Americans in the U.S. Senate, recently declared "America is not a racist country" in the Republican Party's response to President Joe Biden's first address to Congress on April 28, 2021. Oddly enough, President Biden and Vice President Kamala Harris share the same sentiment. Sigh. During the 2008 presidential campaign, then presidential candidates Barack Obama and John McCain were each asked: "What do you believe is the most devastating event in this country's history?" McCain said The Great Depression. Obama said slavery. The divide in this country is wide and deep. Yet, as more and more Black people are elected to public offices and Black voter participation rises, more states, like Florida, Georgia,

---

[39] Emmanuel Acho, "Uncomfortable Conversations with a Black Man;" (June 2020), https://www.youtube.com/watch.

and Texas, design restrictive voting laws to limit Black and Brown people from going to the polls. Where is the fairness in this? Where is the fairness in not restoring the voting rights of those who have served prison time, paid their debt to society, and desire an opportunity to resume normal lives?

There cannot be true "healing" in a country that refuses to honor its promises to all people who claim this land as home, until we acknowledge collectively that racism is indeed a disease that continues to sicken us all.

Is there a balm in the land? I believe there is, but it comes at a price: the willingness of the majority to acknowledge the problem, hold each accountable to work on the problem, with the hope of reconciliation. True healing comes when we can all live freely, without barriers that stifle communities that have been long oppressed and ignored. Until we are all free, we will continue to grapple with race.

What the Water Holds
Ronda Taylor

"All water has a perfect memory and is forever trying to get back to where it was."
Toni Morrison

water holds the weight
of bodies bridled to chattel
devoured into an ocean tomb

water carries us through
being ripped from our home
reborn out of troubled water

waves rage in anguish
belly burdened
by sunken despair
spewed onto strange shore

we unearth the mosaic
language of joy
an anchored breath
they cannot grasp

where they sift like wheat
beating out our being

the waves roar
a jubilee of our becoming

propped on auction block
kneed into concrete

resilience rises
as we shake the earth

the water is wailing

flooding our way Home

"Payne-ful" Business

Illuminating Charleston's Past

Margaret Seidler

*"You may choose to look the other way, yet you can never say
again that you did not know."*
William Wilberforce (1759-1833),
British politician, leader in the abolitionist
movement, philanthropist

Exercising deep curiosity about my family's story brought enlightenment, truth, and a new-found empathy for those they harmed. Imagine yourself, mature, white, female, and a Charleston native searching DNA test results from years back to explore potential genetic health risks. Imagine an unexpected, astonishing finding: cousins of African descent who then ask you to trace your shared ancestry so that they can learn their personal history. Imagine this research journey not only confirms your common ancestor, a sixth great-grandfather and prominent judge in New York, it also unearths a dark and hidden past about your White ancestors and how they made their livings in Charleston. Spawned is an unparalleled personal journey to reveal and make known a more complete truth as a path to racial healing.

The lack of curiosity is perilous; beliefs that are not evidence-based live on as dogma. Traditionally, Charleston's history has regaled the stories of the wealthy, and I lacked connection to prestigious family names. While my father was born in Georgia, my mother had deep Charleston roots. My grandmother, born in 1882, told us that we came from "good people," poor, working-class Germans from Charleston's Eastside. With that narrative accepted, I never explored family genealogy. These were seemingly uninteresting people. That all changed when I revisited DNA test results in 2018 and found a request to connect with an unknown cousin, one of African descent!

My sympathy has evolved into empathy for the African American experience in Charleston. My lifelong experiences were different than most other Whites who came from long-time Charleston families. After leaving a prominent, private girls' school because I felt I did not fit in, I transferred in 1967 to the recently integrated Charleston High School. That broader exposure to people with different life experiences led me to revere the Rev. Dr. Martin Luther King's words and wisdom. Over the decades, I have been involved with Charleston's Black community. In the 1980s, I staffed a federal employment and training program for the economically disadvantaged. More recently, I chaired the Charleston airport's effort to construct the Mother Emanuel AME Church tribute for millions of passengers to see and experience. Also, I led the 2016 Charleston Illumination Project for improving citizen and police relationships. I stood on solid ground in my commitment to help. If you are White, allow me to offer a step you can take. Find one way to engage with members of the Black community on their turf. Consider attending a Black church, mosque, or maybe volunteer in a Black-led nonprofit. The key is to show up as equal, learn what the Black culture has to offer, such as love of family and pride of surviving, even thriving in the face of centuries of oppression.

While I felt my family had been exempt from the past ills of slavery, a more complete truth was right under my nose. It only took a little curiosity to start a revelation-filled journey of shock and horror. One phone conversation with Trish Williams, my Black cousin, who resides near Philadelphia, started a momentous shift. I went from being disinterested to fervently researching with one purpose, providing otherwise inaccessible information on family lineage to my newly-discovered cousins. Incredibly, I already had the information I needed to start. It was all laid out in two pages, hand-written by my grandmother. Since 1983, it had been there just waiting for me. With a first-time keenness, I studied the names and dates. Answers and shock came quickly.

The horrifying truth revealed something that shook my soul to its core. A quick internet search of John Torrans, my fifth great-grandfather, disclosed this summary from the South Carolina Historical Society Library:

"Torrans was a partner in the firm Torrans, Greg, and Poaug (Greg was a London merchant); and later in Torrans, Poaug & Company. Torrans's firms were responsible for bringing a number of Huguenots (1764) to Charleston from England, and hundreds of slaves to Charleston from Africa."

As I read those words, "bringing hundreds of slaves to Charleston from Africa," I literally wailed in pain and disbelief. My family had arrived here in 1758, a hundred years earlier! I was from a wealthy family network in New York who expanded their merchant business to profit from Charleston's thriving economy. Their ships transported both French and Irish immigrants, and later, captive Africans. My family was not poor until the end of the Civil War.

Be prepared for the worst if you conduct a family search. Despite warnings not to proceed after this initial truth, I went deeper. The next revelation was of three generations who were not merely slaveholders in Charleston, they were all slave traders, brokering the sale of thousands and thousands of enslaved human beings from the 1760s through the 1850s. The search turned to the records of John Torrans's daughter, Maria Margaret, who married William Payne, my fourth great-grandfather. Payne was a son of servants to a wealthy family in Ireland named Butler. During the mid-1780s, Payne accompanied their son to Charleston. Young Edward Butler was the nephew of Major Pierce Butler, a strong advocate for slavery and one of South Carolina's delegates to the 1787 Constitutional Convention. Seeking their fortunes in Carolina, Edward Butler and William Payne were quickly accepted into local society because Major Butler had married an aristocrat, Mary Middleton. Payne was soon appointed the major's clerk, though by 1790, both young men had gotten in trouble with him. Major Butler's personal letters reveal his anger with the two young men. He brands Payne an Irishman "well-versed in hypocrisy and falsehood; even though he married the daughter of a respectable good man (John Torrans), he was ever a 'scoundrel.'"

While Edward Butler returns to Europe, William Payne starts a retail business. In 1790, Payne purchased what is today 34 Broad Street, having now combined 32 and 34. These brick buildings stood three stories high and served as both business and residence for the Payne family. Payne's efforts to run a Cash retail store ended in bankruptcy in 1803. Seemingly desperate, Payne sold the 34 Broad building and placed daily ads for months, seeking "any and all" items for sale. The result: a lifelong career in auctioneering and property brokerage.

William Payne's success set the standard for later burgeoning domestic slave trade of the 1850s. His family-owned business brokered sales of commodities, in-town real estate, country plantations, and local enslaved people. Most sales were advertised to resolve personal estates, mortgage debt, as well as tax delinquencies. He also served as agent for the City of Charleston's sheriff, a major participant in the domestic slave trade.

Payne began serving as secretary-treasurer of the Santee Canal Company in 1806. This position played a large role in making prestigious business connections along the South Carolina coast. By 1810, Payne and Charles Cotesworth Pinckney, another South Carolina delegate to the 1787 Constitutional Convention, founded the Charleston Bible Society. Payne served as its first treasurer while Pinckney served as its first president. The Society's advertised purpose was to distribute Bibles to Whites without cost. I am unable to reconcile the hypocrisy of these men of Christian faith.

Follow the money: the domestic slave economy was big business. Payne and his eldest son, John William Payne, built a thriving domestic slave-trading auction house. They sold Africans and their descendants who were brought into the country before the U.S. Congress outlawed the importation of enslaved people in 1808. Payne's biggest slave auction was in February 1819 for the estate of planter John Ball. This two-day auction saw 367 enslaved people sold. With Payne's one percent commission payment of $3,083, we know that the total human sales were roughly the equivalent of $6.5 million in 2021 dollars. Payne held public auctions at a nearby Vendue office on East Bay Street and advertised private sales in the Broad Street office where potential buyers could stop by to "view" the enslaved, likely held in pens. Ads reveal the number and the first names of many enslaved people as well as their work skills and family relationships. Many ads list three generations of families offered for sale.

My humanitarian assumption was that Payne wished to keep the family together. However, there was no such saving grace for the slave trader as local historians explain that enslaved families were more valuable if kept together because they were less likely to run away. I began to imagine the chaos of trying to manage a system of human enslavement. If you tear families apart, humans will seek freedom at any cost.

William Payne's younger son, Josiah, later joined his father and brother in the slave trading business, selling hundreds more enslaved people through 1859. After brother John William died in 1826, followed by William Payne's death in 1834, the business faltered. So Josiah worked both as an auction broker and land developer. On land known as Payne's Farm, he subdivided it into what became Cool Blow Village, east of Meeting Street, along Cool Blow, Conroy, Romney, Isabella, and Williman Streets in today's No Mo District. It was all a family business as the residential survey work was conducted by Josiah's remaining brother, my third great-grandfather, Robert Keith Payne.

This research uncovered Charleston's truth, hidden from sight for two hundred years. Across three decades, Payne & Sons profited from the sale of at least 9,224 local enslaved persons, documented through more than 1,100 newspaper ads. This is likely a conservative number. My research provided a renewed understanding of Charleston's history as 32-34 Broad Street is identified as one of the busiest auction houses of its era. Shining this light creates the opportunity for residents and visitors alike to understand the true nature of Broad Street's bustling slave auction businesses. The revelations about on-premises dealings at 32-34 Broad Street provide concrete evidence about sales and viewings that occurred before and after all public sales were banned on the streets of Charleston in the 1850s. Sales were held inside this historic site, making the story more evident and palpable. Sharing this part of Charleston's story for the first time illuminates the hidden histories of the city's domestic slave economy. Now, we have a renewed opportunity to absorb the intensity of what took place on Broad Street.

Acknowledging truth and affirming suffering can create a new path to racial healing. The research culminated in the placement of a historical marker on the site of Payne & Sons auction house. The marker, erected January 28, 2021, seems an effective way to share these truths for generations to come.

While I am not responsible for my ancestors' actions, I choose to take responsibility for exposing this more complete history to raise awareness and encourage racial healing. Let us acknowledge the whole truth of what happened inside many Broad Street buildings. Let us illuminate what Charleston's White community has ignored while affirming that many in the Black community have labored under the trauma of slavery for generations. Let the healing begin.

Port City

Yvette R. Murray

O, my beautiful, you wear the evening hour
so very well. It hugs all the curves
and loves your cobblestone gams.
Mesmerized, I am, by the mysteries
of you. Closed red lips.
Secrets of indigo and mulatto
that ghosts tell as we stroll
by all manner of metropolis found.
I am lost in the swirl
of steel, blood, and glass.
Phalanges folded intimately.
Your shadow leaping back into azaleas
as if you wish not to be seen
because you do keep secrets from me:
of Coffin-Trees on avenues
and still winds that blow. Still.
My rhythm is yours and yours alone,
my love.
I will not share with the moon
for I am jealous.
Though not a god at all.
A simple man who desires
the complicated love you have to give.

Deliver Us

James M. Brailsford, III

From questioning why we believed in witches,
why we followed teachers,
why we burned young girls
in the zeal of our faith and the whimper of our stupidity;
deliver us, for it is too late to save them,
too late to redeem ourselves.

From questioning why we chained another people
for our profit and comfort,
under the stamp of our righteousness
blotted by our rapacity;
deliver us, for it is too late to save them,
too late to make amends.

From questioning why we dislodged the ancients
from the swamps and plains and mountains,
that they knew how to love far better than we,
why we defrauded them and killed them
in the name of this just and great nation,
the name and the justice and the greatness besmirched by our cupidity;
deliver us, for it is too late to save them,
too late to forgive ourselves.

From questioning why we went to war against ourselves,
following leaders, killing our own,
leaving six hundred thousand dead
for honor and principle and in the sin of our pride;
deliver us, for it is now too late to save them,
too late to revive the squandered spirit of our nation.

But as there is still time to come,
so may there be deliverance tomorrow.
May we screw up our courage and ask our questions now.
May we demand our answers now; and hearing none,
may we give the answers that we know to be true
and do that which we know must be done,
while it is not yet too late to save us all,
while there is still time to save ourselves
and to save this paradisiacal planet.

A Gullah Tradition

"From Freedom's Eve to Jubilee in the Morning" Race, Reconciliation and Atonement in the Gullah Geechee Watch Night Tradition

Heather L. Hodges

Just after midnight on January 1, 1986, Gullah Geechee elder Lawrence McKiver addressed family members and friends gathered in the annex of Mt. Calvary Baptist Church in Bolden, Georgia, as documentary cameras rolled. Mr. McKiver announced they would be "singing a song that our old people used to sing when they came out of slavery." Mr. McKiver clapped and sang out loudly, *"Jubilee, Jubilee!"* and the circle responded, *"Oh My Lord."*

"Jubilee in the morning," he continued.

"My Lord, Jubilee!" the congregation answered. The joyful noise grew as they reached the refrain, *"Shout, my children, you are free! / My God brought you liberty! / Jubilee, Jubilee / Jubilee in the mornin'."*[40]

It was a song of celebration and liberation that called forth their ancestors' elation on December 31, 1862, as they gathered together to await the signing

---

[40] *Down Yonder with the McIntosh County Shouters.* Directed by Clate Sanders. Georgia Public Television, 1986.

of the Emancipation Proclamation on January 1, 1863. To celebrate together their long dreamt-of release from perpetual enslavement on the rice and Sea Island cotton plantations along the sandy Georgia coast. Over 155 years later, it is still the tradition in many communities and churches in the historic Gullah Geechee Cultural Heritage Corridor to host a "Watch Night" service on New Year's Eve and to memorialize January 1 as Emancipation Day.[41] The Emancipation Proclamation Association in Charleston, South Carolina, sustains a New Year's Emancipation Day parade tradition that dates back to 1866.

Together, they mark an inflection point in U.S. history at which the possibility of a healing, racial reconciliation, rooted in Black sacred spaces, was met with a steely commitment to virulent, racial estrangement. An alienation that to this day finds historically Black churches, namely Mother Emanuel AME in Charleston, which maintains the Watch Night tradition, an enduring target for radicalized, racialized, and extremist violence. Watch Night and Emancipation Proclamation commemorations ask us to consider each year where our nation now stands on the long journey to atonement for its original sin.

To be clear, the Watch Night service on New Year's Eve is not a liturgical event. It represents the consensus of a congregation to welcome the new year together, often also extending an invitation to the community to join them in a vigil service. (The word "vigil" comes from the Latin vigil whose meanings include acts of watchfulness.) It is a long-standing, cherished spiritual and folk tradition in some churches, particularly among elders. Occasionally, a church may also newly adopt (or renew) the custom. The preservation of this custom in Gullah Geechee churches is in part due to a larger, historical context. First, there is a long tradition in the Methodist denomination of attending church on New Year's Eve for a Watch Night meeting that was also a covenant renewal service.

Second, late December was also the time of year during slavery when friends and family members could be sold or rented out after the fall harvest to satisfy

---

[41] The Gullah Geechee Cultural Heritage Corridor is a federal National Heritage Area created by an act of Congress in 2006. It extends from Pender County, North Carolina to St. Johns County, Florida, and thirty miles inland. It recognizes the part of the lower Atlantic coastline where Gullah Geechee people have traditionally lived, although subsequent migrations mean many Gullah Geechee people and their descendants live in communities outside the boundary of the federal heritage area.

a slaveowner's debts. January 1 became known as "Hiring Day" (or more sorrowfully as "Heartbreak Day") as the enslaved gathered to pray and console each other in anticipation of separation.

This fusion of history, religion, blood memory, and tradition among people experiencing a range of contemporaneous challenges over the last 155 years helps us understand why their descendants may express different reasons for wanting to attend church on Watch Night. There are freedmen's churches like Mt. Calvary (organized in 1890) that can draw a direct line from their Watch Night tradition back to their enslaved ancestors. That specific memory has been lost in other Gullah Geechee churches although the tradition of going to church for New Year's Eve remains, as does the belief that it is an opportunity to draw strength and solace from each other in difficult times. The Rev. Saint Julian Snider, at the time pastor of St. Paul AME Church in Little River, South Carolina, explained to a journalist in 2004 that "the services have become less about remembering slavery and more about remembering contemporary struggles [his] congregation has survived in the past year. 'We talk about the things that have affected our people.'"[42]

Feelings of gratitude are often expressed by congregants asked to describe why they attend Watch Night, to give thanks for simply surviving. "Thanking God for his love, mercy and grace, for what we can do with the love of the Almighty God," a congregant said. "Although I had my ups and my downs this year, God was always with me and seeing me through."[43] Another recalled that "[t]his time of year was when people gathered all their crops and things and praised God that things weren't any worse … They were looking forward to a better year and knew that the Lord would carry them through if they trusted him."[44] Whether it is recalling the sheer jubilation at the end of centuries of American chattel slavery or testifying to the troubles and triumphs of the year just past, Watch Night remains a time for reflection, gratitude, and

---

[42] Amanda Greene, "Watch Night greets year with prayer, not parties." *StarNews* (Wilmington, NC, December 30, 2004).

[43] Andrew Wigger, "Watch Night rich in history." *Newberry Observer* (Newberry, SC, December 30, 2015).

[44] Dionne Gleaton, "Historic Watch Night offers time of celebration, reflection." *The Times & Democrat* (Orangeburg, SC, December 30, 2013).

expressions of hope among a people whose profound challenges in our nation did not all end with emancipation.

Watch Night services generally begin at nine or ten o'clock at night on December 31. There is remarkable uniformity across congregations and denominations around what happens in the hours leading to midnight. Praise and worship are often punctuated with musical selections, guest speakers, and a homily. Time is also reserved for folks to offer "testimonials," to rise at their pew and address the church in highly personal, sometimes creative, and always meaningful ways. They often share what the prior year has brought them, how faith (and their community) has sustained them, and their hopes for the future. It can be a powerful and very public opportunity for self-reflection, reconciliation, and healing.

Watch Night services provide customs and rituals that have long served Gullah Geechee communities since the days when people gathered in wooden "praise houses," like the still-standing Moving Star Hall Praise House on Johns Island, South Carolina (erected circa 1917), instead of churches. Carolyn "Jabulile" White of James Island, South Carolina, (just outside Charleston) shared some of that history in a 2011 interview:[45]

> [U]p through the 1950s, African Americans on James Island would walk down its dusty roads to the community praise house, pretty much the way they had done since slavery. From about 9 p.m. to midnight, those tiny worship places would be alive with joyful noises. The people would shout, sing, and pray. The structures frequently were built low to the ground with bare floors, and dust would rise when the faithful moved and beat the floor with a stick, keeping rhythm. Back then, they called the event Watch Night. They still do. ... It was strictly coming out to give God thanks for what they'd come through during the year and being glad to see another year.

As Watch Night moved into churches, some of those praise house traditions followed them, including the stationing of "Watchmen" in the church. The Watchmen, deacons or other elders in the community, keep careful time and signal by song to the congregation when midnight is near. "Watchman, Watchman, please tell us the hour of the night," the congregation

---

[45] Wevonneda Minis, "Watch Night: A tradition of hope—African-Americans ring in new year their way." *Charleston Post & Courier* (Charleston, SC, December 31, 2011).

periodically sings. Even those churches that no longer practice this tradition will still dim the lights near midnight to give notice that it is time for silent prayer and reflection.

Pastor Chad Nobles of Lighthouse Christian Center in Beaufort, South Carolina described in 2008 a common set of practices in Gullah Geechee churches that still maintain the Watch Night tradition. "Most African-American churches start around 10 o'clock and have a two-hour service. We also have a period of testimony thanking God for what He has done in 2008. About ten minutes before twelve o'clock, we go into prayer and go into the New Year on our knees."[46]

A few Gullah Geechee churches have also retained the old tradition of reading the Emancipation Proclamation aloud on Watch Night. In others, pastors and guest speakers may deliver messages that remind us that Emancipation Day may have bought freedom but the battle for equality and civil rights persists. Savannah's First African Baptist Church (organized in 1773) has a storied Watch Night and Emancipation Day tradition. In 2018, guest pastor Rev. Reginald T. Jackson brought the church to its feet when he addressed the congregation on the pressing challenges of a nation still beset by the scourges of "violence, hatred, and racism."[47] He called particular attention to the rising numbers of unarmed African Americans who were being summarily executed by police officers and the ways in which movements like Black Lives Matter demonstrated an enduring demand for racial and social justice.

Two years later, on February 23, 2020, Ahmaud Arbery, a Gullah Geechee descendant, was hunted, chased down, and executed by three White men while he was out jogging on a quiet neighborhood street in nearby Brunswick, Georgia. A witness reported that one of them said "fucking nigger" after three blasts from a shotgun left Arbery dying in the road.[48] It caused many in the community to invoke Georgia's history of lynchings and slave patrols. Ahmaud's death echoed another painful and recent memory in Gullah Geechee communities.

---

[46] Mark Allwood, "Area black churches bring in New Year—by marking 'Freedom's Eve'." *Beaufort Gazette* (Beaufort, SC, December 27, 2008).

[47] Jan Skutch, "Pastor Tells Crowd to Seek Out Answers With God," *Savannah Morning News* (Savannah, GA, January 2, 2018).

[48] Nathan Layne, "White defendant used racial slur after shooting Ahmaud Arbery, investigator testifies," Reuters. (June 4, 2020).

The Rev. Clementa Pinckney read the Emancipation Proclamation at Mother Emanuel AME's 2012 Watch Night service, which was internationally covered via Reuters.[49] "It's not just an African American celebration, it's an American celebration, akin to the Fourth of July … It's freedom come full circle," he told the congregation that night.

The lights inside the 194-year-old church were turned off shortly before midnight. In the dark, a succession of singers in a minute-by-minute countdown to the new year called, "Watchman, watchman, please tell me the hour of the night." The minister's response pierced the darkness. "It is three minutes to midnight," then "It is two minutes to the new year," then "Last chance to pray in 2012." Finally, "It is now the new year. Freedom has come."

It was a commemoration that foreshadowed more tragic memorials rooted in slavery to come for this congregation. Rev. Pinckney and eight members of his congregation were executed in their church three years later by a White supremacist and Confederate sympathizer who wanted to start a race war. A killer who had spent part of his time in the weeks leading up to the massacre visiting the McLeod Plantation Historic Site on James Island, and Boone Hall Plantation in nearby Mt. Pleasant—both places where ancestors of today's Gullah Geechee people had been enslaved.

Shared history and blood memory are the potent touchstone at the heart of the Watch Night and Emancipation Day tradition. Testimonials and impassioned homilies serving as the expression of a collective cry for justice, reconciliation, and atonement. In comments published in a local newspaper on New Year's Day in 2013, Charleston's Rev. Joseph Darby very publicly shared his testimony and plea.[50]

"I'm a graduate of the University of South Carolina, where I was thrown off the campus as a sixth grader with a profane warning from a campus policeman that he didn't want to see me there again unless I was wearing a green maintenance uniform. We've come a long way since Lincoln issued the Emancipation Proclamation and since subsequent legal guarantees of equal access and opportunity were enacted, but our national journey to freedom isn't over, because laws can't change hearts, minds or attitudes."

---

[49] Harriet McLeod, "Watch Night marks 150th anniversary of Lincoln's proclamation." Reuters. (January 1, 2013).
[50] Rev. Joseph A. Darby, "Come Together To Honor Emancipation," *The Charleston Post & Courier* (Charleston, SC, January 1, 2013).

The history surrounding the first Emancipation Day in 1863 demonstrates how deep the need for healing goes in light of the many unsung sacrifices and contributions that Gullah Geechee men and women have made since then to preserve the Union and to slowly transform a deservedly condemned slave society predicated on White supremacy into a more just and equal one. Their acts of valor, sacrifice, and unwavering patriotism have been met with violence by far too many of their fellow Southerners.

The depth of the ancestors' patriotism was on full display on Emancipation Day. On January 1, 1863, Gullah Geechee freedmen, White Union soldiers, and many others gathered at the military camp at Camp Saxon in Port Royal, South Carolina, to hear the reading of the proclamation. Colonel Thomas Wentworth Higginson was one of the White officers present when the Emancipation Proclamation was read for the first time. Higginson wrote about that historic day in his memoirs, recalling one particularly poignant event.[51] The audience was stunned into silence when three freedmen began to sing after the reading of the proclamation.

Higginson recalled that "there suddenly arose, close beside the platform, a strong male voice (but rather cracked and elderly), into which two women's voices instantly blended, singing, as if by an impulse that could no more be repressed than the morning note of the song-sparrow:

My Country, 'tis of thee,
Sweet land of liberty,
Of thee I sing!"

Others soon joined them. "Firmly and irrepressibly the quavering voices sang on, verse after verse; others of the colored people joined in; some Whites on the platform began, but I motioned them to silence. I never saw anything so electric."

The transformative power of this moment—of the jubilation of freedom mixed with a stunning patriotism for a country where they had been held in bondage—overwhelmed the audience. "It made all other words cheap; it seemed the choked voice of a race at last unloosed. Nothing could be more

---

[51] Thomas Wentworth Higginson, *Army Life in a Black Regiment.* (Cambridge, MA: Riverside Press. Originally published 1869, reprinted 1900).

wonderfully unconscious; art could not have dreamed of a tribute to the day of Jubilee that should be so affecting; history will not believe it; and when I came to speak of it, after it was ended, tears were everywhere."

The Gullah Geechee Watch Night and Emancipation Proclamation tradition is an opportunity for all Americans to revisit this remarkable history every year. It is a time to collectively reflect on how far we have come as a nation—or not—on our journey of racial reconciliation.

It is notable that an important part of the services are the hymns and spirituals preserved down through the generations and sung throughout the night just as they still are at Mt. Calvary. Spirituals are a uniquely African-American art form with well-documented, deep roots in the Gullah Geechee community. They were songs of Black suffering married to expressions of Christian faith that reflected the desire for freedom from sorrow and bondage. The first substantial collection of Negro spirituals to appear in the United States were collected in coastal South Carolina and published in the *Atlantic Monthly* in June 1867.[52]

One of them, "We'll Soon Be Free," reportedly landed some of the ancestors in a Georgetown, South Carolina, jail after they were caught singing it on the eve of the Civil War. The words of an old song took on new meaning and gave voice to the hope of the Gullah Geechee people for a long-dreamt-of freedom that ultimately would signal only the beginning of the many battles yet to come.

We'll soon be free,
We'll soon be free,
We'll soon be free,

---

[52] Thomas Wentworth Higginson, "Negro Spirituals." *Atlantic Monthly* (June 1857). The songs were collected by Higginson in the Union Army camps where he was stationed. "Often in the starlit evening I have returned from some lonely ride by the swift river, or on the plover-haunted barrens, and, entering the camp, have silently approached some glimmering fire, round which the dusky figures moved in the rhythmical barbaric dance the negroes call a 'shout,' chanting, often harshly, but always in the most perfect time, some monotonous refrain." The Gullah Geechee "shout" and "ring shout" is a religious expression featuring polyrhythmic percussion and call-and-response singing, which is sometimes accompanied by the shuffling movement of the worshipers in a circular (ring) formation. It is believed to be the oldest surviving African-American performance tradition.

When de Lord will call us home.
My brudder, how long,
My brudder, how long,
My brudder, how long,
Fore we done sufferin' here?
It won't be long (Thrice.)
'Fore de Lord will call us home.
We'll soon be free (Thrice.)
When Jesus sets me free.
We'll fight for liberty (Thrice.)
When de Lord will call us home.

The History of New Music in America

Horace Mungin

The first Africans upon the slave ships destined
For the Americas sensed the coming of
A great and lasting catastrophe
They had nothing that would
Protect and fortify them
From the coming centuries of bondage and tyranny
So they sent out an exalting wail
Beseeching God's mercy
God looked down on them and saw
That they had nothing
They were naked and in chains
God in His singular wisdom
Took the very sound of their lament
And turned it into their shield and their weapon
And today we call that sound music
It is those majestic wails
Those cries of despair
That music
In its ever-changing forms
From field holler to hip-hop
That has nourished our spirits through the centuries
A sound that spoke directly to On-high
For sustenance to keep the spirit
Unyielding to the horrors of shackled burdens
Feeble and conquered, music
Became our sacred shield
And our consecrated weapon.

Reconstruction

Black Women Writers as Dark Matter

Yvette R. Murray

Dark matter is more undefined by scientists than it is defined. It is a mysterious substance whose existence is observed only by its gravitational effect on planets, stars, and even entire galaxies. Simply put, dark matter holds our universe together.

The same can be said of our Black women. Our women have been the beating heart of every great movement in this country. We may not be the names remembered or even recognized. Nevertheless, we were there every step of the way, getting the difficult work done.

The arena of American literature is no exception. When a person has to fight so hard for their rights, they never, ever stop fighting. As Black women, all we see are boundaries, glass ceilings, and limitations. So we stay ready to dig our heels in and defy the odds. We achieve greatness in everything we do, from practicing medicine to astrophysics to creating literature. It is a treasured heirloom that we pass on from generation to generation.

Keep the year 1863 in mind. That, of course, is the year the Emancipation Proclamation abolished slavery in the slave-holding states on January 1. We are going on a literary journey through American history to look at some of the major Black female literary giants. Note that for each of the names mentioned herein, a dozen more exist who are unmentioned. These writers provide an intimate view of the totality of the Black experience. Their fiction is truth.

Examination of The Age of Phillis by Honorée Fanonne Jeffers reveals the scope of our literary travels. Phillis Wheatley is the subject. Her book, *Poems on Various Subjects, Religious and Moral*, was published in 1773 before the Revolutionary War, and while she was still considered property. Wheatley was the first person of African descent and the first American enslaved person to publish a book, and only the third American woman to do so. *The Age of Phillis* is a momentous achievement. The book was on the 2020 long list for the National Book Award. It represents a triumph in subject matter as well as form.

As research began, one of the most awe-inspiring truths discovered was the sheer number of Black woman writers at the beginning of our timeline. Some of these women had been born into slavery. Frances Ellen Watkins Harper, however, was born free in Baltimore. She lived from 1825 to 1911, and authored several books of poetry and a collection of short stories. She was also a prominent abolitionist and women's suffrage activist. In 1915, Myra Viola Wilds published her poetry collection, *Thoughts of Idle Hours*. Other notable Black woman writers of this period include Carrie Morgan Figgs, Carrie Williams Clifford, Olivia Bush-Banks, Hannah Crafts, Julia C. Collins, Harriet Ann Jacobs, Elizabeth Hobbs Keckley, and Harriet E. Wilson.

Moving forward we arrive at one of the most romanticized eras: the Harlem Renaissance. Lasting roughly from 1917 to 1937, it was a period of intense social and cultural development that began in Harlem, New York. Although it was centered there, the influence of these writers, poets, and activists had a global reach.

The Ku Klux Klan was founded in 1866 by ex-Confederate soldiers and other Southerners opposed to Reconstruction. Their membership and activities died down a little as Reconstruction progressed. However, they added others to their hate list — Catholics, Jews, and foreigners — and in the 1920s membership in this heinous organization ballooned into the millions. What a difficult time to tell Black stories. Did that stop our ladies? Not at all.

The Black women of the Harlem Renaissance were writers, poets, playwrights, essayists, literary critics, social critics, and editors. The sheer volume of their work is dizzying, and they often wrote in multiple genres.

Zora Neale Hurston's name is always mentioned in the same sentence as the great Langston Hughes when one speaks of the Harlem Renaissance. Her most famous work is *Their Eyes Were Watching God*, the story of a young Black woman's journey from her teenage years to womanhood. Attention to her many writings slacked after the Harlem Renaissance cooled. However, *Their Eyes Were Watching God* resonated with familiar themes of self-discovery, struggle for independence, and personal triumph. In the late twentieth century, there was renewed interest in her work. Then in 2005, the celebrated book became a movie of the same name starring Halle Berry and Michael Ealy.

Another major player was Jessie Redmond Fauset, born in 1882. She was a novelist and the editor of *The Crisis*, the official magazine of the NAACP. The first female graduate of Cornell University, one of eight Ivy League campuses noted for academic excellence, Fauset was also the first Black woman accepted into that university's chapter of Phi Beta Kappa, the nation's most prestigious academic honor society. Fauset published four novels, and her writing skill was said to parallel that of Hurston.

Angelina Weld Grimké, born in 1880, also was instrumental in the Harlem Renaissance. A poet, teacher, and playwright, Grimké penned *Rachel*, a play that dealt with the theme of lynching in America. When it premiered in 1916, it was the first play by an African-American woman to be publicly staged.

Against the horrifying backdrop of Jim Crow laws, frequent lynching, and overt racism, the writings of these phenomenal women bring many words to mind: bold, daring, poignant, and intense are just a few. They were not afraid to say what they had to say, standing toe-to-toe with their male contemporaries.

The foray into the modern era begins with another marvelous poet, Gwendolyn Brooks. She authored more than twenty books of poetry and a novel, *Maud Martha*. She was the first Black poet (and not the last) to win a Pulitzer Prize, and she served as the Illinois poet laureate for thirty-two years. Brooks was also the first Black woman appointed a poetry consultant to the Library of Congress.

Alice Walker arrives. A bestselling author, she wrote *The Color Purple*, which won the 1983 National Book Award and the Pulitzer Prize for fiction that same year. This fine piece of literature became an iconic movie of the same name. Walker wrote seven novels, four short story collections, four children's books, and volumes of essays and poetry. Covering themes of female struggle and liberation, her catalogue has been translated into more than two dozen languages and sold more than fifteen million copies.

In 2019 the world became a much more shallow place when we lost the literary genius, Toni Morrison. Morrison was a novelist, essayist, book editor, and college professor. She was brilliant and wove complicated tales that move effortlessly between reality, imagination, history, and the present day as if they were one. Morrison authored eleven novels, seven children's picture books with her son, the late Slade Morrison, and numerous short stories and essays.

Her novel, *Beloved*, won a Pulitzer Prize and was a National Book Award finalist. Her critically acclaimed book, *Song of Solomon*, won the National Book Critics Circle Award. She won the Nobel Prize in literature in 1993, and was the first Black woman to do so, and the first American woman to have won it in fifty-five years when she did. In 1996, the National Endowment for the Arts awarded her the Jefferson Lecture, America's highest award for achievement in the humanities. President Barack Obama awarded her the Presidential Medal of Freedom in 2012, and in 2016 she received the PEN/Saul Bellow Award for Achievement in American Fiction.

Ushering in Afro-futurism with a double-edged sword was Octavia E. Butler. Half writer, half prophet, Butler's books *Parable of the Sower* and *Parable of the Talents* seem to come from current headlines. We lost Butler in 2006, so we know these great works came from her immense imagination. Her writing is at once arresting, horrifying, and engaging. Her characters and themes touch chords of humanity that pull us in like luxurious literary quicksand.

Butler's novels garnered many awards. *Parable of the Sower* was a *New York Times* Notable Book of the Year in 1993. *Parable of the Talents* won the Nebula Award in 1995. She won both the MacArthur "Genius" Grant and the PEN West Lifetime Achievement Award, among many others. Butler was a visionary, and as such, her work is in high demand. More than two hundred universities use her novels and short stories in their curriculums. A graphic novel adaptation of her book *Kindred* is a *New York Times* bestseller, and her novel *Dawn* is currently being adapted for television. White male writers dominate the field of science fiction writing, yet this Black female writer brought her Black protagonists and Afrocentric themes to life with such precision and verve that the world had to notice. Through the door which she knocked down, many Black female sci-fi writers entered and have established themselves as luminaries. Nalo Hopkinson, Tananarive Due, and Nnedi Okorafor are three who immediately come to mind.

The idea of truth-telling with a capital "T" shines brightly in the 1619 Project created by *New York Times Magazine*'s journalist Nikole Hannah-Jones. Her opening essay, "Our democracy's founding ideals were false when they were written. Black Americans have fought to make them true," won the 2020 Pulitzer Prize. Other articles in the project showed the tremendous influence slavery has on politics, diets, criminal justice, healthcare, and even traffic patterns in Atlanta. The project contends that systemic racism is still alive and flourishing within every single American institution. Moreover, Black people deal with this every day. They drew the lines and connected the dots that nobody ever wanted to discuss.

Here's why Black women writers are dark matter. We were there on every step of the journey of the African in America, writing, creating, teaching, and advocating. Dark matter is invisible as many try to make us. However, the presence of dark matter is undeniable, as are we. Black women writers kept writing through slavery, Reconstruction, Jim Crow, and beyond Donald Trump. We never waited for anyone to lead us or ask us to help. We did the hard work. We do the hard work. We tell our stories. We are here holding this America together with our Black woman selves. And we will never stop doing that.

Good Troublemakers

Tim Conroy

Modjeska Simkins
December 5, 1999-April 5, 1992

Modjeska Simkins strategized change
from a small wood frame
on Marion Street, Columbia, South Carolina.

Hell-raiser, street fighter, insurgent
against the wrongs of the world.
"If it wasn't right, it needed to get right!"

No patience for the "ain't ready yet conclave."
Not a meek push but a shove for rights.
She poked her fingers into clavicles.

Modjeska Simkins churned out good
in a state as evil as homemade sin,
poured molten truth on lie, man, and Klan.

Forever today's reminder,
"We have a job laid out for us,
…this is no sitting-down time."

Now!

2.

"We shall not be moved"
(Edwards v. South Carolina)

On March 2, 1961
from Mt. Zion's holy doors

marched two hundred students of the light.
"All of whom were black."

Two-by-two from higher ground,
tyranny on their backs.

To shoo away the State House Crow,
close the cawing minstrel show.

"Down with segregation"
"You may jail our bodies, but not our souls."

Arrested for their truthful tongues,
breach of the peace for prophets' lungs.

It's unnerving to visit history
to feel the pain created

when people felt no wrong
to accept as right a sin.

These students sang the hymn
though hate will never end

unless all believe the song,
"We shall not be moved."

3.

Sarah Mae Flemming
Columbia, South Carolina

Sarah Mae at twenty
heroine of the city
conservator of dignity
of hard-working women
before brave Rosa Parks
sat in front of time
the invisible moving line
of a segregated city bus
knocking on equality
June 22, 1954

Notes: A version of "Sarah Mae Flemming" appeared in a booklet for a project
organized by Ed Madden, the poet laureate of Columbia, South Carolina, for their
bus system, The Comet. A version of "Modjeska Simkins" appeared on the South
Carolina Progressive Network's website.

The Womanist Blueprints of Reconstruction

Sara Makeba Daise

I've always known my subjectivities shape the questions I ask. As a queer Black Gullah Geechee woman, and the child of two griots, or storytellers, I have unique vantage points from which to explore how I got to be who I am, and how I might survive within, or imagine outside of this white supremacist patriarchal capitalist society. Loving myself fully has always required not only looking inward, but also acknowledging that the narratives I've been given to view the past and present are crooked[53] at best, spiritually bankrupt at worst. Furthermore, this rigid scope and forced linear timeline limits the future I believe I can hope for.

In the introduction to *All the Women are White, All the Blacks are Men, But Some of Us Are Brave*, Akasha Hull and Barbara Smith explain:

"Like any politically disenfranchised group, Black women could not exist consciously until we began to name ourselves.

"Merely to use the term 'Black women's studies' is an act charged with political significance. At the very least, the combining of these words to name a discipline means taking the stance that Black women exist—and exist positively—a stance that is in direct opposition to most of what passes for culture and thought on the North American continent."[54]

---

53 Melissa Harris-Perry, Sister Citizen: *Shame, Stereotypes, and Black Women in America* (New Haven: Yale University Press, 2011), 28-29.
54 Akasha (Gloria T.) Hull, Patricia Bell-Scott, and Barbara Smith, *But Some of Us Are Brave: Black Women's Studies*. (Old Westbury, N.Y.: The Feminist Press at CUNY, 1982), xvii. https://search-ebscohost-com.proxy.myunion.edu/login.aspx?direct=true&

It is with this focus that I engage the period known as Reconstruction. Much of what we understand about ourselves is sculpted through lenses of whiteness and maleness, excluding the minds, hearts, bodies, and actions of Black people, and non-cisgender heterosexual men.[55] Through these limited vantage points, we miss the many examples of resilience, choice, risk, and agency that Black people—namely women—embodied in the name of freedom. I recall learning a lot about different Black male leaders in my college African American history courses. It wasn't until finding my mother's copy of *In Search of Our Mothers' Gardens* that I began to realize there were far more perspectives and experiences than I'd been taught to search for, points of view that affirmed my own. My search for womanist praxis among Gullah Geechee women's resistance during Reconstruction stems from the safety, solace, and limitless possibilities I found in Alice Walker's and others' interpretations of womanism.

In *The Womanish Roots of Womanism: A Culturally-Derived and African-Centered Ideal*, Dorothy Randall Tsuruta claims that "womanish," an African American colloquialism Walker evokes in her definitions of womanism, confirms that the ideology is specifically and especially for Black women. "Womanish" carries images of Black girls with "wit, will, grit, smarts, empathy, curiosity, thoughtfulness, loyalty, risk-taking, trustworthiness, active not passive, pensiveness, and stubbornness as necessary to remain strong against attempts to undermine her intelligence or kill her spirit."[56] Tsuruta explains, "As a culturally-derived concept, womanish ... is rooted in the social practice of Black adults, especially Black women, setting boundaries for Black girls, but simultaneously recognizing their coming into their own as women ... but it also affirms the value and validity of African culture and is in the emancipatory and creative interest of African women and African people as a whole."[57]

Womanism is self-determination. It is care and accountability. It is self-love. It is acknowledging your reflection in the faces of your community. By

---

db=nlebk&AN=1158354&site=eds-live&scope=site.

[55] Patrick Garvin, "What does 'cishet' mean?," *The LGBTQ+ Experiment* (April 2019.)

[56] Dorothy Randall Tsuruta, "The Womanish Roots of Womanism: A Culturally-Derived and African-Centered Ideal (Concept)," *Western Journal of Black Studies* 36, no. 1 (Spring 2012): 4.

[57] Ibid.

gleaning our historical archives with this understanding, we are more likely to uncover expansive, unexpected examples of our resistance, survival, and constant community care.

Prioritizing my personal experiences in my historical research allows the ancestors to reveal affirmations of my complex lived reality and our collective, ever-present desires to be free. Regarding the years leading up to and following the gradual "end of slavery," Black women have loved fiercely, resisted violence, articulated desire, advocated for the political, spiritual, and physical well-being of themselves and their communities, and envisioned and manifested versions of freedom where they could be whole.

I am both a historian and an Afrofuturist, fully committed to non-linear time. To center the descendants of enslaved Africans presently known as Gullah Geechee people, I'm going to stretch the liminal boundaries of Reconstruction to include The Port Royal Experiment. Beginning in 1861, this era is often referred to as the Rehearsal for Reconstruction.

My father, Ron Daise, is the youngest of nine children of two Penn School graduates, and was raised on St. Helena Island, a Sea Island along the Atlantic coast of Beaufort County, South Carolina. In *Reminiscences of Sea Island Heritage*, he writes:

> Following the capture of St. Helena and the surrounding Sea Islands by Union troops during the Civil War, about 10,000 black inhabitants remained on the land deserted by the plantation owners and their families. The newly-freed slaves ... bought small farm plots of land, which had been confiscated for taxes. The White population steadied at about fifty residents for many years. The isolation of the island fostered a people with a unique language, Gullah, and a unique heritage, which includes being the source of the Union's first all-Black regiment, organized in 1862.

Black-and-white photos in both Leigh Richmond Miner's *Face of an Island* and Daise's *Reminiscences* illustrate the important roles the midwife and nursing class held in the community. "These members are prepared to search out illness or other special needs, offer first aid where indicated, give instructions on home management and food care, etc. Twice each year every home on the island of 6,000 people was visited through the combined efforts of this group, the nurse and her midwives or training class, and the agriculture instructors under the farm agent."[58] Of St. Helena Island's annual Baby Days, my grand-mother Kathleen Daise recalled:

"That was the day mothers took their babies to the Penn School campus to be weighed and measured. All the midwives were there. All the healthy babies received blue ribbons; others, honorable mention ... it taught mothers to try to keep their babies healthy. There were always a number of blue-ribbon babies because the mothers would try to live up to what the midwives were teaching them: how to care for the baby, how to bathe him, and what kind of food to give him."[59]

It is apparent that when given the resources (and honestly, even when we're not), we have always cultivated and nurtured our communities and acquired the tools needed to best do so. In Baby Days, I see remnants of the communal care and accountability common among Sea Islanders during the Rehearsal for Reconstruction. This annual initiative also directly addressed poor Black maternal and infant mortality rates.

I uncovered other examples of Gullah Geechee women's self-determination. In "Sweet Dreams of Freedom: Freedwomen's Reconstruction of Life and Labor in Lowcountry South Carolina," Leslie Schwalm includes an anecdote from former slave owner Charles Manigault. He writes of a formerly enslaved woman named Peggy. Manigault, like many other Lowcountry planter families, abandoned his plantation as Union General William T. Sherman's troops approached. Numerous plantations along the coast were virtually free of Whites, as the formerly enslaved flexed their freedom muscles for the first time. Planters have shared stories of Gullah Geechee people raiding the big house in their absence. Manigault wrote:

"Peggy 'seized as Her part of the spoils my wife's Large & handsome Mahogany Bedstead & Mattrass & arranged it in her own Negro House on which she slept for some time'... Peggy also confiscated from the Manigault residence 'some Pink Ribands, & tied in a dozen bows the woolly head of her Daughter, to the admiration of the other Negroes.' "[60]

Manigault's account paints an image of an audacious woman. When he and his son, a former overseer and Confederate officer, returned to the plantation

---

[58] Leigh Richmond Miner, *Face of an Island*, (Columbia: The R. L. Bryan Company, 1970).

[59] Ronald Daise, *Reminiscences of Sea Island Heritage: Legacy of Freedmen on St. Helena Island*, (Orangeburg, SC: Sandlapper Publishing, Inc., 1986), 54.

[60] Leslie A. Schwalm, "'Sweet Dreams of Freedom': Freedwomen's Reconstruction of Life and Labor in Lowcountry South Carolina," *Journal of Women's History* 9, no. 1 (1997): 9.

to collect their confiscated belongings, "Only Peggy ... tried to intervene: placing her arms akimbo, said, 'She would go off to the Provost Marshal in town & stop our unlawful proceedings with their property in their own homes.'"[61] Tsuruta would likely describe Peggy as "womanish."

Women like Peggy worked to shape their freedom both before and after the Civil War. At no time were women of African descent the silent, passive characters in the transition to freedom as scholars once claimed. For example, southern freedwomen refusing to return to the fields in order to align themselves with the femininity of White women was a commonly accepted narrative. Schwalm, however, offers a more nuanced interpretation. She writes, "In Lowcountry South Carolina, freedwomen escalated the battle to define black freedom when they sought autonomous control over plantation lands, when they negotiated and reconstructed plantation and domestic labor, and when they defended the new autonomy of their families and household economies from exploitation by planters and unwelcome intervention by northern agents of Reconstruction."[62] Labor contracts brokered by the Freedmen's Bureau support the claim that freedwomen were strategic about the work they did, and when and how they did it. They preferred to be at home with their families, attend to their homes and their loved ones. They were concerned with reuniting lost family members, engaging in politics, and access to education.[63]

Unsurprisingly, Black women continued to resist and survive sexual violence at the hands of men—regardless of race, status, or political association—even after slavery. Due to President Abraham Lincoln and the Republican Party broadening the scope of rape to include violations of Black women, "U.S. military courts prosecuted at least 450 cases involving sexual crimes during the war, many of them brought by black women."[64] Black women took advantage of the limited safety they had under the law before the federal government pulled the Freedmen's Bureau out. They would also take time off from work to participate in politics. Although Emancipation didn't give freed women the

---

[61] Ibid.
[62] Ibid.
[63] Kate Côté Gillin, *Shrill Hurrahs: Women, Gender, and Racial Violence in South Carolina, 1865-1900.* (Columbia, US: University of South Carolina Press, 2013): 21.
[64] Crystal N. Feimster, "The Impact of Racial and Sexual Politics on Women's History," *Journal of American History 99*, no. 3 (December 2012): 258.

right to vote, they'd travel to the polls to ensure their men voted appropriately and in favor of the whole.[65] In the case of an election riot in Macon, Georgia, a newspaper reported, "The Negro women, if possible, were wilder than the men. They were seen everywhere, talking in an excited manner, and urging the men on. Some of them were almost furious, showing it to be part of their religion to keep their husbands and brothers straight in politics."[66] The freedwomen took advantage of every opportunity freedom offered.

I offer two more blueprints for Black women's ownership of their bodies and potential relationships. Tera Hunter writes of a freedwoman who lived with "each of her two husbands for a two-week trial before making a decision … in one case, perhaps unique, a wife resumed her relationship with her first husband, while the second husband, a much older man, was brought into the family as a 'poor relation.'"[67] The domestic slave trade forced marital separation. In some cases, ex-slaves had more than one spouse, as marriages during slavery weren't considered legal, and spouses who were sold were often presumed dead.

With these stories, we see freed women taking the "awkward dilemmas" into their own hands and deciding for themselves with whom they'd share their time, hearts, and homes.[68] We've always had options. And we deserve to be choosy.

Whether engaging in politics, feeding families on unfair wages, intentionally choosing their partners, or decorating their daughters' hair, freedwomen refused to be limited. This is the truth of who we are. And these miraculous manifestations of freedom are our birthrights and legacies. While the violent White supremacist patriarchal capitalist opposition continues to morph, exploit, and consume—century after century—it is our responsibility to tap into the expansiveness of our power, and our ancestors' dreams for us. We must engage the timelines that affirm we have always been free, and we can only do so if we are listening for and seeking out all of our voices. We came before these oppressive systems, and if our free, and enslaved, and liberated,

---

[65] Tera W. Hunter, *To 'Joy My Freedom: Southern Black Women's Lives and Labors after the Civil War*. (Harvard University Press, 1997.): 32.
[66] Ibid., 33.
[67] Ibid., 39.
[68] Ibid.

and repatriated, and willfully traveling, and ever-mobile, ever-present ancestors didn't see limits, why do we? With a fuller picture and deeper dive into the archive, we see examples of Black women re-imagining and reconstructing freedom for all of us in every timeline, at every turn.

The Reconstruction

Horace Mungin

She was black
Her dress was black
Her aura was black
A familiar blackness
An all-knowing blackness
Everything about her was that
Blackness that provokes awakening.

She flew in from the East
Her destination was all-encompassing
Every heart and every soul
And from her eyes an inborn
Truth scattered
Her smile was love—shared
And her voice roared like a teardrop.

We stood there in silent and complete
Submission
To the axiom of the Universal
Host
Our hearts merged to one
As we sailed to a new and different
Harbor
The words of our souls
Became a song of a
Sameness.

And the reach of her supremacy
Covered the earth
And all the galaxies
As we sailed to a peace and
Oneness.

And it is on the wings
Of this spirit
We shall all have arrived.

Lynching

Confronting Lynching in South Carolina. Finally.

Stephen G. Hoffius

In the fall of 2016, a large group gathered in Abbeville County, South Carolina, to dedicate an historical marker to the memory of Anthony Crawford. Crawford wasn't a noted politician or Civil War general, not an award-winning scientist or musician. He was a successful Black farmer, fifty-six years old, owner of more than four hundred acres, who in 1916 dared to question the price of cottonseed. For his impertinence, he was beaten, stabbed, shot, and hanged.

Normally, Crawford then would have been forgotten by the historical record. He was one of about 180 South Carolinians who have been lynched since the end of Reconstruction, about 90 percent of them African Americans. Almost none of these victims are remembered by more than a handful of family members. (One of the few who gained widespread attention was Willie Earle, the last to be lynched in South Carolina, in Pickens County in 1947. His case drew national coverage, though none of the thirty-one men who were tried for his murder was ever sentenced.)

In many cases no trial was ever held, though in most instances (nearly all the lynchings took place in small towns or rural areas) the perpetrators, who often felt no need to conceal their identities, were surely known. Often the victim was already arrested; a group of men knocked on the door of the city jail and announced they had a prisoner to deliver; the sheriff or one of his men opened the door and was then pushed aside while the crowd took the victim into the night. One wonders how much resistance the law officers offered.

Sometimes the crowd of killers was small and sometimes it was huge (several hundred wasn't uncommon).

Sometimes the victim was lynched because a jury trial didn't deliver as harsh a verdict as the local mob expected. For instance, Jack Williams was pulled from the Orangeburg jail in 1881 because, although a jury had found him guilty of "an outrageous assault" on a ten-year-old White girl, the jurors asked for mercy for him; that is, life in prison rather than the death penalty. A crowd of 150 broke him out of jail and hanged him. In 1926 in Aiken County three Lowman siblings, Bertha, Demon, and Clarence, the latter who was fourteen at the time, were murdered because they were either found not guilty of possession of illegal whiskey or were expected to be acquitted.

Sometimes the crime for which someone was murdered was serious, like murder or rape. Sometimes it was trivial, as in the case of farmer Anthony Crawford in Abbeville. Robert Pope of Hampton County was shot and then his throat was slit in 1890 because he was considered "obnoxious." His 11-year-old son, Willie Pope, just happened to be with his father; he ran away, was captured, brought back to his father's corpse, and his throat was "cut to the bone." Isaac Lincoln of Oconee County was murdered in 1893 for insulting a White woman; Hardy Gill was murdered in Lancaster in 1894 when he struck a White woman while having a seizure; a Black man in Spartanburg County was murdered in 1894 because of a sexual incident two years earlier, though the woman in the case apparently became infatuated with him and wanted to run away with him; "General" Lee of Dorchester County was murdered in 1904 because he knocked on a woman's door, frightening her, then ran away (or, rather, someone knocked on her door, as the woman, who knew Lee, never identified him as the knocker); Kitt Bookhard was murdered in Berkeley County in 1904 for quarreling with a White friend; Arthur Davis of Florence County was murdered in 1909 for injuring a mule; Joe Brinson and Frank Whisonant of Cherokee County were murdered in 1912 after an evening of drinking and oral sex with a White man; Willie Green of Florence County was murdered in 1914 for sneaking under a house, apparently intending to steal chickens, and frightening a white woman; and W. T. Sims of York was murdered in 1917 for harboring "antiwhite sentiments."

Sometimes there was one victim, but other times many people were killed. For instance, five men were murdered in York County in May 1887 because they supposedly had killed a young man while stealing cotton. Eight men were already imprisoned in Barnwell on December 28, 1889, and were dragged from the jail and shot to death before they could be tried; two of them were charged merely with having witnessed a murder. And eight men (possibly twelve, no one knows) in the town of Phoenix, in Greenwood County, were murdered over several days in November 1898 because they insisted on their right to vote; no one was ever charged for these murders. In addition, John Hammond Moore explains in *Carnival of Blood: Dueling, Lynching, and Murder in South Carolina 1880-1920*, "During the height of lynching, the decades from 1880 to 1920, there were at least ten double lynchings, and on four occasions black trios that included one female were killed almost simultaneously…."

In 1921 Bill McCallister was lynched in the Black River section of Williamsburg County for having a consensual relationship with a White woman. After his murder he was found to have in his pocket a letter from the woman in question, who wrote him, "I thought of you all during the show last night, and wanted you with me. It is too bad that we cannot be together always. My love for you is greater than you can imagine. Sometimes I become so disgusted with conditions in Florence that I want to leave and go some place where people are sensible, where I can at least walk the streets with you in the daytime without danger and fear. You often impress on me the fact that you are Colored and can't take any chances. I know that, darling, but love is greater than color in my case, and we must do the best we can until both of us are in position to leave Florence." It was signed, "Devoted." The murder was exceedingly controversial, but not because of the nature of the crime; a Williamsburg newspaper claimed, "Officials here state that it is an injustice to have this affair laid at Williamsburg when it actually happened in Florence, five miles from the Williamsburg county line."

In 1933 Norris Dendy, a Black truck driver, was beaten, shot, and strangled after he and a White truck driver argued, supposedly about whose truck was faster, after driving crowds to a Fourth of July picnic at Lake Murray near

Columbia. The state grand jury refused to indict the five men who were thought to be leaders of the mob responsible for the lynching.

Almost none of these crimes is noted in county histories, certainly not in most state histories (though Walter Edgar's *South Carolina Encyclopedia* has an entry for "Lynchings" and tells us of the 1898 Phoenix massacre and the Lowman siblings' lynchings, both mentioned above).

But the Equal Justice Initiative (EJI), founded by attorney Bryan Stevenson and based in Montgomery, Alabama, has sought to draw attention to the issue and, more specifically, to the victims of lynching. At the group's very moving National Memorial for Peace and Justice, each of the eight hundred counties in the country in which a lynching has taken place is represented by a monument, similar to a coffin, and has inscribed on it the names and dates of its lynching victims. The memorials are all hung from the ceiling, and the floor rises and falls, like a hill, so the viewer seems to lift up to them, and then drift away. EJI encourages local communities to erect markers to their own lynching victims.

Not many South Carolina counties have stepped forward, but a few have.

The Anthony Crawford memorial in Abbeville County was installed as part of EJI's Community Remembrance Project, which engaged the people of Abbeville in extensive activities meant to acknowledge a part of their history long hidden. School children wrote essays on racial justice, and four of them received $5,000 scholarships. Church services and seminars were held. Crawford's descendants gathered dirt from the site where he was murdered and placed it in a glass jar to be displayed at EJI's Legacy Museum in Montgomery. (Few of his descendants still live near Abbeville because, according to EJI, "Days after the lynching, Abbeville's White residents 'voted' to expel the Crawford family from the area and seize the property. When South Carolina's governor declared himself powerless to protect the family from violence, most of the surviving relatives fled to destinations as distant as New York and Illinois, fragmenting the once strong and close-knit family.")

Other communities in South Carolina have also reached out to EJI in hopes of tearing off the blinders that so many of us have worn when the subject of lynching turns up.

In researching the murder of Andrew McKnight in Union County in 1889,

I found an account posted by the Union County Community Remembrance Project (UCCRP), which "seeks to document and recognize the history of lynching and racial terrorism in Union County. We seek to foster ongoing collaborative education, justice, and healing." (The Equal Justice Initiative recognizes four lynchings in Union County, while the UCCRP has identified twenty-two, "from the Union County Jail Raid in 1871 which was one of the largest Klan jail raids in the southeast through lynchings as late as 1934.") With the help of EJI, the Union County group has erected one marker to the lynchings and hopes to set up another.

The Community Remembrance Project of Greenville County has been working for four years to address Greenville's lynching history. The project is a partnership between a diverse collection of organizations in the Upstate, including churches, schools (Furman University and the University of South Carolina Upstate in Spartanburg, among them), civil rights groups, and more. At least four individuals were lynched in Greenville County, including George Green, a tenant farmer in Taylors, in 1933. Green's landlord tried to kick him off his land, and when Green challenged that decision, the landlord reached out to the Ku Klux Klan. A group of men broke into Green's house and shot him to death.

The markers and other recognitions of lynching in South Carolina will never undo the horrors that took place in the state, but they are first steps in acknowledging one of the darkest parts of the state's history.

A good introduction to lynching in South Carolina is John Hammond Moore, *Carnival of Blood: Dueling, Lynching, and Murder in South Carolina 1880-1920* (Columbia: University of South Carolina Press, 2006). Moore includes an appendix that lists about 180 different lynchings in the state, from 1880 to 1947. He describes many of the lynchings cited in this essay: Hardy Gill, 65; the 1894 Spartanburg murder, 69; "General" Lee, 70-71; Kitt Bookhard, 72; Arthur Davis, 75; Joe Brinson and Frank Whisonant, 76-77; W. T. Sims, 80-81; the five lynchings in York County in 1887, 64, 206; the eight lynchings in Barnwell County in 1889, Moore, 61-62; and the Phoenix lynchings, 52-53, 56, 58. The quotation "During the height of lynching..." is from 58.

The Jack Williams lynching was described in *The Charleston News and Courier*, October 10, 14, 15, 1881; as was the Isaac Lincoln lynching, June 2, 1893.

The State (Columbia) covered the Willie Green lynching on December 5, 1914.

The Lowman lynchings are described in Walter Edgar, ed., *The South Carolina Encyclopedia* (Columbia, SC: University of South Carolina Press, 2006), 570, as is the Phoenix riot, 719.

The Robert and Willie Pope lynchings are described on the website "Strange Fruit and Spanish Moss," which covers many other murders as well, in South Carolina and across the country. (originally from the *Atlanta Constitution*, February 28, 1890; posted June 20, 2015; consulted January 6, 2022)

The Bill McCallister lynching is cited in Ralph Ginzburg, *100 Years of Lynchings* (Baltimore, Maryland: Black Classic Press, 1962), quoting the *Memphis Commercial Appeal*, January 14, 1922.

The Norris Dendy lynching has been described in detail in a report by Rieko Shepherd, "The Lynching of Norris Dendy, May 29, 1900-July 4, 1933," Civil Rights and Restorative Justice, repository.library.northeastern.edu (consulted Apr. 26, 2021).

The Anthony Crawford historic marker dedication is described in "Hundreds Dedicate Lynching Marker to Anthony Crawford in Abbeville, South Carolina," Oct. 24, 2016, eji.com (consulted April 21, 2021).

What Blinded Eyes

Tim Conroy

When Sgt. Isaac Woodard was discharged in 1946
and rode a bus home to South Carolina,
I was not born and had no eyes for him.

When Sgt. Woodard still in uniform
asked the driver to use the washroom,
and reasoned "I am a man just like you,"
I was not born and had no eyes for him.

When the police chief of Batesburg
blackjacked Sgt. Woodard's eyes to craters,
I was not born and had no eyes for him.

And when Jim Crow America saw
African American World War II veterans
pin their medals to ragdoll jobs,
I was not born and had no eyes for them.

But what of my sight now?

I never viewed myself as the White
bus driver angered at how Sgt. Woodard
held his gaze and liberated himself.

I never viewed myself as the White
soldier who did nothing
when Sgt. Woodard was ordered off the bus.

And I never viewed myself as the White
police chief who gouged Sgt. Woodard's eyes
and bloodied him.

Though I must see I am them—
privileged, obedient, blind
turning off the latest lynching on TV
never doing enough— not then, not now.

What blinded eyes must see of me.

Note: Details of the Sgt. Isaac Woodard blinding came from the true account, *Un-exampled Courage: The Blinding of Sgt. Isaac Woodard and the Awakening of President Harry S. Truman and Judge J. Waties Waring* by Judge Richard Gergel. "What blinded eyes..." is after a line in "Staggerlee wonders" by James Baldwin.

The Lake City Lynching Sermon

Ernest L. Wiggins

Today's message is taken from the Book of Ida. And we read:
"Feb. 22d. 1898, at Lake City, SC, Postmaster Baker and his infant child were burned to death by a mob that had set fire to his house. Mr. Baker's crime was that he had refused to give up the post office, to which he had been appointed by the National Government. The mob had tried to drive him away by persecution and intimidation. Finding that all else had failed, they went to his home in the dead of night and set fire to his house, and as the family rushed forth they were greeted by a volley of bullets. The father and his baby were shot through the open door, and wounded so badly they fell back in the fire and were burned to death. The remainder of the family, consisting of the wife and five children, escaped with their lives from the burning house, but all of them were shot, one of the number made a cripple for life."[69]

As we consider our present circumstances, let's take a moment to look back through the prism of history and reflect on earlier travails. Our purpose is to glean wisdom from those who have gone before.

We are all aware that Ida B. Wells-Barnett, who lived from 1862 to 1931, just shy of seventy years, is set in the panoply of human rights champions and Black liberation. Her scrupulous accounts of the murderous treatment of Blacks around the country in the decades after Emancipation are evidence

---

[69] Ida B. Wells-Barnett, *On Lynchings* (Mineola, NY: Dover Publications, Inc. 2014), 79.

that she was one of the bravest and most trusted of our nation's early African American scribes. Her companion in that brilliant array of justice warriors, abolitionist and author Frederick Douglass, wrote of her work: "There has been no word equal to it in convincing power. I have spoken, but my word is feeble in comparison."[70]

Wells-Barnett's accounts of lynching, mostly of Black men, are an invaluable record of the systematic oppression of African Americans, how members of a nation conceived in liberty conspired to dominate others and annihilate those it could not control. From Wells-Barnett's reports we learned that "America was failing to confront the lingering injustices left by chattel slavery or the morbid practices of white supremacy and legalized racial segregation." We argue the same today.

There is abundant evidence of America's early failings, but we need look no further than today's reading, taken from Wells-Barnett's report on mob rule published in 1900. The account of the lynching of duly authorized postmaster Frazier Baker and his infant daughter, Julia, and the White mob's attempt to entrap and burn alive all eight members of the Baker family, is horrifying and shocking, made even more so because it is indisputable.

Uncontrollable white resentment had poisoned the little town of Lake City, South Carolina — and towns and cities all over the South.

Before that tragic night, Baker, his wife, Lavinia, and their six children lived in Effingham, South Carolina, a predominately Black town where Baker was postmaster. Historians[71, 72] tell us that President William McKinley's appointment of Baker in July 1897 to run the post office in Lake City was supported by Republicans in the South Carolina State House, but, looking back, it is seen

---

[70] Frederick Douglass, *Letter from Frederick Douglass to Ida B. Wells; October 25, 1892.* In Shaun L. Gabbidon, Ph.D.; Helen Taylor Greene, Ph.D.; Vernetta Diane Young, Ph.D. (eds.). *African American Classics in Criminology and Criminal Justice.* (Thousand Oak, CA: Sage Publications), p. 25.

[71] David Carter, *Newspaper Reactions to Baker Lynching.* (Unpublished Paper, 2012) http://racialviolenceus.org/Articles/carter_lake_city_reactions_20130323.pdf. Accessed April 23, 2021.

[72] Trichita M. Chestnut, "Lynching: Ida B. Wells-Barnett and the Outrage over the Frazier Baker Murder," *Prologue Magazine*, Fall 2008, Vol. 40, No. 3 (College Park, MD.: National Archives).

by many as just a bone thrown to those insisting on more positive action on behalf of Black people. White Lake City residents who loudly opposed Baker's appointment harassed and undermined him and called for his removal. They filed bogus claims against him, charging incompetence and mismanagement and demanding he be fired. They charged him with being disrespectful and exhibiting inappropriate behavior toward White women. Baker's supervisors dismissed the allegations as groundless. In response, a White mob burned down the post office.

What you can't achieve by lying, you get by violence.

Baker did not give in to intimidation. He moved the post office to his home. Harassment intensified; Whites resented having to go to Baker's home — on the edge of town in the Black community — to get their mail. Further efforts to slander and sully him were also rebuffed, so the mob torched the Baker home. The remains of the postmaster and his daughter Julia were recovered from the rubble; Frazier Baker had been Lake City postmaster less than a year.

News of the night of terror rang out across the country. The attackers were called animals. The Southland tossed on the ash heap as barbaric and unsalvageable.

We all know that for all of its promise, Reconstruction failed to unite the nation or improve the lives of Black people in any real way. National leaders failed to recognize or respond to the determination of the enemies of Black progress to undercut the very oath the nation supposedly rallied around— liberty and justice for all. Loyalty pledges and solidarity oaths meant nothing to those who committed to acting in bad faith. So, what is this bad faith?

It is lying and misleading when dealing with others to gain advantage over them. It is promising with no intention of making good on your word. It is going through the motions solely for the sake of appearance.

And bad faith snaked through the aftermath of the Lake City lynching.

Thirteen White men, described in *The New York Times*[73] as merchants and farmers of Lake City and the vicinity, were identified and arrested in connection with the Baker deaths. They were charged not with murder but with conspiring to deny Frazier and Julia Baker's civil rights. The charge, while

---

[73] "The Lake City Lynching: Thirteen Men Indicted in a Federal Court for the Alleged Murder of Negro Postmaster," *The New York Times*, (Saturday, April 8, 1899) 1.

certainly true, is unspeakably reductive of the men's murderous actions. The trial was held in Charleston, South Carolina, but despite the judge describing the case as "the blackest ever perpetrated in South Carolina,"[74] the jury could not decide unanimously to convict, mainly because of the absence of compelling eyewitness testimony. The judge ruled a mistrial and all of the accused were freed. Federal prosecutors later said finding reliable witnesses in Lake City would be impossible so they chose not to go to trial again. Bad faith denied the Baker family justice.

Lavinia Baker and her surviving children found shelter in the Black community for a time and eventually moved to Charleston and then Boston. Even though Frazier Baker was lynched for executing his duties as postmaster, his family received no remuneration from the government. Wells-Barnett pleaded with McKinley and members of Congress to make it right. But congressional bills introduced by northern delegates were squashed by their southern counterparts.

The Bakers were essentially abandoned by their government, which was busy from April to August in 1898 warring with Spain.

A monumental display of bad faith.

In 1899, the famous abolitionist and author William Lloyd Garrison posted an appeal in *The New York Times* asking for private support for the "pitiable" Baker children, who needed shelter and schooling.[75] As providence would have it, Lavinia Baker and her family remained in Boston, but over the course of the next twenty years, her children would be taken by the ravages of tuberculosis. The mother would return to South Carolina after the death of her last child in 1942. Lavinia Baker, herself, the last survivor of Lake City lynching, would die in 1947.

Yes, we are too far removed in time from 1898 to say absolutely but it looks like Frazier and Julia Baker were sacrificed on the altar of political expediency. We might well ask if President McKinley saw little benefit in coming to the aid of the small-town Black postmaster in South Carolina whom he had placed in jeopardy. The stakes were too low to merit his intervention. We

---

[74] Ibid.
[75] William Lloyd Garrison. "To Aid the Baker Family," *The New York Times*, (Saturday, September 23, 1899) 6.

might also ask why Baker's superiors did not suspect tensions and animosity would continue to build and authorize more protection, especially after White residents' demands for Baker's removal were denied. Were postal chiefs that vain or that naïve? Why did they abandon Baker's family after he was taken from them so horribly? Was it because Baker's widow and children were of no political use to the government?

But we look about us today, at the resurgence in White supremacist activity, at callous indifference among elected officials, at leaders abandoning the most vulnerable who suffer because of the incompetence or misdirection of their leaders, and wonder if we really are so far removed from our ancestors.

The great American lawyer Clarence Darrow was a famous agnostic, but he was also an ardent defender of civil rights. In the Sweet Trials of 1925 and 1926, Darrow defended a Black Detroit dentist, Ossian Sweet, and eleven of his friends who were charged with conspiracy to commit murder after shots were fired and a man killed while Sweet and the others were defending the dentist's home from threatening Whites who opposed Sweet moving into their neighborhood.

Darrow's successful defense of Sweet depicted the nation's justice system as mired in racial imbalance and prejudice. Darrow, who had been enlisted by the NAACP to lead the defense, is reported to have said, "History repeats itself, and that's one of the things that's wrong with history." I take Darrow to mean this: history can hardly be called history if it is indeed the present.

Amen and Amen.

What Mama Says

Elizabeth Robin

Don't think I'm haunted, 'xactly, not haunted, no
but I cain't get one picture outta my mind. Truth
mean seein' clear, 'n here what I see: a mother shot
jus' watched her husband die, the bullet what wounded
her kilt the baby in her arms, pieces of brains 'n blood
staining her shoulder, she lookin' back, see her man 'n baby
burn, her house collapsin' on 'em, sky bright past midnight
wit' their flames, 'n she turn, rushin' her three bleedin' chillen
'cross the street, push 'em under bushes, where they crouch
untended by doctor or friend or food or drink for three days
whilst she wonder where her other two chillen be

Mama say the Truth will set you Free
 But I's feelin' trapped inside this Truth

Amongst thirteen men charged, my great grandfather big 'n bold
on that list, indicted, tried 'n acquitted on all charges, including
killin' the Postmaster 'n his baby — a father and his baby

So I ain't feelin' free, just full 'o questions —
 Did my Mama know this story? My Granma?

'Course they musta knowed, thinkin' Lake City history ripe in
atonement —
The year my granddaughter born, we voted, in 2011 to build a science
museum
in Ron McNair's name — 'N the year her mama gradiated high school,
whole town,

74

in 2003, placed a historical marker on the empty South Church Street lot
to tell the story of Frazier and Julia Baker's lynching, 'n you knows since
1986 Ron McNair Boulevard crosses South Church Street — honorin' him.

Why? Atonement, maybe. Late as 1955 — Thas the year I's born — the
Greater St. James AME Church, set on the site of that 1898 fire and
lynching, burned,
I hear 'cause their preacher talkin' civil rights. T'ain't a pretty hist'ry, but
it our'n.

— in 1950 Ron McNair born here, becomes
valedictorian, MIT graduate, laser specialist
renaissance man, Challenger astronaut
'n the town's favorite black son — All them what saw the fire, musta heard
the shots: All them Christians —
Where was they? We got sixty-one churches in Lake City—sixty-one

congregations maybe gone blind? Why didn't they petition for gov'ment
pensions due, get 'em Christian charity? Ain't Christian, but Lake City

folk did it in 1898 'n before 'n after, and ain't nobody serve justice —
Remember the *Maine* but not Frazier Baker, 'n the stain spreads, don't it?

Mama say the Truth will set you Free
But if'n we cain't see it, we won't never be free.

I still can't get that picture outta my head, outta my dreams, haunts
as sure as that shootin' happened. Does a sign, a museum, atone enough?

Saved by the New Deal, Killed by the New Deal: Benjamin J. Rivers of Wadmalaw Island

Kerry Taylor

Before sunrise on April 29, 1938, Benjamin J. Rivers spent his last hour alive singing hymns in his cell on death row at the state penitentiary in Columbia, South Carolina. It had been nearly two years since the 46-year-old Black maritime worker had survived an exchange of gunfire with a White Charleston police detective that left the officer, Purse A. Wansley, dead. "Tell Mother and Father I will meet them in heaven," Rivers said to a guard before walking unassisted to the death chamber. "As far as I know I have told the truth," he whispered as he was strapped to the electric chair. "I've told all I have to say." The state electrician administered the fatal shock and Rivers was pronounced dead three minutes later.[76, 77] A long ordeal ended for Rivers. Over the previous twenty-two months, he had survived a vicious assault, a botched arrest, and a

---

[76] "Rivers Pays with his Life," *Charleston Evening Post* (April 29, 1938) and "Negro Dies for Police Slaying," *Orangeburg Times and Democrat* (April 30, 1938). One hundred and thirty-five men preceded Rivers in the South Carolina death chair beginning in 1912 when the state adopted electrocution as a more humane and efficient alternative to hanging. The author thanks Ariel Washington for joining him in the search for Benjamin Rivers at the earliest stages of this study.

[77] Sam W. Cannon served as state electrician from 1919 to 1957.

serious gunshot wound. He had eluded a week-long manhunt and two Charleston lynch mobs and endured disorienting police interrogations while being shuttled around jails in Charleston and Columbia. He had been convicted of murder and sentenced to death by an all-White jury. And in his final days, Rivers had lost his case on appeal and his last-ditch bid for clemency was rejected.

In its outlines, the story of Benjamin Rivers's state-sanctioned murder is the story of most of the 465 human beings legally executed in South Carolina since the Civil War. Eighty percent of them have been African American and have had little chance for a fair trial in South Carolina's racist criminal justice system.[78] The vast majority have also been poor and had no means to finance an adequate legal defense. A closer look at Rivers's case makes the likelihood of his guilt improbable while exposing a legal process compromised by its "overt attention to the emotional satisfaction of the white majority."[79] At the same time, Rivers's ordeal reveals complexities and contingencies that emerged from South Carolina's shifting political terrain in the 1930s. It highlights the promise of Black activism and New Deal reform even as it haunts us with painful reminders of their lethal limitations.

In the early evening of Monday, July 13, 1936, Rivers finished work as a "mess boy" in the galley aboard the Charleston-based *Cypress*, a United States Lighthouse Service tender that maintained coastal buoys and lighthouses from the New River in North Carolina to the Hillsboro Inlet in Florida. The Charleston resident and Wadmalaw Island native had worked on the *Cypress* with few interruptions for about thirteen years. Rivers met up with his neighbor Isaac Brown and several acquaintances at a second-floor apartment on the corner of Magazine and Logan Streets.[80] The group played cards and shared pulls from a pint of whiskey through the late evening hours until playful "bull-dosing" or teasing turned to threats of violence and brought an

---

[78] Since resuming executions in 1985, South Carolina has killed 26 White people and 17 African Americans. This recent shift reflects political sensitivity to criticisms regarding racial disparities and the death penalty. All data related to the death penalty is drawn from the Death Penalty Information Center. https://deathpenaltyinfo.org/executions/executions-overview/executions-in-the-u-s-1608-2002-the-espy-file

[79] The phrasing is borrowed from historian Seth Kotch's study of the death penalty in North Carolina (see Kotch, *Lethal State: A History of the Death Penalty in North Carolina* [Chapel Hill, NC: University of North Carolina Press 2019], 205).

[80] Brown is alternately referred to as Isaiah Brown.

end to the gathering. As he exited the apartment, Rivers was assaulted from behind by partygoer Francis Middleton who struck him with a metal object that opened a bloody gash on the top of his head. Vowing revenge, Rivers and Brown headed home to retrieve a pistol. Fearing backlash, Middleton and his uncle Lymus Simmons sought protection at police headquarters at Vanderhorst and St. Philip streets about seven blocks away. Simmons may have been more inclined to seek police assistance than most Afro-Charlestonians. Simmons, like Rivers, was a maritime worker and at least casually acquainted with police commissioner and alderman Henry W. Lockwood, who worked as a tugboat engineer. Possibly through Simmons's connection to Lockwood, he was also on friendly terms with several Charleston police officers, including Wansley.[81]

Detective Wansley had been at work for about three hours when Simmons and Middleton arrived at the police station. He took their report and attempted unsuccessfully to radio a patrol car with orders to apprehend Rivers and Brown. Frustrated by the delay, Wansley left the station in his car with the two Black men in the back seat. Within a few minutes, they spied Rivers and Brown on Montagu Street approaching Pitt Street on foot. Wansley attempted to take the men into custody. The three men scuffled as Simmons and Middleton watched from the car. A few moments later, gunshots broke the late-night silence. Wansley and Rivers exchanged fire and Wansley collapsed near the side of Wohlers grocery store. The four Black men, including a wounded Rivers, fled the scene in separate directions. Police appeared quickly in response to neighbors' reports of gunfire, but Wansley was pronounced dead on arrival at Roper Hospital. Purse Wansley was forty-seven years old and had been on the police force for twelve years. He was survived by his wife and daughter.[82]

In pursuit of the suspects, the police placed Black Charleston under

---

[81] Many of the details of the case are found in the trial transcript, see "The Trial of Benjamin J. Rivers, September 24-25, 1936," Governor Olin D. Johnston Papers (1935-1939), Pardons, Paroles, and Commutations Files: Box 6, Folder 1. State Department of Archives and History, Columbia, South Carolina. In December 1938 Lockwood became mayor of Charleston when he was elected by his fellow city council members to replace Burnet R. Maybank, who resigned to become governor.

[82] "Trial of Benjamin J. Rivers, September 24-25, 1936." In the five years prior to his death, Wansley wounded several Black suspects, killing at least one. He was charged with murder in that case and exonerated.

occupation. Within hours of Wansley's death, detectives searched the rooms where Rivers and Brown stayed on Clifford Alley and detained Middleton and Simmons for questioning. Police arrested at least twenty additional Black people believed to have connections to the suspects and detained many others. In a strong show of blue and White solidarity, officers from dozens of area police agencies spent the better part of the week scouring Charleston's alleys and tenements, rounding up any African American with the surname Rivers.[83] Meanwhile, county police concentrated on the rural Black communities surrounding the city. They erected blockades on the major roads leaving Charleston and searched "all suspicious cars." The fevered atmosphere generated more than a few false leads and inspired dangerous and unnecessary raids and maneuvers. Two Black men fishing from a small boat on the Ashley River were mistaken for the fugitives, and were overtaken by a Coast Guard vessel as a cluster of detectives watched excitedly from the bridge. In another incident, officers, responding to what they thought was a hot tip, burst into a grocery store with drawn pistols. They were quickly informed that someone had merely dialed the wrong number for a taxicab. Acting on other false information officers were diverted to Beaufort, Columbia, and Savannah, Georgia. However ill-focused the efforts, the massive police response led to the first major break in the case when Isaac Brown, tired of hiding, turned himself in at police headquarters after two days on the run. Brown confirmed earlier reports that Rivers was the gunman, but he offered no information regarding his whereabouts.[84]

On Monday afternoon July 20, the *Evening Post* reported that the police "were no longer taking much interest in reports that Rivers is hiding in the city" and were shifting focus to Wadmalaw and other surrounding sea islands south of Charleston. As the paper hit the streets, police were arresting Rivers after following a tip that he was hiding under a house on Duncan Street. He had spent the week there less than two blocks from the police station. Famished,

---

[83] The 1934 city directory for Charleston lists 135 African American adults with the surname Rivers.

[84] "Police Search for Suspects," *Charleston Evening Post* (July 14, 1936), "Manhunt Extends Over Lowcountry," *Charleston News and Courier* (July 15, 1936), "Isaac Brown Surrenders," *Charleston Evening Post*, July 16, 1936 and "Two Man-Hunting Detectives Called by Youth Seeking Taxi," *Charleston News and Courier* (July 22, 1936).

exhausted, and in considerable pain, he surrendered and was brought to the station without resistance. Rivers was badly in need of food and medical attention, but commissioner Lockwood, solicitor Robert McCormick Figg, Jr., and a rotating team of police officials bombarded him with questions aimed at eliciting a confession.[85] In the face of the orchestrated confusion and intimidation Rivers proffered a statement that investigators touted as a confession. But Rivers was steadfast in asserting that he had not recognized Wansley as a police officer and that he fired at him in self-defense. Those assertions later provided the basis for his legal defense.

Over the course of the interrogation the police threats may have diminished in Rivers's mind as he listened to the loudening noise from outside the station, where a vocal crowd had gathered to express their rage. The clamor proved disconcerting to the police as well, who began to doubt their ability to prevent the police station from being overrun. They suspended questioning and removed Rivers under heavy guard to the county jail on Magazine Street. There, an even larger and angrier White crowd gathered, swelling to more than five hundred people and "uttering threats of violence." The county sheriff requested backup from the U.S. Marines, but was informed that such a request could only come from the governor. Into the morning, a contingent of city and county police "armed with rifles, shotguns, clubs and tear gas, guarded the massive entrance to the jail" while commissioner Lockwood and other officials negotiated unsuccessfully with the mob's masked leaders. In the early morning the police subdued the crowd with clubs long enough to slip Rivers into a car and transport him to Columbia for safekeeping. He entered the city jail there at 6 a.m. to await admittance to the state penitentiary.[86]

Charleston officials—most notably Mayor Burnet R. Maybank and

---

[85] Figg later distinguished himself as advisor to Governor Strom Thurmond's 1948 presidential campaign and the States' Rights Party, legal strategist behind the state's defense of the White primary and opposition to school desegregation, and Dean of the University of South Carolina Law School from 1959 to 1970.

[86] On the arrest and interrogation, see "Removed to County Jail," *Charleston Evening Post* (July 20, 1936), "Rivers Captured in Hiding under Duncan St. House," *Charleston News and Courier* (July 21, 1936), "Two Lodged in Columbia Jail," *Charleston Evening Post* (July 21, 1936), "Ball Chase Ends Hunt for Rivers," *Charleston News and Courier* (July 22, 1936), and "Healy Plans Second Quiz," *Charleston Evening Post* (July 22, 1936).

Lockwood—had strong motivations for protecting Rivers from mob violence. They understood that a lynching in Charleston would give momentum to proposed federal anti-lynching legislation, which President Franklin D. Roosevelt had declined to support for fear it would alienate his southern base and harm his bid for reelection in the fall. A staunch supporter and personal friend of the president, Maybank viewed any threat to the New Deal coalition — especially its southern White base — as potentially disruptive to the steady flow of federal money to South Carolina. It had already totaled almost $533 million and much more was on the way.

But if the political imperatives of the New Deal kept Rivers safe from the lynch mob, they may have also written his death warrant. Charleston's New Dealers saw the Rivers case as a test of the legitimacy of their leadership and the local criminal justice system. Any outcome other than a conviction and death sentence would redound to the lynch mob and the proponents of popular justice. Their challenge then was to stage a plausible trial for Rivers, while knowing they could not risk a fair one.[87]

For the most part, everyone played their role as the trial began on September 24, 1936. Solicitor Figg called Wansley's widow and seven of his coworkers to the stand mostly to remind the jury that a husband and police officer had been killed. Simmons and Middleton provided their eyewitness accounts identifying Rivers as the gunman. Another witness for the state — a medical official — stated that Rivers's wound was self-inflicted — an allegation that fell apart under defense scrutiny. Rivers took the stand in his own defense, testifying for 80 minutes. He held up admirably until the close of Figg's rapid-fire cross examination. Figg pressed

---

[87] Maybank was elected in 1931 and was an early convert to the New Deal as he realized that federal monies allowed him to deliver much needed improvements to the city, while putting people to work and fortifying his political base. Working closely with his mentor, Senator James F. Byrnes, he helped deliver a large share of South Carolina's appropriation to Charleston. For more on Maybank, Byrnes, and South Carolina New Deal politics, see Marvin Leigh Cann, *Burnet Rhett Maybank and the New Deal in South Carolina, 1931-1941*, Ph.D. Dissertation, University of North Carolina at Chapel Hill (1967); David Robertson, *Sly and Able: A Political Biography of James F. Byrnes* (New York: W.W. Norton and Company 1980); Jack Irby Hayes, Jr., *South Carolina and the New Deal* (Columbia, SC: University of South Carolina Press 2001); and Kieran W. Taylor, *Charleston and the Great Depression: A Documentary History 1929-1941* (Columbia, SC: University of South Carolina Press 2018).

Rivers into acknowledging he had once brutally assaulted his estranged wife. Figg repeated the details of the assault to underscore that Rivers was prone to fits of drunken rage.

Though they were tasked with representing Rivers just a few days before trial, court-appointed attorneys B. Allston Moore and Frank H. Bailey provided a spirited defense. Under their questioning, the physician who performed the autopsy on Wansley stated that it would be near impossible for the detective to have returned fire after receiving the fatal shot, thus boosting Rivers's claim of self-defense. The attorneys also established, contrary to early press reports, that Wansley was dressed in street clothes, displayed no badge, and drove an unmarked car when he approached Rivers. Moreover, Wansley had no arrest warrant, a circumstance that weighed in favor of Rivers's claim that he was defending himself from what he reasonably thought was an unlawful attack.

Twelve White male jurors played the most important role in the trial. They appeared attentive and, importantly, they looked the part. Their foreman, Colonel Harry O. Withington, had commanded National Guard troops responding to the national textile strike in 1934. The others were drawn almost exclusively from the ranks of Charleston's professional class. They deliberated thirty minutes before breaking for dinner, reconvened for twenty-five more minutes to deliver a guilty verdict with no recommendation for mercy. Juror Thomas H. Frampton nearly broke character when he exchanged knowing nods with Lockwood before the verdict was announced. The defense attorneys motioned for a mistrial but were castigated by the judge for impugning the reputations of such well-respected men.[88]

Charleston's Black community had no speaking role in the Rivers courtroom drama. They nevertheless received notice. Press reports registered surprise at the overcrowding in the section of the courtroom reserved for Black people and

---

[88] On the trial, see "State Calls 14 Witnesses to Tell of Wansley Slaying," *Charleston News and Courier* (September 25, 1936), "Rivers Convicted in Wansley Case," *Charleston News and Courier* (September 26, 1936), "Rivers Will Die in Chair," *Charleston News and Courier* (September 27, 1936), and "Trial of Benjamin J. Rivers (September 24-25, 1936)." *News and Courier* reporter Samuel A. Cothran later offered details that are not included in the daily press account and the trial transcript. Those include explicitly racist comments from Figg's summation (see Samuel A. Cothran, "First Come, First Serve," in Beatrice St. J. Ravenel, ed. *Charleston Murders* [New York, Duell, Sloan, & Pearce, Inc. 1947]), 191-216.

noted they far outnumbered their White counterparts. Perhaps, reflecting the growing spirit of hope and restiveness, Black Charleston anticipated a different outcome for Rivers. Earlier in the week Black longshoremen skirmished with police as they tested their right to organize a union under the new labor law. Black women at the Charleston Bagging Mill had done much the same three years earlier as they demanded a living wage under the New Deal industrial codes. Changes were afoot and Black worker militancy offered hope in the possibility that collective action could bring about more change. The realists in the courtroom, still embittered by the occupation, may have attended the trial to defy the heavy police turnout. Whatever their motivations, Afro-Carolinians continued to fight for Rivers's life through his failed appeal and the rejection of his request for a commutation.

Charleston's Black ministerial leaders issued their final plea for mercy three days before the execution. Scores of Black people across the state did likewise. In the end none of it was enough. The Black-owned *Palmetto Leader*, which had campaigned to save Rivers, lamented that "things are so one-sided in some things that one must some time wonder if God is still in His high heaven." At least for a moment, it seemed that grief was the only option.[89]

---

[89] Large numbers of Black Charlestonians also attended Isaac Brown's trial at which he was convicted of murder and sentenced to life (see "Brown on Stand in Murder Trial," *Charleston News and Courier* [December 11, 1936], and "Brown Gets Life Term for Killing," *Charleston News and Courier* [December 12, 1936]. On the Black worker protests, see "Police Disperse Gang," *Charleston News and Courier*, September 20, 1936 and "Bagging Mill Shut as Women Strike for Wage of $12," *Charleston Evening Post*, August 27, 1933. On the failed appeals and the campaign to save Rivers's life, see "Trial of Benjamin J. Rivers, September 24-25, 1936" and "The Chair Only for Negroes," *Palmetto Leader* (May 7, 1938). Rivers's attorneys continued to represent him through the appeals. Moore's son later described his father as haunted by the Rivers case. He reportedly sought an audience with the governor on the night before the execution, but he was turned away from the governor's mansion (Benjamin Allston Moore, Jr., interview by author, March 27, 2015, notes in author's possession).

The Insurrection

Horace Mungin

I am not crazy, nor mad or insane
Still I must die this death to vindicate my humanity
Within myself there is harmony
Still the antagonism on my outer world
Has drawn me to this suicide
When they come I will fight
Why else have I come this course but
To have the world recognize that
I have for too long been maligned

I know who and what I am
And there is peace
Yet there remains the compulsion
To have the world concede
My calamity and suppress this affliction
When they come I will fight
Even when their awakening comes
By way of my death

I take up arms as a martyr
For the future of my son's son
And his son's son.
That they will live free
In America and know
A genuine American Justice
When they come I will fight.
The Healing Influence of Music

A Gullah Jazz Aesthetic | Our Gift to American Culture

Karen Chandler

"It is no wonder that so much of the search for identity among American Negroes was championed by Jazz musicians. Long before the modern essayists and scholars wrote of racial identity as a problem for a multiracial world, musicians were returning to their roots to affirm that which was stirring within their souls...And now, Jazz is exported to the world. For in the particular struggle of the Negro in America there is something akin to the universal struggle of modern man. Everybody has the Blues. Everybody longs for meaning. Everybody needs to love and be loved. Everybody needs to clap hands and be happy. Everybody longs for faith."[90]

The vocal and rhythmic utterances of enslaved Africans that survived the Middle Passage and isolation in the Gullah Geechee region of Charleston and the South Carolina Lowcountry, and that were sung, shouted, clapped, and stomped in praise houses, were among the first distinct syncopated sounds and rhythmic lilts in the New World. With tonal and song-like influences from West African speech and dialect, and the visceral sensibility and feeling that inform musicians' jazz style and practice, these and other Africanisms are the

---

[90] Martin Luther King, Jr., "On the Importance of Jazz" (Berlin: Berlin Jazz Festival, September 1964). This quote was included in a speech Dr. King gave at the first Berlin Jazz Festival in 1964.

soul of a Gullah aesthetic, and may be the purest African assessment in musical language in the United States.[91] Though little known or embraced fully in the jazz canon, this Gullah (or Charleston) rhythm is the inventive contribution of a people and their heritage, one that is inherently and authentically Gullah, and undeniably, an American living artifact. These pronouncements represent the search for Charleston's jazz identity by the Charleston Jazz Initiative (CJI).

CJI was called into existence March 25, 2003, at the Avery Research Center, the former school that began educating Black Charlestonians in 1868, by the daughters and sons whose stories the initiative is uncovering. It is a loosely organized network of colleagues engaged in unearthing hidden and fragmented stories and discovering new narratives and interpretations of Charleston's contributions to early jazz. They are jazz musicians, journalists, writers and critics, archivists, ethnomusicologists and historians, visual and design artists, photographers, video producers and filmmakers, arts educators and managers, family members of the musicians we're studying, and a universe of other folk interested in this unfolding jazz story. Each brings their own colorful lens (particularly CJI video producer and photo-documentarian Tony Bell's peering and up-close perspective) to inform the scholarship, teaching, artistry, and creative dissemination of the initiative.

I have been meaningfully engaged with those from this Gullah soil in contributing to a narrative that has questioned prevailing notions of jazz historiography and Charleston's role in the origins of this American art form. Jazz history is often told by focusing on clear geographical centers that blur the real complexity of a music which, after all, was not just "invented" over a hundred years ago but is the result of cultural negotiations between people of different origins, in different places, at different times, and under different conditions.

If we accept the premise that jazz or any cultural product, for that matter, has not had a static birth nor has its journey followed a specific footprint, then we, in turn, must question traditional views of the roots of jazz history, expand our discourse about when, where, how, and by whom complex rhythms and other musical Africanisms were heard and practiced, and debunk that old

---

[91] This statement represents the research that the Charleston Jazz Initiative (CJI) has been examining since 2003. It is a defining premise of our work.

jazz history cliché that this art form originated in New Orleans, traveled up the river to Chicago, then to New York and over to Kansas City, and finally made its way to Los Angeles. This great American music has its inception in these and many other places and has been shaped by myriad cultural influences and traditions that are the result of place and memory on both sides of the Black Atlantic—and the Gullah Geechee coastal region is one such place. Without inserting Charleston in this dialogue or embracing a Gullah Geechee aesthetic sensibility, our understanding of jazz and its origins is narrow at best and largely undefined.

The pulse of CJI began with its co-founder, the iconic Jack McCray, Charleston's jazz aficionado who gave us all so much—his love of music, notably jazz, his words and voice, limitless discoveries, and all cultured things. Jack guided our work until his untimely passing in 2011. He penned an essay, yet unpublished, titled "What Is This Thing Called Jazz?" to contextualize CJI's vision:

"The practice of this jazz craft is not limited to enslaved Africans and their descendants. It's a quest that has as its goal humanity, the pursuit of which is at the bottom of all African culture, which makes its practice accessible to everyone. It's a human response to life's circumstances that attempts to turn obstacles into opportunities. It's the only art form that seeks perfection in real time. Jazz is a blues response to the travails of life, mundane and extraordinary, that has evolved as the signature American artifact." The practice of jazz by musicians from Gullah soil is the subject of a chapter in an American jazz story that's yet to be fully told. Many of these musicians learned their craft at a Charleston orphanage. Established in 1891 by the Rev. Daniel Joseph Jenkins, a patriarch of this country's Black leadership movement, the Jenkins Orphanage was chartered by South Carolina as the Orphan Aid Society, Inc. in 1892. He was a visionary leader who gained a worldwide reputation for his charitable benevolence, and with fundraising and entrepreneurial acumen he developed the orphanage. For several decades, the Jenkins Orphanage Bands (there were five over the life of the orphanage) were the orphanage's primary revenue stream.

Some of the Jenkins Orphanage and other musicians from the Palmetto State include inventive multi-instrumentalists, band leaders, vocalists, composers, and arrangers who not only innovated musical techniques and sounds that were used in compositions in the *Great American Songbook* but transmitted this characteristic sound worldwide through touring, big band concerts, and recordings. Some of these musical stories include Jenkins' resident Cat Anderson, Duke Ellington's high-note trumpet player; Bubber Miley, the trumpeter who helped create the signature jungle sound heard in many Ellington tunes, including "East St. Louis Toodle-Oo" and "Black and Tan Fantasy"; Charleston native Chippie Hill, a blues vocalist who led ensembles with Louis Armstrong on cornet in 1920s Chicago; Georgia native and Jenkins orphan Jabbo Smith, a prolific songwriter and recording artist of the 1920s and 1930s and most known for his trumpet duels with Louis Armstrong; Jenkins band musician Geechie Harper, who Langston Hughes dedicated his autobiography, *The Big Sea* to; Julian Dash, an Avery graduate, who was the tenor saxophonist with Erskine Hawkins and co-wrote the jazz standard "Tuxedo Junction"; Tommy Benford, the ace drummer who remembers playing with the Jenkins Orphanage Band as a kid in 1913 and "swinging" the music, and whose Gullah-styled approach to drumming can be heard on Jelly Roll Morton's recordings of the late 1920s; James Jamerson, an Edisto Island native who was the innovative bass player for the Funk Brothers, the Motown studio band and musical engine behind those great Motown hits; and of course, Cheraw, South Carolina, native Dizzy Gillespie, the trumpeter-bandleader and innovator of bebop and Afro-Cuban jazz.

This seminal story continues with orchestral composer Edmund Thornton Jenkins, Reverend Jenkins's son, who used Gullah-inspired motifs in his "American Folk Rhapsody: Charlestonia." Active in London's Black political and cultural scene beginning in 1914, he founded the Coterie of Friends and organized cultural programs at events for people of African descent including the 1921 and 1923 Pan-African Congresses, for which W.E.B. Du Bois was a delegate. Jenkins was also a jazz instrumentalist and prominent player in Paris at the height of the 1920s Jazz Age.

And there was Charlestonian Freddie Green, a pioneering figure of the swing era and a revolutionary contributor to the Gullah jazz aesthetic. Though not an orphan, Green studied music at the Jenkins Orphanage and was Count Basie's rhythm guitarist for nearly fifty years. According to Basie, he defined swing with his steady and driving rhythmic pulse with the best rhythm section of the jazz ages. Wynton Marsalis praised Green's unprecedented rhythm guitar technique by referring to its constant and metronomic pulse as "the guts of the music" in a discussion of how he adapted it for the seventh movement of his "Blues Symphony."[92] Green's rhythm guitar was the heartbeat of the Basie band that provided the foundation upon which Basie and his band members could romp around and improvise on top of.

Charleston's jazz story is not just a historic one. It lives today in Ranky Tanky. "Get funky" is the loose translation of this quintet of native South Carolinians, four Gullah descendants, and one disciple, who are 2020 Grammy winners in the Best Regional Roots Music Album category. This ensemble infuses original and refreshingly imaginative interpretations of Gullah shouts, game songs, and spirituals, and maintains an active tour schedule of high-energy performances around the globe. Nurtured by their own lived experiences, they are preserving this regional sound with present-day innovations not unlike what their Gullah descendants did centuries earlier. Gullah rhythm, then, is representative of both a past and living history, making it a historically novel and contemporary artifact of American cultural heritage and a gift to the world.

CJI colleague and Ranky Tanky percussionist and jazz drummer Quentin Baxter, who grew up in a Pentecostal church in Charleston (with a mother who played drums in that church), tells us that it was there "the Gullah language, its strong rhythmic characteristics and quick syncopations, [and] the aggressive sound of its vocabulary" affects the way he approaches the practice of his instrument even today. "I grew up in a community which informed my feeling of pitch, rhythm, timbre, and micro-form. My music is heavily influenced by a translation of such aspects of [Gullah] language."[93]

Baxter's Ranky Tanky partner, trumpeter-vocalist Charlton Singleton, added that there is a personal sensibility that shows up in the playing of Gullah rhythm by individual musicians. He explained that though one can notate Gullah rhythms, the playing of them can vary significantly among musicians. One example is the rhythmic motif in "Gullah Suite," a three-movement work by

---

[92] Wynton Marsalis, "Talking About Blues Symphony: Movement VII" (2009), https://www.facebook.com/wyntonmarsalis/videos/239032991330045/
[93] Wolfram Knauer, ed., *Gender and Identity in Jazz* (Darmstadt: Jazzinstitut Darmstadt, 2016), 24-25.

trombonist Slide Hampton.[94] The rhythm in the first measure, the dotted quarter, eighth note, quarter rest, quarter note, is how most musicians would notate this Gullah rhythm but not necessarily how one would feel and play it.

Singleton explained: "That is how the rhythm looks on paper. However, there is a feel to it that I don't think can be notated. An accent in some places is brought about from that feel and that is purely in the moment." [95] This individuality and in-the-moment sensed quality in the performance of Gullah rhythms is just as distinct as the rhythm itself.

It is shortsighted that the predominant ways many have come to understand Charleston's contribution to American culture is Gershwin's *Porgy and Bess*, spirituals, and the dance, The Charleston. Gullah rhythm and song have been retained and shared with the world by Jenkins Orphanage musicians, Ranky Tanky, and countless other descendants of the craft with inventiveness as its soulful core. Little did we know that CJI's journey would unearth a fuller story of the little-known contributions from yesterday and today that Gullah descendants have made to the American jazz canon.

---

[94] In 2010, CJI commissioned Slide Hampton to compose "Gullah Suite." It is the title track on *Legends*, CJI's first CD that received major funding from the National Endowment for the Arts (NEA). Hampton was recognized in 2005 with the Jazz Masters Award, the highest honor given to a jazz musician in the United States by the NEA.
[95] Charlton Singleton, Text interview (October 16, 2016).

Jazz Men (remembering Jack McCray)

Portia Cobb

In this Holy City,
we pour libations
& drink dranks of pure shine from a flask
fetched deep from the bosom of Black
Joy

In speakeasy spirit houses
we toe tap on creaking wood floors
to Pizzicato double bass strings

I once saw jazz man Jack McCray
dash across rain-slick streets
& back-alley cobblestone corridors
headed to meetings of this profound
sound

   (an image suspended in time)

He could translate the lingo of brass
& drum
speaking in tongues

might offer his own pocket square
to dab away salty droplets rolling
from the temple of a brethren
drummer setting trembling cymbals in
counterclockwise spirals
on music hall stages

In Charleston,
we gather in these parlors
of Remembrance
witness trickster spirits trance dance
on the faces of jazz men
holding us
in an eternal embrace

Holding us

Awakening of the Ancestors through Music

DeMett Jenkins

As the director of education and engagement for the International African American Museum being built in Charleston, South Carolina, I have the honor and privilege to have created educational programs related to faith, spirituality, and religion. I developed "Awakening of the Ancestors through Music." This program highlights the music of Lowcountry spirituals throughout the Gullah Geechee region from Wilmington, North Carolina, through South Carolina and Georgia to St. Augustine, Florida. The program presents the music of Lowcountry spirituals, Negro spirituals, songs of strength and encouragement, funeral and home-going celebrations, songs of equality, and Sunday morning worship.

Christal Brown Heyward, a music educator and well sought-after psalmist, facilitates the program, offered at least twice annually in partnership with faith communities across South Carolina. Christal grew up with the spirituals common to the Lowcountry, specifically on Johns Island near Charleston. At an early age, Christal served as a musician at various churches. The program includes songs from the Gullah Geechee cultural heritage to evoke the spirit of those who made it possible for us to be here today. These songs, which gave our ancestors strength, continue to encourage, empower, and motivate us. Through these songs, communities learn of our ancestral music, its styles, meaning, and purpose.

We also provide an educational component to explain the music and lyrics with the accompaniment of foot stomping, the syncopated Charleston-style double clap, and the instruments, which include the washboard, pots, glasses, and other common household items.

"That's Alright," a familiar song in the Gullah Geechee community, refers to the sovereignty of God, recognizing God as being in full control, and, when our earthly life ends, we will be grateful for a place in heaven. No matter what happens in this life, in the kingdom is where the singer wants to be. The song's repeated line "That's alright," is an acknowledgment that the soul is at rest and knows its destination.

That's alright
That's alright
That's alright
It'll be alright
Since my soul has a seat up in the kingdom
That's alright

One of these mornings it won't be long you'll look for me and I'll be gone
Since my soul got a seat up in the kingdom that's alright

Hush little baby don't you cry you know your momma been born to die
Since my soul got a seat up in the kingdom that's alright

My my mother how you walking now your feet may slip, and your soul may long
Since my soul got a seat up in the kingdom, that's alright.

Singing singularly and collectively strengthened our ancestors daily. They sang in the field, after they were pulled apart from family, beaten, and raped. "Wade in the Water" and "Go Down, Moses" were songs that hoped for freedom in this life, while songs such as "Swing Low, Sweet Chariot," "Sit Down, Servant," and "That's Alright" rested in freedom at last in heaven.

The only source of comfort was a trust and belief in God that freedom would come in the sweet by and by. This is a true reflection of worship today as we continue to see and experience injustices, heartbreak, and incivility. When confronted with pain you cry out to God or cry out to your mother as George Floyd did while he was being murdered. Songs provide a way to evoke trust that God hears your prayers, that's worship! When you believe God will turn things around, despite the circumstances, that is worship!

Music speaks a language that words can't convey. Music has the ability to stir the emotions, elevating us to a place of calm, joy, and peace. German theologian Martin Luther wrote that music frees the heart from "the weight of sorrow, and the fascination of evil thoughts."

I love music, and I am drawn to the scholars' analysis of it. I recall one scholar who said this: "Music is the language of emotions in the same way speech is the language of the intellect. It can express the inexpressible. When words alone or musical notes alone are insufficient, the simple song can blend melody and lyrics to create an eloquent statement of glorious praise." Therefore, Awakening of the Ancestors Through Music was created. Music connects our souls with those of others. We are also reminded of the ministry of our ancestors then and now. Yes, I say ministry because they endured what they experienced yet they still trusted that God would free them from this hard life. That is ministry at its best!

The Awakening of the Ancestors through Music program is an homage to those who endured travesties. We awaken those ancestors to thank them for all they did to allow us to be here now as a result of their sacrifices. We sing these songs so they can rest.

Often music is the sermon. Sometimes the spoken word or message does not grab you like the music does, and sometimes music supports the message. Music facilitates the worship. Praise and worship go hand in hand, and ultimately are about the heart. The heart, filled with love toward God, is our offering. When we praise God, we acknowledge that God is holy and righteous, and we are grateful for our life and breath.

Worship is how we show love. Praise is the relationship and worship is the demonstration. They are mutual in our daily honor and reverence through our love, trust, and belief in God. Nothing else matters. Romans 12:1 in the New International Version of the Bible confirms this: "Therefore, I urge you, brothers and sisters, in view of God's mercy, to offer your bodies as a living sacrifice, holy and pleasing to God this is your true and proper worship."

Music evokes powerful emotional responses. It serves as a cue to recall and reflect with a language that evokes emotions to elevate us to a place of calm, joy, and peace.

On the Two and Forever

Savannah J. Frierson

to the untrained ear it sounded
lament-like
grief-like
agony-like
woe

the notes on top, a tune they
only wanted to hear
a song they wrote for us
with relish
without regret
for greed at
humanity's expense

but for the enslaved and
their ancestors and
their children
the words hit different
the moans and groans and wails
ain't about shackles, degradation, dehumanization
but the birth of a new people
a new resistance, a hewed resilience
sowed in fields of rice and indigo and tobacco and cotton
toiled on lands that ain't belong to us neither by law nor birth

the rhythms demand our rights
to exist
to live
to thrive

We make opera of our defeats and triumphs
the horns of our joy
the percussion of our rage
the strings of our serenity
the voices of our ingenuity

we ain't never needed no sheet music
no recording machines
no studios
no Grammys or billboards

just us
for the culture
when and where we gather
we gonna sing till the spirit moves in our heart
because we here, we always gon' be here
and ain't no stoppin' us now

Social Justice

"A First Child of School Desegregation Reflects on the Goals of Those Actions and Their Unintended Consequences Affecting Black Communities Today"

Millicent Brown

In the middle of the twentieth century throughout the nation, the South, and certainly in South Carolina, public school desegregation was but one aspect of a much larger set of actions designed to extend fundamental rights of access and inclusion for African Americans. Expensive lawsuits, ongoing street protests, economic boycotts, as well as individual stands of courage and determination all represent the multiple attacks designed to stop injustice and racial discrimination. But all political and social protests face the danger of being misunderstood, and consequent misunderstandings may foster interpretations that are far from what activists championed.

This is a cautionary tale offered by a seventy-three-year-old former first child of desegregation, and lifelong advocate for human rights. I write it out of frustration and pain in recognition of how confused and misguided the telling of the peoples' history can become. Such a history demands that great care be taken as time goes by to teach not only the acts and processes used in seeking social change, but also clearly presented explanations of "why?"

This essay speaks to what many were trying to do to improve Black life in Charleston, South Carolina, the state and nation, but also warns of what happens when actions go without critique, and when assumptions of progress are made without deeper scrutiny. To be sure, it has taken decades to appreciate how my participation in unraveling the segregated school systems of South Carolina would take so many turns and affect so many minds long after 1963.

By 1960, our activist family of six, crossing three generations, had openly supported, participated in, encouraged, identified with, and often led local efforts to end the legal mistreatment of Black people (respectfully and preferably called "Negroes" at the time). By current twenty-first century standards, I'm not sure if my grandmother, parents, siblings, and an extraordinary group of supportive Charleston warriors for justice would meet the very high bar set by that word: activist. Television cameras, mobile phone photos, social media memes, frequent, dramatic confrontations with battalions of police and national guards are not the images defining the majority of the ongoing Lowcountry protests that spanned not days or weeks or months, but all the years of my youth.

My family's involvement between the mid-1950s and mid-1960s seemed so regular, ordinary, and expected on most days that in retrospect, it seems indulgent, even self-serving, to describe us in such heroic terms, but active we certainly were. We attended mass meetings at all-Black Baptist, AME, AME Zion, R.M.U.E.[96], Methodist, Congregationalist, non-denominational, and eventually even Episcopal churches. The fact that our family was affiliated with the Episcopal church created an eventual showdown between my father, J. Arthur Brown, a local and state NAACP leader, and his St. Mark's Episcopal Church vestry. Lots of people asked why no mass meetings in support of civil rights demands had ever been held inside those hallowed walls. But even churches such as ours, reluctant to embrace the demand for long overdue social change, eventually opened their doors to a broader group of locals than had ever before been welcomed. This quest for fairness was bringing people of all ilks together (even if only temporarily in ways many found uncomfortable and unfamiliar, but oh so necessary and impossible to ignore).

---

[96] Reformed Methodist Union Episcopal

Over the years, our family joined with hundreds, then thousands of justice-seekers in Charleston and throughout the state turning out for protests, boycotts, marches, and demonstrations. People of all ages and backgrounds placed hard-earned and sometimes scarce dollars into the collection plates, and thereby supported in the most fundamental way the growing impatience with the brutality of racial bias with which we had become so familiar and painfully adjusted. Many who were not openly associated with such gatherings and actions contributed money to support the movement with no one the wiser.

Eventually, local and state beaches, golf courses, parks, playgrounds, theaters, lunch counters, and yes, public schools, all ended their legally-sanctioned rebuke of the race, and by extension of our family and circle of allies. The 1964 Civil Rights Act and 1965 Voting Rights Act validated what we had been saying for so long: that our tax dollars mattered and must benefit us, not only others who had always used our money with no intention of sharing the goods. These pieces of federal legislation declared that the color-of-your skin game was over, at least in the openly discriminatory way accepted for decades that deemed race-mixing in public spaces taboo. We all (family members and others) who had stayed the course until the laws caught up with our demands took our actions and results of those actions very, very personally. Generations coming behind us have not always been taught the motivations keeping us going. Many today do not know how the press ignored us, elected city leadership warned us not to move "too fast," the number of those in our community who shunned us, how social club and church circle members who seemed to be embarrassed by such advocacy avoided us, and that those who understandably could not summon the strength to risk losing their jobs politely tolerated us.

We operated primarily out of commitment to the cause. We were race men, women, and children in the truest sense of the word, meaning we understood deeds and sacrifices were intended to improve conditions for the Black community. Our actions would open gates not only for ourselves, but also for those who passively let us act on their behalf—motivated by principle, not self-gain. To be sure that this legacy of struggle is understood correctly by future generations we can use the example of school desegregation to apply the following three criteria for how civil rights movement history must be taught:

First, admit the frustration in not achieving all for which we fought so hard and so constantly; truly democratic learning environments with access and opportunity for all children—neither color nor class nor caste being an issue. Tragically, we are far from where we thought we would be. Many all-Black schools have closed, Black faculty are sorely missing, and schools with high poverty rates have become over-policed, if not direct pipelines to prison.

Second, we must acknowledge the difference between winning legal battles against segregated public schools and bringing about our emergence from the subordinate social stratum that we have been limited to for so long. Racially unbalanced and differentiated curricula separate students under the same roofs. Standardized testing reflective of White-privileged values and exposure disproportionately designate Black, Brown, and poor children as deficient.

Getting into the schools was, and continues to be, only a step benefitting some and forsaking many others, while not achieving the goal of an equal and equitable environment. Masterfully executed plans that fall within the law allow for continued discrimination, just not based on color, rendering earlier legal battles insufficient in achieving equity.

Third, we must explain it never was our intention to encourage fellow citizens of color to move away from our own kind. Abandoning community businesses, neighborhoods, and institutions in the name of integration was not a part of the freedom plan. For sure, the successful elimination of color-based segregated public schools proved that changing laws is not easy, changing patterns of behavior not easy, convincing people to put aside their fears, not easy, but can be done. As a result of that resolve, thousands upon thousands of Black children nobly and admirably gave up the innocence of childhood to advance the race by participating in the grand experiment to eliminate White supremacist notions once and for all. We believed that once we got together in the classrooms, it would become clear that all groups of children have a range of intellectual abilities that public schools are commanded to nurture and develop. Black children and teachers took their gifts along with them into the bastions of all-White misconceptions and prejudices.

The first children deserve our gratitude not only for their actions in stepping forward into frequently hostile classrooms, cafeterias, and gyms; but they also deserve our apologies because the adults, lawyers, parents, and justice-minded community advocates had no idea if such sacrifices could actually make southern and U.S. society more accepting of people of color. We are still not sure, but data and current national conditions suggest that goal is a long way from completion.

Well into my adulthood, as a member of a generation that had lived both inside segregated schools and legally desegregated ones, the problem of not specifically teaching the why we did it became painfully apparent. The following account summarizes the regret I feel about those unintended consequences of the desegregation process that drive present-day parents and children to look outside and beyond their communities and themselves for educational excellence and standards of achievement.

Thirty-five years after being one of the first eleven K-12 grade students to desegregate South Carolina's public schools, I was proudly positioned in my first full-time assignment as a professor of U.S. history at Bennett College, a highly respected historically Black campus in Greensboro, North Carolina. I shared memories of my pre- and post-school desegregation classroom experiences. Students appreciated my incorporating personal reflections into information about ever-emerging Black liberation philosophies, motives, and actions of the era most had only romanticized notions about. ("Negro" by the end of the twentieth century was permanently eliminated from our political and cultural vocabularies.) The day a seriously engaged coed sheepishly approached me after class forever changed my idea of how I should present my front-seat view of this part of civil rights history.

"Dr. Brown, when you talk to us about all-Black schools that you attended, we think 'ghetto.'" Hearing this literally caused my jaw to drop in disbelief, and it took an hour's conversation with this young woman to really make sense of what she was sharing. My students, mostly from North and South Carolina or at least the southeastern U.S., were all born approximately between 1990 and 1994. Most had attended integrated but definitely White-majority elementary, middle, and high schools. They listened intently to my reflections of decades well before their birth, but could not understand my seeming praise and regard for the single-race (segregated) schools with which they had no personal experiences.

Their automatic concepts of all-Black schools had been shaped by endless references to the need to leave or avoid poorly financed and resourced physical structures as the way to achieve a quality education deemed synonymous with White. They had been told directly and indirectly that integration was the saving grace for minority students with high aspirations, abilities, and commitments to achieve beyond the limiting all-Black environments experienced by most of their parents and grandparents. They were to get away from those environments holding them back and the historical reality of underachievement based on race. They had not been taught the difference between inferior school resources and inferior students and communities. The concept of all-Black academic excellence was unknown, as were examples of supportive teachers who looked like them, lived on their streets, saw beyond their parents' economic level, and so many other factors that had shaped me before 1963. Arguments against being forcibly segregated as a race had been compressed into tales of despair, loathing, and desperation to get out and away from our own people.

Aware now of the importance of telling our civil rights history more accurately, it is with a heavy heart but ongoing determination that I, and many other first children of school desegregation call upon all who are able, to correct while we can, the misconception of why we demanded entry into all-White schools. Our children must stop being taught that they, or their communities, were ever or are now the problem.

In the Spirit of the Movement
Horace Mungin

The assassination of President John Kennedy on November 22nd elevated
The tone for the turmoil yet to come in the young decade of the sixties from
The activism for racial justice gathering steam from the Montgomery Bus Boycott
Of the 1950s taking the tenet to the realm where the truly unimaginable could be
Entertained

The activism of the sixties started when four college students took a stand
Against segregation in Greensboro, North Carolina when they
Refused to leave a Woolworth's lunch counter without being served
Over the next several days, hundreds of people joined their cause in
What became known as the Greensboro sit-ins.

Gov. George W. Wallace's 1962 campaign promise to defend
Segregation at all costs, he stood in the schoolhouse door where
He declared segregation now, segregation tomorrow, segregation forever
The White Knights of resistance were forming

Martin Luther King, Jr. had become a shining icon of hope for the future
Negroes around the country were organizing to combat local issues
Unemployment
School Segregation
Low wages
Jim Crow codes
Voter participation
From Birmingham, AL to Jackson, MS to Albany, GA to Charleston, SC
There hung above the Negro community a halo of hope through activism

The spirit of the movement was palpable everywhere throughout the land
Negroes, young and old wore activism like a suit of armor ~

The storm of change was amassing all over the South
An avalanche of amendments to address the grievance
Of activists came in the form of the Civil Rights Act and
The Voting Rights Act and the Equal Rights Commission

This national spirit of the movement infused local actions
There were many individual acts of bravery and sacrifice
On the local level that carried national implications and
Brought real change to substantiate the meaning in the motto
Of the Civil Rights Movement:

We Shall Overcome.

March Forth:
Pat Conroy's Last Act as a Teacher

Jonathan Haupt

"I'm living proof that Penn Center can change a White boy's life. You changed me utterly and I'm forever grateful to you. Yes, I was fired, humiliated, and run out of town because I believed what Martin Luther King believed. Yes, they got me good, Penn Center, but on this joyous night, let me brag to you at last: Didn't I get those sorry sons of bitches back?"

—Pat Conroy, from his 2010 acceptance speech when inducted into Penn Center's 1862 Circle

Pat Conroy—the beloved author of *The Water Is Wide*, *The Great Santini*, *The Lords of Discipline*, and *The Prince of Tides*—is integrating a cemetery. Conroy (1945-2016) is the only White person, Roman Catholic or otherwise, buried in St. Helena Memorial Gardens, an African American cemetery on the outer edge of the Penn Center Historic District. Understandably, this outcome took some special permissions—efforts that began in earnest in 2010 when Pat was inducted into Penn Center's 1862 Circle, recognizing national advocates for the Gullah Geechee culture of the Sea Islands. But this story begins much earlier than that, and it continues to this day.

The Conroy family arrived in the Lowcountry in 1961, when Pat's father, decorated fighter pilot Col. Don "the Great Santini" Conroy, was assigned to the Marine Corps Air Station in Beaufort. This was the twenty-third time the family had moved since sixteen-year-old Pat Conroy had been born, and Beaufort High School was the tenth school he attended, completing his junior and senior years there.

Conroy's junior year English teacher Gene Norris became an empowering and essential mentor to the burgeoning writer, inviting him into the larger world of literature, introducing him to the first living writers Pat ever met—state poet laureate Archibald Rutledge, and accomplished novelist and short-story writer Ann Head—showing him the possibilities of becoming a teacher and writer, and educating young Conroy about the myriad ways words could be used to challenge and change the world.

One such lesson was to introduce teenaged Pat Conroy to Penn Center on St. Helena Island. Originally founded as the Penn School in 1862 to educate the newly-freed, formerly enslaved people of the Sea Islands, in the 1960s Penn embarked on a remarkable second life as one of the few places in the nation where Blacks and Whites could safely gather together. As such, it became a haven of activities during the civil rights movement. It was there at Penn, under the guidance of his teacher Gene Norris, that Pat met Dr. Martin Luther King Jr., Julian Bond, Jesse Jackson, and other members of the civil rights leadership.

Pat was more open than most southern-born young White men might have been to the teachings and advocacy he encountered at Penn, where meetings and community sings immersed him in the chorus of voices seeking to preserve the Gullah Geechie heritage of the past and reshape a brighter future for people of color. Pat's mother Peg taught the family that her people, the Peeks, had survived the Great Depression through the generosity of neighboring Black sharecroppers. And Pat had experienced integrated education in Roman Catholic schools prior to his arrival in Beaufort, experiences he shared in lunchtime conversations at Harry's Restaurant with his Beaufort High principal in what Pat would later call his "Bill Dufford Summer." Those dialogues, along with other realizations, helped begin the transformation of Bill Dufford from a scion of the White supremacist Jim Crow South into a stalwart champion of education equality, which Dufford himself recounted in his own inspirational memoir, *My Tour through the Asylum*.

Young Pat's heart and mind were already open to what he experienced at Penn Center, and Penn helped Pat advance on the path to his destiny as a social justice advocate and truth-teller.

In the spring of 1968, when King was assassinated in Memphis, Pat Conroy was teaching at Beaufort High School, following his 1967 graduation from The Citadel. Beaufort High was not yet integrated, but through freedom of choice, a growing number of Black students were on campus. Following school desegregation, freedom of choice became a popular method in the South to skirt the law by giving all students the freedom to choose where they want to attend school. In practice it mostly maintained the status quo across the south. Following King's death, several Black students approached young, liberal Conroy about serving as faculty advisor to the school's first Afro-American Culture Club, a student organization. Pat readily agreed to the role.

But Pat also wanted to incorporate these students, their history, and their future into the curriculum. So, he proposed an Afro-American history class, a first for the county, and perhaps a first for the state. Pat was given approval to teach the class, but with the stipulation that it could only be offered if both Black and White students signed up. Pat had become so popular among the students as their progressive-minded psychology and government teacher that White students did indeed sign up for the class and made possible a transformative moment in public education. Several of Pat's Beaufort High School students later became teachers themselves, counting Pat among their inspirations toward lives of service in education.

In 1969, Pat became the first White schoolteacher and the first male schoolteacher on the isolated Sea Island of Daufuskie. He had considered going into the Peace Corps, but discovered he could have a Peace Corps-like experience without even leaving the county. On Daufuskie, at the two-room Mary Field School, Pat became the life-altering teacher to eighteen native island children, grades five through eight. Some of those students later became teachers, inspired by their year under Pat's tutelage. Upon realizing that separate had never been equal in the lives of these students, Pat devoted himself fully to their education, transforming their lives through immersive, experiential learning on and off their island and, in the end, giving them an education that was superior to their White counterparts on the mainland.

As those familiar with Pat's 1972 teaching memoir *The Water Is Wide* or its two film adaptations know, his reward for his heroic efforts on behalf of his students was to be fired by the school district for conduct unbecoming a professional educator. After losing a wrongful termination suit, which in turn became a national news story, the spark was lit for Pat to tell the truth of his experiences in book form instead. And so began his ascension to internationally-acclaimed author with a remarkable writing career that spanned nearly fifty years, during which he continued to inspire and mentor his fellow writers, outside of the traditional classroom setting.

In 2010, when Conroy was inducted into Penn Center's famed 1862 Circle, Barack Obama was in his second year as the nation's first African American president. Those leaders and organizers who had gathered at Penn in the 1960s had been proven to have been on the right side of history, and Conroy welcomed his own recognition at Penn, a place he had so admired as a boy. It was that night, and through his friend and fellow 1862 Circle honoree Roland Gardner, that Pat began seeking special permission to be buried in the Penn Center Historic District.

I have since come to think of this choice as Pat's last act as a teacher. Because he had been in the habit of visiting the graves of writers he admired, he knew his own readers, who number in the millions, would be compelled to visit his gravesite as well. He was right. But these literary pilgrims cannot get to Conroy's final resting place without driving through the heart of Penn Center and learning at least a little bit of its vital role in the still-unfolding history of race relations in this country.

On March 4, 2016, Pat Conroy left this world for the next. And by the fall of that year, the nonprofit Pat Conroy Literary Center was established in Beaufort, the result of the thoughtful planning and spirited fundraising of Pat's family and friends, honoring Pat as writer, educator, and generous spirit. Pat, who had so often been referred to as "larger than life," proved to be larger than death as well.

As the Conroy Center's first two staff members, Maura Connelly and I created the inaugural March Forth Day of Learning, a collaboration with Penn Center, on March 4, 2017, the first anniversary of Pat's death. My vision was to honor Pat's memory not with a day of mourning, but with a day of immersive education into some of the major themes that had defined Pat's teaching and his writing life: social justice, conservation, and storytelling.

The original March Forth event in Penn's Frissell Community House brought together about sixty attendees, mostly from Beaufort County, to participate in a nature walk of the grounds led by master naturalist, poet, and memoirist J. Drew Lanham; a presentation on the history of Penn Center by Victoria Smalls, a screening of a panel discussion by Pat and his family; and a conversation between Lanham and *Lowcountry Weekly* publisher and columnist Margaret Evans, Pat's former assistant. A catered lunch by Debbi Covington, a food writer and friend of Pat's who had also catered his funeral reception, rounded out the day.

The first March Forth proved to be a deeply emotional and engaging experience, remembering our beloved friend and advancing his legacy as advocate and educator. That this needed to be an annual event was immediately obvious. The following year, attendance doubled, reaching the full capacity of Frissel Community House, with participants from eleven states.

In 2019, March Forth grew to include a bold partnership with Beaufort High School, the same Beaufort High where Pat had once been both student and teacher, now located on a larger campus on Lady's Island. In generous collaboration with the Beaufort County School District—the same district that had fired Pat Conroy—all 1,300 students at Beaufort High were given copies of *Dear Martin*, the social justice-themed debut young adult novel by March Forth keynote speaker Nic Stone. Following months of reading and discussing the novel, BHS students had an opportunity to meet Stone in an all-school assembly in which they asked thoughtful questions about the novel's themes and characters and about the novelist's writing life.

Students were also encouraged to respond artistically to *Dear Martin*, and the young artists and writers who crafted twenty-four of those pieces were selected by their teachers to have a lunch discussion with Stone—reminiscent of the lunches Pat had as a student with his principal and mentor Bill Dufford. Among those twenty-four students was freshman Holland Perryman, winner of the school's short story competition inspired by Stone's novel.

Less than two months later, inspired in part by her March Forth experience, the ambitious and multi-talented Miss Perryman was in the Conroy Center, meeting with me to propose a student internship for herself as an opportunity to pursue her burgeoning interests as a young writer. Honoring the ways in which Pat had been mentored by his BHS teachers—including his unorthodox off-campus writing mentor, the novelist Ann Head—I accepted her internship proposal.

As I write this, two years later, sixteen-year-old Holland Perryman is now the same age Pat was when he arrived in Beaufort in 1961 to meet his destiny as teacher, writer, and man. She has quickly become an essential member of our Conroy Center team and the great pride and joy of my entirely unexpected teaching life. Holland has also been my co-host of our annual March Forth event, serving masterfully as on-camera interviewer for YA novelist Kalynn Bayron, author of *Cinderella Is Dead*, an empowering novel of diversity and social justice, and the subject of March Forth's 2021 student engagement collaboration with Beaufort High School.

Inspired in part by her March Forth experiences and by the larger and more diverse experiences of her Conroy Center internship, Holland has now created a new student organization at Beaufort High—DAYLO: Diversity Awareness Youth Literacy Organization, which uses a book club model to learn and teach inclusivity and social justice themes. More than fifty BHS students have already signed up to participate in the club, and DAYLO will be an essential partner in the Conroy Center's upcoming public programs, including the 2022 March Forth partnership with Penn Center.

Pat Conroy believed wholeheartedly in the power of circles, the gravitational forces at work in the world that bring people, places, ideas, and memories back to us, like the Lowcountry tides, when we were meant to return to a task incomplete. That Conroy Center intern Holland Perryman, inspired by her experiences through the center, has taken up the mantle as a young social justice peer leader is such a circle honoring Pat's last act as a teacher. It is one of many ways in which the good work of Penn Center and the great love of Pat Conroy for all of humankind continues to resonate in new generations.

May we continue to March Forth together.

Conrack

Horace Mungin

Conrack was an American author
A good man and a great teacher
His life is lived in his many memoirs
He was the eldest of seven children
Five boys and two girls
He did not have a hometown until
His family settled in Beaufort,
South Carolina

Conrack taught English in Beaufort, South Carolina;
Before he then accepted a job teaching children in a
One-room schoolhouse on remote Daufuskie Island
An experience that developed in the memoir *The Water Is Wide*
The book won Conroy a humanitarian award from the
National Education Association and an Anisfield-Wolf Book Award.
The Water Is Wide turned into the feature film, *Conrack*

Conrack rummaged the people, the places, and the trauma
Of his childhood and young manhood for his sparingly
fictionalized novels and a series of memoirs that captivated
Readers with their openly emotional tone, lurid family stories
And lush prose that often reached its most affecting
Lyrical pitch when evoking the wetlands around Beaufort, S.C.

Conrack wrote in *The Prince of Tides*,
"I would have to take you to the marsh on a spring day, flush the great
blue heron from its silent occupation. Scatter marsh hens as we sink to
our knees in mud, open you an oyster with a pocketknife and feed it
to you from the shell and say, 'There. That taste. That's the taste of my

childhood.' I would say, 'Breathe deeply,' and you would breathe and remember that smell for the rest of your life, the bold, fecund aroma of the
tidal marsh, exquisite and sensual, the smell of the South in heat, a smell
like new milk, semen and spilled wine, all perfumed with seawater."

The St. Helena Memorial Garden cemetery belongs
To historic Brick Baptist Church, out on the main road
Across from Penn Center; Brick Baptist is an elegant place
Built in 1855 by slave labor. When slave owners fled
Federal occupation, the church became one of the earliest
Symbols of Reconstruction, and was recently included in
The new Reconstruction Era National Monument in Beaufort County

See that beam of light shining down from the heavens above
On the old historic Black Cemetery
You won't need a flashlight to find Conrack's final
Resting place even on the darkest of nights.

Blue vs. Black: A Brief History of Policing in the U.S.

Adam Parker

In the beginning, there was mob rule, along with the imperative to view your enemy as less than human—as savage, filthy, immoral, and heathen. The irreligious and sacrilegious were to be converted or condemned. The social hierarchy, atop which sat wealthy White landowners, merchants, and industrialists, was to be maintained at any cost.

As colonial-era settlements grew along the East Coast of North America, White men crafted stratified social structures along with conventions to keep the peace—and maintain power. As the nascent United States sought to expand westward, aspects of these social protocols were exported to the frontier, though modified to accommodate a different set of circumstances. Meanwhile, in the Antebellum South, White slavers crafted their own system of control.

Policing in the United States, then, initially relied on three main approaches. In the early days of the urban North, a constable performed essential public functions, such as land surveys, marriage announcements, and verifying weights and measures. He also dealt with criminals and vagrants, administering physical punishment as required and overseeing a schedule of watches. By the 1880s, all major U.S. cities had established public policing. These departments became instruments of social and labor control wielded by prominent politicians and others upholding the economic order.

Out West, lawlessness was combatted with lawlessness: vigilante justice. Citizens became "regulators," banding together to assert authority and fight crime. In the South, the first slave patrol was established in Charleston in 1704. This was a version of vigilante law enforcement designed to instill fear and to control the growing population of enslaved Black people. Unlike policing outside of the South, where constables and vigilantes responded to unrest, slave patrols were designed to stop rebellions, escape attempts, and other transgressions before they occur.

Today, the police patrol is a cornerstone of modern law enforcement. Officers in cruisers regularly drive through certain neighborhoods that have a reputation for criminal activity to deter misconduct and signal that help is available to those willing to collaborate. Indeed, the tactics and purpose of the old slave patrols live on in contemporary policing in a variety of ways. People of color too often continue to be on the receiving end of police violence committed with impunity and informed by history.

These early systems of law enforcement—the constable, vigilante, and slave patrol—and modern policing share a problematic core attribute: confrontation. Police, then and now, are meant to maintain the social order as it is. When workers across the country went on strike in the 1920s and '30s to demand better wages and fair treatment, they faced down the police. When Black Lives Matter protestors organize marches or rallies to demand justice and fair treatment, they are met with batons and tear gas.

Police, then, perform a function that is fundamentally conservative. They are meant to defend the status quo, no matter how unjust it is, and to silence calls for reform. No wonder police in the U.S. have found it so difficult to abandon old regimes and embrace a new model of public safety and service.

Policing the enslaved and the free

Initially, the slave patrol, whether required by the state or authorized by local officials, was part of a quasi-improvised system to protect the interests of slaveholders. Patrols consisted of a captain and a few other armed men who committed to work for a defined period, then return to their regular lives as others rotated into duty. They monitored the roads for runaways and other suspicious figures, and they visited the plantations to ensure no enslaved person was out of line. Patrollers also stopped Black people in transit to check for the required passes. No pass? Then twenty lashes were laid on a traveler's back. This frequent brutality caused dissent not only among the targeted Black population but also among the masters who observed disruptions to the plantation's daily routine caused by an aggrieved workforce.

Citizen patrols eventually gave way to larger, better armed militias, formed and maintained in response to the threat of insurrection. All in all, there were hundreds of slave revolts in North America and the Caribbean between the beginning of the transatlantic slave trade and the start of the American Civil War. Some were small and spontaneous, others ambitious and well-planned. All but six were suppressed.

Law and order, no matter the region, always has been largely about quelling unrest. In the South, policing was meant to control a restive and abused slave population. In the North, increasingly, it was meant to assist the mercantile class and control laborers. In the West, it was meant to defeat Native American resistance to expansion. In each case, policing fundamentally was a way to protect economic interests. Crime was but an inevitable consequence of urbanism and addressed only insofar as it disrupted conditions that ensured a stable and productive workforce and the free flow of goods.

Maintaining social order, though, could be better accomplished with a centralized system that shifted the costs and logistics from private industry to government. Beginning in the 1830s, municipal police departments were established across the country, quickly emerging as an intrinsic part of the political machinery. In the rural South, White planters continued to rely on slave labor—and the imposition of laws that enabled it. "Slave Codes" severely restricted or forbade group assembly, movement outside of the plantation, the exercise of free speech, the ability to bear arms, opportunities to learn to read and write, and the chance to testify against White people in court. In the first couple of years following the Civil War, those regulations persisted in the guise of "Black Codes" designed to suppress economic power among people of color and ensure that White farmers had access to cheap labor. The Black Codes included penalties for "vagrancy," enabling the arrest of Black men on nearly any pretext. These men then became part of the emergent convict leasing system, which required them to serve their sentence providing free labor to White farmers. This was, as author Douglas A. Blackmon declared, "slavery by another name."

After the Reconstruction period, such restrictions persisted and intensified, now under the guise of Jim Crow laws set in place across the South. These laws upheld segregation and relied on a "separate but equal" doctrine that federal Judge J. Waties Waring of Charleston, South Carolina, refuted in 1951. "Segregation is per se inequality," he famously said. Yet where there are laws, there are those who enforce them. White authorities in the South eagerly cited their matrix of legal justifications to deny Black people access to the polls, to capital, to public services and more. When Black people protested injustice, vigilante mobs often burned their homes and churches, seized or destroyed their farms, or threatened their families. Racial terrorism was not restricted to property damage. Between the Reconstruction period and World War II, more than 4,400 black men and women were lynched in the United States. Many of these killings were conducted with law enforcement's tacit approval.

During the direct-action phase of the civil rights movement, between 1954 and 1968, nonviolent protests provoked extraordinary violence—fire hoses and attack dogs, Ku Klux Klan murders, church bombings, campus shootings—mostly committed by law enforcement or, at least, with its knowledge. Rarely were White perpetrators prosecuted; rather, Black protestors and their allies were arrested, jailed, threatened, and killed.

The Black Power movement of the 1960s and 1970s, whose participants sought not only equality under the law but self-determination, was deemed so radical and threatening to the status quo that government forces (federal, state, and local) aligned to crush it. The FBI launched a Counter Intelligence Program (COINTELPRO) to assassinate Black leaders, and the White House deployed the National Guard to crush domestic rebellions. Police across the country stepped up confrontational tactics. Officers were encouraged to view Black people, especially young Black men, as threats. Long-standing institutional discrimination, which ensured that a majority of Black people remained economically and politically disadvantaged, led to attitudes about Black people that permeated all of society: poverty was equated with corruption, depravity, and lawlessness and was effectively criminalized.

President Richard Nixon, an adherent to the Southern Strategy to boost the number of White voters in the South, launched the so-called war on drugs, which disproportionately impacted people of color. That "war" intensified under presidents Ronald Reagan and Bill Clinton, leading to the phenomenon of mass incarceration. Increasingly, Black men were given harsh sentences for nonviolent petty crimes, including low-level drug possession. The effect was to fracture Black families, reduce their ability to accumulate wealth, and entrench entire populations in cycles of nearly inescapable poverty. This was what attorney and author Michelle Alexander called, for reasons that ought to be evident, "the new Jim Crow."

Empowering the police

The fragmented nature of U.S. policing requires each municipality or county to determine its own policies and practices, and this makes it difficult to achieve meaningful reform. The federal government is alternatively complicit in police brutality and critical of it, depending on who is in office. State and local police agencies, including some in small communities, have received over the years billions of dollars' worth of surplus tactical military equipment through the 1033 program from the U.S. Defense Department. After Michael Brown was killed in 2014 by police in Ferguson, Missouri, and law enforcement responded to protests with armored vehicles and other military gear, President Barack Obama imposed limits on the 1033 program. Just two years later, Attorney General Jeff Sessions, acting at the behest of President Donald Trump, rolled back the reforms and again began distributing tactical military vehicles, grenade launchers, night-vision goggles, and riot gear to local agencies, which continue to put such equipment to use in the streets.

The Supreme Court determined in 1985 that disparate policies regarding use of force required some degree of consistency and control. In *Tennessee v. Garner* the court ruled that police officers only could shoot a suspect if they had probable cause to believe the individual could injure or kill officers or others nearby. Four years later, in 1989, a more conservative court ruled in *Graham v. Connor* that claims of excessive use of force must be assessed using the "objectively reasonable" standard of the Fourth Amendment. Facts and circumstances, not intent or bias, would be considered henceforth. Split-second decisions to shoot and kill were to be understood as reasonable responses to perceived threat, regardless of the presence of actual threat, or the precise nature of that threat. Police, therefore, were granted a certain license to kill, along with a high degree of protection against any consequences.

This relative freedom enabled law enforcement agencies to pursue without much accountability a variety of discriminatory practices and apply controversial ideas such as "broken windows" theory, which held that crime begets crime, no matter how minor the infraction, and that petty offenses such as loitering, vandalism, fare evasion, and jaywalking ought to be punished. This approach led agencies such as the New York Police Department to implement dubious crime-preventative programs like "stop-and-frisk" and tended to encourage racial profiling—often as part of seemingly benevolent "community policing" efforts.

African Americans learned long ago that law enforcement was no ally, and that injury and death were possible outcomes of any interaction involving police conditioned by training, social expectations, and history to favor confrontation over public service. "Tough-on-crime" stances assumed by politicians found significant support among the public. The tendency of Whites to perceive Black people, especially Black males, as suspicious, dangerous, or predisposed to crime is part of a feedback loop that cycles between the populace and the police, reinforcing biases and encouraging discrimination.

Policing the police

The Black Lives Matter movement got its start after the 2013 acquittal of George Zimmerman, a lone vigilante in Florida who fatally shot 17-year-old Trayvon Martin. Three Black women—activists Alicia Garza, Patrisse Cullors, and Opal Tometi—began to post "#BlackLivesMatter" on social media and to call for mass action that affirmed Black lives and confronted institutional racism. The hashtag quickly caught on, providing the movement with its battle cry. The Black Lives Matter Global Network Foundation soon was established, along with another organization, The Movement for Black Lives. Though, for the most part, the Black Lives Matter movement is a loose coalition of activist groups, and its decentralized structure means there is no clear hierarchy, no single leader, and no uniform ideology.

The goals can differ, to a degree, depending on each community's particular circumstances. Some groups are solely committed to protest; others work on social issues such as education reform, economic development, and criminal justice reform. Because two of the women who started the movement have expressed affinities to Marxist theory—which asserts that we live in a material reality whose contradictions are generated and explained by real-world conditions such as class, work, and economic interaction—critics of the Black Lives Matter movement often tend to dismiss it.

"Marxist" is a slur well-known to anyone familiar with the history of civil rights in the U.S. The NAACP was linked to communism by its opponents. The Student Nonviolent Coordinating Committee and the Rev. Martin Luther King's Southern Christian Leadership Conference were linked to communism by the FBI. Marxism and communism long have been favored pejoratives of the political establishment, and have provided a degree of justification, however faulty or immoral, to law enforcement agencies tasked with putting down legitimate protests and marginalizing social justice advocates.

But the demonization of political activists does not start with law enforcement. Rather, it is fostered among those who hold power and common citizens convinced that advocating for more democracy and inclusion is somehow problematic. Those who object to visible Black Lives Matter slogans, or discussion of the movement's purpose, typically cite policies against the display of "political messages," or concerns about "one-sidedness"—implying that there is a legitimate opposing side of the debate that deserves equal time.

In response to eight years of mostly peaceful Black Lives Matter demonstrations that began after Trayvon Martin's death and intensified after George Floyd's murder in May 25, 2020, the nation has undertaken a tentative reckoning on the subject of race. Many White people have acknowledged the transgressions of the past, their own privilege and complicity, and the deeply rooted nature of racism in the U.S. They have joined Black people in the streets, on the airwaves, in the schools and elsewhere to decry mistreatment, police violence, and various forms of institutional injustice, calling for systemic reform. Companies are hiring diversity officers and committing to anti-bias training. Organizations large and small are issuing statements in support of racial justice, and sometimes contributing significant amounts of money to the cause.

At the same time, as always, the backlash has gained momentum. "Blue Lives Matter" and "All Lives Matter" are used to counter legitimate claims of discrimination. Calls for reform are met with resistance. In a sense, law enforcement is caught in the middle (along with the protestors): a potentially dangerous place to be, for this is where confrontation can devolve into violence. To escape the violence, Americans must reconsider what sort of society they want, and what role they want the police to play.

So Out of Words

Marjory Wentworth

In a world where too many people
have their fingers on the triggers

of guns aimed directly at Black people,
we have borne witness, time

and time again, to executions
filmed on tiny cameras—

Which allow us to see too much
Which allow us to see not enough.

Judge, jury, executioner—
It's due process in the suburbs

and the city streets, on winding
country roads and highways, sidewalks

in front of the convenience store,
where the streetlights don't shine

in the back corner of a parking lot,
on the playground, behind the fence

in a field near your children's school
on the street in front of your house.

This interminable spectacle
of Black death playing on a loop

over and over again until
we become numb to something

that is now a permanent part
of the American memory.

How could these grainy videos
not translate into justice?

I just don't know how to believe
change is possible

when there is so much
evidence to the contrary.

I am so out of words
in the face of such brutality.

Black lives matter, and then
in an instant, they don't.

(Published in *Sojourners* June 2017)

This poem is inspired by Roxanne Gay's editorial "When Black Lives Stop Mattering" *The New York Times* (July 16, 2016).

"When you shoot us, can you shoot us with rubber bullets instead of real bullets?"

Treva Williams

I say to people all the time that everything the Rev. Nelson B. Rivers III says should be framed and hung on every wall throughout Charleston. The first thing he ever said about me? "What is a White girl from Kansas going to be able to do in Charleston, South Carolina?"

When these words were relayed to me following my interview for the lead organizer position of the Charleston Area Justice Ministry (CAJM), I smiled to myself. I remember thinking, "He makes a very good point. No matter what I did or didn't do, I would be forever labeled a 'come yah' and never a 'bin yah'." I also knew that Charleston, South Carolina, was not short on community leadership and there would never be anything I could say or do that would ever be any better or wiser than what was already being said and done, so my work here has been to assist in amplifying the voices of local people. That is what I am attempting to do here.—Treva Williams

On June 1, 2020, six-hundred community leaders and members gathered online to lay out CAJM's strategic vision to create a community where justice and equity prevail. Less than a week had passed since the brutal murder of George Floyd, and Charleston's protests over his murder became a riot. One hundred years had passed since Charleston had experienced a riot—one of dozens of such riots that happened that Red Summer of 1919 that destroyed Black businesses and killed and terrorized Black people across the country.

Now, many in the Charleston community feared what might happen as their neighbors took to the streets in pain and anger. The Rev. Nelson B. Rivers III, an outspoken Civil Rights icon in Charleston, addressed us that night. Here is some of what he had to say, and some of the stories of Charleston, which form the context in which he said it.

"When they asked me yesterday, a couple of days ago, how did I feel about young people, especially young White people doing so much marching, leading the movement?

"I told them, I said hallelujah. I thank God for 'em ... I am overwhelmed with excitement. I tell you why, because this is the first time, that I'm aware and I got more years than most of you in the movement, that White people have been in the movement, not at my invitation only, not to walk beside me, but to lead it, to go whether I go or not.

"That is powerful. And I am grateful to these young people who have contradicted their parents, their grandparents. They have looked at this now for all these years and they realize that they are guilty if they are silent. They are guilty if they're compliant by being silent or complicit, so they raise their voices and sometimes it gets violent. So folk want to know, yes I'm against violence, not just because I think it's the right thing to say, I believe it.

"But let me be clear. America responds to violence more than anything, definitely better than morality. We are a violent nation. We rarely ask for what we want. We just take it."

Charleston attorney Jerod Frazier told me a story right after I moved to Charleston. His great-great-grandfather and great-great-uncle, William and John Frazier, were both fishermen. William owned his boat and spent many days fishing off the shores of Edisto Island, a Sea Island south of Charleston. It's how he made his living. A White man from Charleston wanted to buy his great-great-grandfather's boat, but his grandfather refused to sell. The White man made multiple offers and became visibly angry at being told "no." Some days later, the boat was set on fire with Jerod's great-great-grandfather and great-great-uncle on board. Both men perished in the fire. While it was well known in the community at the time that this White man had set fire to the boat, local authorities refused to press charges. The Rev. Rivers:

"We are a violent nation. We rarely ask for what we want. We just take it."

"I want to lift up the context of the present struggle we're under now, these protests, which are so vital and for me, so encouraging. I had to remind my own members and colleagues and friends, there was a lot of consternation a couple of days ago with the violence and a lot of folk were concerned about, are protests effective and should we continue? And of course, the answer for me is yes, because I think it's important for us to understand how we got here. I say with deference and without trying to offend, America was born of violence. America has been sustained through violence. In a lot of ways, you could call America the original thug nation.

"I've had people tell me that all lives matter when they see the sign or hear the refrain Black Lives Matter. Well, that's patently not true. In America all lives do not matter. I would challenge anyone to tell me when that was the case? All lives matter? From the Native Americans whose land was taken, their lives didn't matter, from the enslaved Africans who came to America by force and brutality, the worst form of slavery the world has ever known, chattel slavery. Their lives didn't matter.

"When America expanded, it took territory that belonged to somebody, namely a lot of folk from what was known as Mexico. And their lives didn't matter.

"Now there is a group of people in America whose lives have always mattered. But to be honest about it, for the rest of us, our lives have always been a question. So what does that have to do with where we are today?"

Charleston is home to social justice warriors and sisters Minerva King and Millicent Brown, and they too have told me stories. In the 1950s and '60s their father, J. Arthur Brown, was the president of the local NAACP chapter for five years and later became the organization's state president. Brown was very vocal about the city's injustices. As a result, their home was targeted for many racist acts, including two cross burnings and many threatening phone calls.

In the 1960s the city built the "Crosstown Expressway"—one piece of a nationwide effort at urban "renewal," a.k.a. "removal." As happened elsewhere, the Crosstown Expressway cut through historic Black neighborhoods and business districts. The road was too dangerous to cross on foot and literally severed generational community connections. More than 150 houses were destroyed to create it. In 1978, the City of Charleston and the South Carolina Department of Transportation renamed the expressway the Septima P. Clark Parkway, after a notable Black Charleston educator and activist. Why? Perhaps to pacify conscience, but no matter—not only did the expressway divide and destroy a historic Black neighborhood, but many in Charleston will tell you that there is an unnecessary curve in the expressway that was built into the plan to ensure the expressway removed the Brown's family home. Today it is still referred to as The Joe Brown Curve. The Rev. Rivers:

> "America was born of violence. America has been sustained through violence. In a lot of ways, you could call America the original thug nation."
>
> "South Carolina ... is the granddaddy of all of the recalcitrant rebel Confederate states.
>
> "They talk about Mississippi and Alabama and South Carolina but South Carolina got it on lock because we learned in this state you don't have to be violent if you are brutally in charge. That's why the lynching numbers may be low in South Carolina, because when you control everything, you don't have to kill people, you just choke them."

Following the murder of Michael Brown in Ferguson, Missouri, a Black Lives Matter chapter sprang up in Charleston in response. Hundreds of young people flooded King Street, Charleston's central shopping district, and marched, chanting, "Hands up, don't shoot!" I joined a planning meeting to create posters for that march and sat and listened to a discussion around the Confederate flag and the hate it symbolizes. One organizer said, "The Confederate flag, the American flag, what's the difference? This country will never be our home."

I remember leaving that space stunned. What would it be like to live in a country where my ancestors had to fight to be freed from daily terror and savagery only to be still bound by laws that prevented them and eventually me from thriving, from safety? In Charleston, it's common knowledge that federal Community Development Block Grants were used to renew/remove historically Black communities, transforming the Charleston peninsula from 80 percent Black to 80 percent White. Today, if you are Black in Charleston, you are three times more likely than your White neighbors to be stopped by police for a minor vehicle violation like a tag light being out, three times more likely to experience use of force by a police officer. As a Black child in Charleston, you are nine times more likely to be arrested or suspended by the school district. Housing costs are rising, wages are stagnant, and healthcare is unaffordable. The Rev. Rivers:

"When you control everything, you don't have to kill people, you just choke them."

"Dr. King, when he wrote that fantastic letter from the Birmingham jail, he wrote that letter out of a strategy 'cause he had gone to jail trying to get Black adults in Birmingham to rise up and go to jail. They wouldn't do it.

"So he went to jail and the Black folk didn't get him out. And they didn't go to jail either. So they had a rally at 16th Street Baptist Church where the young four little girls were murdered. They had a rally in '63 at the church and at that church, he asked that group, who was willing to go to jail. Not one adult stood up. A 16-year-old Black girl stood up and said, 'I'll go,' and like popcorn, the children and the youth popped up all over the room. So they started going to jail before their mothers and fathers and before their pastors, and the children filled up the jail. So much so, that somehow or another, a little four-year-old boy got into a jail cell. And they asked him, 'How did you get in here and what do you want?' And he said, 'I want f'eedom.' They said, 'What did you say?' And he said, 'I want f'eedom.' He couldn't say it as well. But he understood it very clear that he wanted freedom. Four years old, in jail.

In 2015 the city of Charleston sought to improve relationships between the community and law enforcement by meeting with community members and asking them what improvements could be made. In one meeting in a local school, facilitators asked, "How can things be made better between you and police?" One child raised his hand and said, "When you shoot us, can you shoot us with rubber bullets instead of real bullets?" I was stunned, again. He spoke of being shot as a given. Not, if there's a time when you might shoot us, but WHEN YOU SHOOT US. The Rev. Rivers:

"I want f'eedom."

"The way I know I matter, is if you speak for me, if I am absent, if I don't have to be there. That's how I know Black Lives Matter ... and understand this, there's a lot of people who want to go to Brunswick, they want to go to Minneapolis, they want to go to Louisville. You don't have to go anywhere. You can fight where you are. North Charleston and Charleston have plenty of work to be done in the field of justice, but I am happy that I don't have to be present always to be fought for.

"Sometimes, my life matters by what you do and what you say without me having to say a word. That's why I'm encouraged, that's why I'm not sad and I said to my family and my friends and my church members who said, 'Let's go pray.' I told 'em no matter how long you pray, when you get up, you put some feet to your prayers and some arms to your faith.

"I'm glad the young people are up, and I encourage them and I thank them and I'm grateful to them because they've embarrassed some folk. Because while we've been talking, they've been walking. God bless them, God bless you.

"Don't be discouraged. Friends and family, the best is yet to come. We're so close. We're much closer than we've been in a long time."

Music of Doves Ascending

Marjory Wentworth

Yellow crime tape tied to the wrought-iron fence
weaves through bouquets of flowers
and wreaths made of white ribbons,
like rivers of bright pain flowing through the hours.

Weaving through bouquets of flowers,
lines of strangers bearing offerings
like rivers of bright pain flowing through the hours.
One week later; the funeral bells ring;

lines of strangers still bring offerings.
Nine doves tossed toward the sun.
One week later; the funeral bells ring,
while churches in small towns are burning.

Nine doves tossed toward the sun.
Because there are no words to sing,
while churches in small towns are burning,
a blur of white wings, ascends like music.

Published in *Illuminations*, 31, Summer 2016.

"The Lowcountry: Whose Story to Tell?"

On Documentary as Witness

Vicki Callahan

As a film historian and media practitioner, I have spent countless hours and pages of script on what sort of documentary project *The Lowcountry: Whose Story to Tell* should be. The project began in June 2016 as an effort to capture a range of perspectives from the Charleston, South Carolina, community on the possibilities of racial justice and conciliation in the aftermath of the Mother Emanuel AME Church massacre the previous year. Although I was then living in California with many years of residence across the United States and abroad, I had grown up in Charleston, frequently visited close family members in the area, and still considered the city "home." Despite these familial and emotional ties, I realized as a White academic coming back into Charleston it was critical to consider the lens and the objectives of the project that I was undertaking. Documentary films, like their fictional counterparts, come in many genres, with the key elements defined by point of view and assumptions about the kind of knowledge generated. There is a sliding scale of subjective-versus-objective perspectives and a similar variation in the certainty of the information and argument relayed by a work. Some documentaries are about the revelation of a singular true story and some weigh in on the side of multiple truths or the uncertainty about any truth in a given context. None of these seemed to fit Charleston's story or indeed the story of racial injustice in the United States. I had no desire to show "both sides," but I also recognized my Whiteness and that my long-time absence from Charleston meant I had much to learn about the state of Black and White relations in the city and the material conditions across racial differences.

Complicating all of this is the story, or rather, more precisely, the history of Charleston, which in its more (White) tourist-friendly variant has glossed over racial inequities and tensions. A "golden haze of memory," as the historian Stephanie Yuhl has described it,[97] still seemed to envelope much of Charleston's "official" history. This "history" painted an essentially benign and benevolent past and one largely absent in acknowledging enslaved African people and the material realities of their lives and labor that built the city and enriched the local economy. Sundering the haze, however, other voices and stories that countered and corrected this "official" history were also in circulation, such as those histories that centered on African-American experiences at McLeod Plantation Historic Site, The Old Slave Mart Museum, and the Borough Houses, to name a few.

The intersections and divergences of these narratives were daunting to consider, and I knew that my approach and ensuing genre of expression needed to explore the city's complicated past, present, and future. In line with a documentary based in the "Holy City," I thought it best to begin with the area's faith-based communities. My process drew inspiration and its foundation from the welcoming and open conversations and connections that were shared by members of church groups, including the New Francis Brown United Methodist Church, the Charleston Area Justice Ministry, Mt. Zion AME, Mother Emanuel AME, and Grace Church Cathedral. Drawing on these experiences, I began to understand that my role in the process was neither to be "objective" nor "subjective," but rather to follow the path of "witness" as mapped out by the several guiding sources, but especially as found in the works of James Baldwin and Bernie Glassman.

The notion of witnessing straddles a grey zone between observation and activism. It begins for Bernie Glassman, founder of Zen Peacemakers and a

---

[97] Stephanie E. Yuhl, *A Golden Haze of Memory: The Making of Historic Charleston* (Chapel Hill: The University of North Carolina Press, 2005).

Buddhist teacher, with a commitment to "unknowing," or a lack of assumptions about what we know, and deep listening.[98] Glassman challenges us to push the process of "unknowing" and "listening;" the outcome is not ambiguity or doubt but a broader understanding and a movement toward compassionate action.[99] "Bearing witness" is essentially an endless process rather than a space of closure and from this arises not a particular didactic turn but an ever-expansive vision and healing. Interestingly, for Glassman, the opposite of "witnessing" is denial, a refusal to listen or learn.[100] Coming from a different religious background, Christianity, the writer James Baldwin has a similar evocation of the term, akin to truth-telling but not as an exhortation: "I have never seen myself as a spokesman. I am a witness. In the church in which I was raised you were supposed to bear witness to the truth. Now, later on, you wonder what in the world the truth is, but you do know what a lie is."[101] As the "golden haze" from Charleston's histories dissipates with corrective histories, Baldwin's words are instructive.

The late College of Charleston professor Ade Ajani ("Dr. O") Ofunniyin and Ms. Johanna Martin-Carrington of the Gullah Society led our film team[102] through the "sacred burial ground" at the end of Monrovia Street in the Neck area of Charleston. Here, just down the street from the Washington United Methodist Church and graveyard, in an overgrown area directly adjacent to Interstate 26, is an African-descendant burial site the Gullah Society is working to document, restore, and maintain. There are blue and red tags everywhere marking artifacts, graves, monuments, and crypts that need clearing, care, and recording of information related to those buried there.

As Dr. O pointed out as we arrived at a densely overgrown back area of the site: "This tombstone over here, it's leaning up against the fence [and] that tombstone was lying face-down. So my class ... we were out here cleaning

---

[98] Bernie Glassman, *Bearing Witness: A Zen Master's Lessons in Making Peace* (Blue Rider Press, 2013), 889, Kindle.

[99] Ibid, 893.

[100] Ibid, 910-939.

[101] James Lester, "James Baldwin: Reflections of a Maverick." *New York Times* (May 27, 1984) (https://archive.nytimes.com/www.nytimes.com/books/98/03/29/specials/baldwin-reflections.html.

[102] Our film team for the December 2018 filming included Dianne Farrington, Tony Bell, Lewis Porcher, and Noa Kaplan,

this up and my students they got together and they raised the tombstone up so that the person's name can be seen.... And you should have seen the joy on those students' faces, it was like they released this soul from obscurity.... It was an amazing experience, you know. But, I mean, this is our ancestors. These people gave so much to our world here in Charleston. They gave so much to the world and this is how they are left to rest. It's not acceptable. It's not acceptable, and just look at these markings, these people had to have been ... even if they weren't significant, even if they didn't have these tombstones signifying their significance, they're significant!"[103]

Ms. Martin-Carrington continued with this important moment of instruction about our surroundings: "You know, one of the things about the difference in graveyards and cemeteries—graveyards are burial sites for family, organizations, churches, and the like. Cemetery, it's a commercial place where everyone gets buried. And there's that difference. ... There's kinsmanship in a graveyard. And a cemetery is just a place to lay bodies and they're commercialized.

Whereas he [Dr. O] speaks about this site ... you see these people, who had a connection, whatever that connection was; whether it was familial as in family or familial as in clubs and organization, or familial as in places of worship that they were into ... and that's what we are standing on. We call it 'standing on holy ground' because that is the kind of ground that we're standing on ... and there's a need to recognize and clear these places up and make them, places that our ancestors would be proud that we've done. It's what they'd want."[104]

While the cold December weather and the noise from the wind and highway were bracing, this moment with Dr. O and Ms. Martin-Carrington was transformative for the project. I realized we were not there to "document" in the sense of a simple transcription or recording of events, but rather as a "witness," as someone to help share evidence of people and places obscured or lost in the "haze" of the official history. The "sacred burial ground" project is one part of the invaluable work of the Gullah Society to preserve and am-

[103] Dr. Ade Ofunniyin, founding director for the Gullah Society, interviewed for *The Lowcountry: Whose Story to Tell?* (filmed in December 2018). Professor Ofunniyin passed away in October 2020.

[104] Johanna Martin-Carrington, board member of the Gullah Society, interviewed for *The Lowcountry*, December 2018.

plify the history and culture of African descendants in the Lowcountry. This is the arduous work of corrective history, challenging entrenched narratives and revealing difficult truths. It is also a history as noted by WiBi Ashley, the organization's wellness coordinator, closely linked to issues of health and healing for the community.[105]

As our documentary project, *The Lowcountry*, moves forward, my goal is to keep in the foreground the responsibilities of the witness to broaden vision, listen, and generate restorative practices. Although the time to build this project has been lengthy, I know there is much I still need to hear and learn. Beyond the specific uses referenced here, within global contexts the media scholar Sandra Ristovska has argued that witnessing has undergone a shift in recent years from a witnessing of to a witnessing for, that is, a turn to explicit action in response to the evidence presented, a movement toward activism.[106]

The role of witness as activist has also been a key element within the African-American church and the civil rights movement, with a sense of close connection between divine encounter and practical actions.[107] As religious scholar Rosetta E. Ross notes in speaking about Black women's civil rights work, this tradition was an important corrective history to the dysfunctional and destructive myth of American individualism:

> These women's persistent practices of organizing, teaching, and agitating bore witness to their understandings of human mutuality and relationship as divine gifts and to their understanding of divine calling to affirm human community. By testifying about and witnessing to the value of human community, they brought to public debate a norm of relatedness that challenged the notion of individual rights as a value that trumps every other value confronting it.[108]

The story of our trip to the Monrovia Street sacred burial site with Dr. O and

---

[105] WiBi Ashley, community wellness coordinator for the Gullah Society, in discussion with the author, April 2021.
[106] Sandra Ristovska, "The Purchase of Witnessing" in *The Routledge Companion to Media and Activism*, ed. Graham Meikle (New York: Routledge, 2018), 221.
[107] Rosetta E. Ross, *Witnessing and Testifying: Black Women, Religion, and Civil Rights* (Minneapolis: 1517 Media, 2003), 224
[108] Ibid., 235.

Ms. Martin-Carrington was just one of the many opportunities our five-person crew had to bear witness to the new histories being written in Charleston. My hope is that *The Lowcountry* will provide a space where others can view and hear the stories with a sense of "unknowingness" that might amplify and increase the many acts of witnessing for already well underway in the city. *The Lowcountry* takes as inspiration the many efforts toward building the "beloved community" throughout the Charleston area, and hopes that by highlighting these practices of healing, it might offer a model for the rest of the country.

The Witness

Horace Mungin

It all happened quite suddenly
Man's fury turned against him
The air became dense
The sky mushroomed
The flowers wilted and died
I stood the only witness.

Death raged
Death raged like an angry beast
And hope proved to be death by radiation
The human will is dispirited
City dwellers crawled into the streets to die
People died however they could
People killed themselves
And murdered each other
And with the world in the midst
Of all this madness
Willie across the street
Screwed himself to death.

No longer were there trees
Building crumbled/the rivers dried
And when all things were dead
There standing for a witness
Stood I.

Now all living things cease to be
There was never a baby born
And Jesus didn't die on the cross

If I forget
The poet's lyrics never sweetened the air
And all of man's majesty
None of it is real
Ain't none this stuff real without a witness.

Land Lost

Heirs' Property: "The Biggest Problem You've Never Heard Of"

Dr. Jennie L. Stephens

When the late Johnnie Rivers was a boy, the houses in Pinefield had long porches, places to gather late at night when it was too hot to sleep. Patrolling mosquitoes from the nearby marsh found warm bodies with fresh blood. Smoke from piles of burning dried grass repelled these pesky intruders. In 1883, Hector Rivers, Johnnie's great-grandfather, paid $250 to purchase fifty acres of land along a deep-water stream to the Cooper River near Cainhoy, South Carolina. He called this land, the Rivers family compound, Pinefield.

A century later, Hector's descendants continued to live in a cluster of homes at Pinefield. However, by the late-twentieth century, the land had been reduced to seventeen acres. Despite this, Johnnie never left Pinefield; he raised his family there. In 2001, Johnnie lost the remainder of this land because of an heirs' property dispute, a legal issue across America that ProPublica called: "The biggest problem you've never heard of."

Johnnie's family became involved in a legal dispute with his sister, another heir of Hector's, over Pinefield because she wanted her monetary share of the land's value. The seventeen acres of land was not easily divisible by the numerous heirs and there was no agreement among them. Consequently, this issue was eventually tossed into state court where a judge ordered the land sold and the money divided among the family. In September 2001, Johnnie and twenty-five members of his family, children, grandchildren, and great-grandchildren, were evicted. Johnnie and his wife remained until the land was sold. An investor purchased Pinefield for $910,000. Eight months later, after title to the land was resolved, the land was back on the market for $3 million.

Pinefield's story and the loss of family-owned land is not just a problem with African Americans in the South. "Fractionalized land," "tangled titles," or whatever you may call heirs' property impacts both rural and urban communities—for both Blacks and Whites—across the United States. As in the case of the Rivers family, much of this land has been passed down through the generations without a will so that the land is owned "in common" by multiple heirs. This unstable form of ownership puts this land at high risk for loss because any heir can sell his or her ownership interest to another or demand the monetary value for that share, as in the Rivers family example, which leads to a forced sale of the entire property in the courts.

The current Covid-19 pandemic and the highly publicized killings of Black Americans last year by police have pushed forward a national conversation around systemic racial inequities. Black land loss and heirs' property are now mentioned in legislation, discussed as political priorities, and targeted as injustices. At the heart of what we do at the Center for Heirs' Property Preservation is to pursue justice. You cannot separate justice from the land or from economics. Justice is education. Justice is a job. Our mission is to ensure that people realize those possibilities.

Heirs' property is a significant issue in South Carolina, especially in coastal communities and on the Sea Islands. The mosquito-infested marshlands along the coast that were once deemed undesirable are now the waterfront lands that are in high demand. It is thought that in the Lowcountry of South Carolina, most heirs' property is land that was acquired by African Americans after Emancipation. With an increase in commercial and development interest, heirs' property is a prime target, and many heirs' property owners have lost their land for lack of a clear title or timely tax payments.

Additionally, many rural landowners in South Carolina lack the knowledge and services that would help them realize the economic value of landowner-ship. To help address both issues, the Center for Heirs' Property Preservation provides legal and forestry education and services to protect heirs' property and to promote the sustainable use of land to provide increased economic benefits to historically underserved families.

Heirs' property is not just an African American issue in the South. Other vulnerable landowners throughout the country—especially, women and the poor—have involuntarily lost family property through contested claims, unaffordable high transaction and legal costs, forced sales to speculators, and outright fraud. Wherever there are large communities of underserved people, such as in Appalachia or Native American lands, so are the dual problems of fractionated ownership and the inability to collateralize land wealth. Although historical origins may differ, heirs' property and reservation trust lands both share consequences of high legal and transaction costs due to fractionated claims (multiple owners) and the inability to collateralize land wealth.

Heirs' property is also not simply a rural issue either. A 2007 study by Philadelphia VIP, a nonprofit legal services agency, found that nearly fourteen thousand city properties had heirs' property issues or what they call "tangled titles." The Pew Charitable Trusts plans to release updated urban numbers. Advocates feel that the 2007 figures have not changed much.

Preserving intergenerational family wealth is key to closing the racial wealth gaps. Whether rural or urban, most family wealth is based on a family's largest assets, their homes. Heirs' property disproportionately affects people of color, according to housing advocates, partly due to racial gaps in estate planning that transcend education. According to Thomas Mitchell, a MacArthur fellow and professor at Texas A&M University School of Law, roughly 75 percent of college-educated White people in the U.S. have a will, compared with only 33 percent of college-educated Black people. Inheritance and land use can be difficult conversations. Impoverished people do not sit around the kitchen table to talk about estate planning. Unfortunately, because of this, they often are taken advantage of.

In South Carolina, many rural landowners have been unable to access the knowledge and services that would help them realize the economic value of land ownership. To address both issues, the Center for Heirs' Property Preservation was created as a 501(c)(3) non-profit organization in 2005.

Property matters. It's more than just a parcel of land. It's also window to the past that tells the story of a family, a community, a way of life. Knowing your family's history and culture creates a sense of place and belonging. The loss of heirs' property has impact on the entire community, not just one family.

The center builds trust in the rural African American communities where distrust and fear of authority and the legal system are pervasive. Once trust is established, these communities are open to receive information. Knowledge increases confidence, self-determination, better decision-making, and an ability to take action to change positively a family's circumstances.

Sixteen years ago, many people thought the problem of land loss was just too complex to solve. In contrast to this, we saw opportunity. We also knew that prevention and solving the legal aspects to clear title was simply not enough. Hurricane Hugo in 1989 highlighted the plight of heirs' property owners and their inability to access Federal Emergency Management Agency (FEMA) funds and proceeds from their insurance policies. Heirs' property holders are often denied FEMA disaster assistance because they do not have clear title to their land. And due to global warming, disasters like hurricanes, flooding, and storm surges are more commonplace and severe.

In an April 17, 2021 article, "FEMA: Don't drive the Gullah-Geechee from their land," published in The Hill, George Albert, *founder of the Resilience Initiative for Coastal Education (RICE),* discusses Hurricane Matthew in 2016. He reports that more than eighteen thousand disaster-assistance claims were denied in South Carolina counties, with a high concentration of those claims concerning heirs' property. Janiece Glover with South Carolina Policy, Engagement, Advocacy and Research analyzed that the counties with the highest prevalence of heirs' property saw half of FEMA aid applications denied.

Property owners often tell us they are tired of working for their land. We knew that once families received clear title to their properties, we needed to reverse that statement, so the land works for them. Through a sustainable-forestry program and other efforts we have created a landowner movement that has the power to unleash the cultural and natural resources of land.

Most African American landowners have owned their family property for generations. Therefore, their land-management decisions are sometimes driven by family legacy, rather than economic factors. Without realizing any economic value for their owners, however, the property faces the risk of becoming a liability, rather than a managed asset. African Americans have faced additional challenges due to heirs' property, smaller land holdings, and mistrust of the forest industry and federal programs. Since 2013, the center has been involved with the Sustainable Forestry and African American Land Retention (SFLR) Program. Forestry is more than a $21-billion-a-year industry in South Carolina. Chances are, if you have property in South Carolina, it has trees on it. The SFLR program provides a way to keep deep ties to family land while promoting wealth creation.

We serve 22 of the 46 South Carolina counties. Our legal and financial expertise has been sought on a national level. We've pushed the heirs' property issue to the forefront in national legislation and even to a part of Congress's COVID relief bill. Along with robust landowner advocates, we have started an economic and conservation movement that creates intergenerational wealth among historically underserved landowners.

In this country, researchers estimate that Black families have lost hundreds of billions of dollars in land value over the last century. The U.S. Department of Agriculture considers heirs' property the "leading cause of Black involuntary land loss." The prevention of continued loss of Black farmland and investing in generational family wealth is one practical way to address this inequity.

Since its inception through the first quarter of 2021, the center has provided nearly 3,260 persons with free one-hour "advice and counsel," with 777 clients receiving direct legal services to clear title. A total of 1,225 simple wills have been drafted at free community wills clinics, and 285 titles have been cleared on family land with a total tax-assessed value of $16.6 million. On the forestry side, more than 503 families own in excess of twenty-six thousand acres. Landowners have received nearly $2 million dollars in financial assistance from the U.S. Department of Agriculture/Natural Resources Conservation Service programs and thirty landowners have realized $2 million in timber sales.

It has been the center's mission to help families protect their property. It is the history, the family dynamics, the opportunity to help people and their communities now, as well as future generations that has motivated us for the past sixteen years and what will propel us as an organization into the future. By expanding our services, the center hopes to assist even more families like Johnnie Rivers's keep their land and expand their wealth.

Following Dorothy In Her Wheeler Hill
Aïda Rogers

It's the four o'clocks that get me. They bloomed bright red alongside the elephant ears in Bertha Lewis's yard. That's "Old Bertha Lewis," long gone, with her plants and well-tended home in Columbia, South Carolina. "Hers was the best house," Dorothy Perry Thompson remembers in "Pickens Street," her poem about the neighborhood where she grew up. "It looked just like a white folks place."

Bertha Lewis's place wasn't the only landmark on Pickens Street. There was a pink concrete house where the taxi driver lived with his wife and the gray-green house where the plumber lived with his. There was the store where you could buy pickled pig's feet and hear Lionel Hampton on the Piccolo, and if you knew where to look, you could see where "Big Book Kitt/ Let himself ooze/ All over the sidewalk/ Through a big hole/ Left by a shotgun."

Colorful—that was the Pickens Street of Dorothy Perry Thompson's child-hood. It played a big part in her neighborhood, Wheeler Hill. I'm embarrassed not to have heard of her before, but then again, I'm White. I didn't grow up in a neighborhood White people called a slum. Nobody would have used the words "insidious cancer" to describe my family's paved street of brick ranch houses and rectangular green yards. But that was Dorothy's reality. Wheeler Hill, with its wooden shotgun houses and unpaved roads, its dearth of parks and modern plumbing, didn't suit the vision of Columbia's leaders. To use their word from the 1970s, it wasn't "compatible" with what loomed over it. That was the University of South Carolina.

Dorothy was six in 1950 when her father brought her from Charlotte to live with her mother and stepfather in Wheeler Hill. It didn't take her long to learn the rules. No crossing Wheat Street, which ran perpendicular to Pickens Street at the bottom of the hill. On the other side and up another hill was the university, where "colored" students hadn't been allowed since 1877, when Reconstruction, the era that allowed newly freed Black men to vote and scholars to continue their educations, was killed. For Dorothy and her neighbors, the campus was definitely off limits, and so was whatever was behind the vine-covered fence with the KEEP OUT sign. Dorothy wrote about that sign in "Wheeler Hill:"

> *But I got to the top of that fence once.*
> *Saw another sign reading MYRTLE COURT.*
> *There was a fountain circled by four huge houses.*
> *The whole place was paved.*
> *Wonder where the white kids played?*

I love that she climbed that fence. And I really love that she wrote about it.

Dorothy Perry Thompson, Ph.D., died too soon. She was 57 in 2002 when the breast cancer she'd survived four years earlier came back. I can't talk to her, but she talks to me, through her three books of poetry and writings collected elsewhere.

Anyone with internet access can learn about her: the daughter of a carpenter and a laundry presser, she's included in the *South Carolina Encyclopedia* and the South Carolina Academy of Authors. Maybe the most about her can be found at Winthrop University in Rock Hill, South Carolina, where she taught English and writing, started its African American Studies program, and where her papers are kept. She had been promoted to full professor just months before she died. A book of her poetry, *Priest in Aqua Boa*, and another she edited, *Out of the Rough: Women's Poems of Survival and Celebration*, were released in 2001.

I'm lucky I can read her poems. While *Fly with the Puffin* and *Priest in Aqua Boa* are out of print, copies are available through the University of South Carolina, where I work. With a half-minute of online searching and two keystrokes, I can have them waiting for me as soon as a librarian can retrieve

146

them from the shelf. The hardest part is walking to pick them up.

Not so for "Dot," as she was known. Unable to cross Wheat Street at the bottom of the hill, she couldn't even consider coming to the University of South Carolina. Having graduated from the highly regarded and much-loved Booker T. Washington High in 1962, right on Wheat Street in her neighborhood, she went instead to the AME-supported Allen University about two miles away, graduating in 1968. She started her teaching career and married her high school classmate, Johnnie Thompson, with whom she'd have two sons and a daughter.

If she'd waited a year after high school she could have applied at the so-close-but-so-far-away University of South Carolina, because it integrated, with three students, in 1963. Dorothy enrolled later, earning her Master of Arts in Teaching in 1974 and her Ph.D. in 1987. She was the second Black person to get a Ph.D. in English at the university and the first to complete a dissertation in creative writing, with celebrated poet and novelist James Dickey as her dissertation-committee chair.

"Wheeler Hill and Other Poems," like other dissertations and theses written by university students, is available at the library. For me, tracking Dorothy just as she tracked Zora Neale Hurston in *Hurrying the Spirit: Following Zora*, that dissertation is pure gold. It's my map to a community that pulsed with life and people, crime and peace, schools and churches, four o'clocks and a café that sold fish sandwiches on Fridays, and a little girl who was taking it all in, holding it until it was ready to spill out. It's all there, in her dissertation.

"The poem 'Wheeler Hill' expresses much of my frustration at USC's eventual take-over; but the physical domination is secondary to what I saw later as the psychological crippling, especially to the young people," she writes in her introduction. "I know that part of that crippling was made easy because of the social conditioning of our parents. They taught us as they were taught: White folks got the power; work hard and don't make waves. Those who believed this directive suffered the consequences; those who didn't, who 'made waves' … suffered the consequences."

By the time she was writing those words her Wheeler Hill was becoming a memory, thanks to the university that dominated and then, bit by bit, demolished it. Dorothy watched bulldozers at work from her fifth-floor campus window; she had already taught courses in the high-rise dorms that were built earlier, the ones that blocked her grandmother's view not too many years before. Did she feel she was being sucked into the institutional machine that had dictated much of her life? Was writing her dissertation her way of preserving her neighborhood, even as it changed from working-class Black to high-income White? She was certainly following that old writer's rule—writing about what she knew.

In her poems she's made her neighbors immortal. A skinny girl named Pig slept with another woman's man and took a bullet for it. Big Pink, a bootlegger "in a sharkskin suit and alligator shoes," operated in high style until he got arrested. Benjamin Jefferson whistled "in spurts/ Of exaggerated life/ To the rhythmical pop/ Of his shoeshine rag." Sisters Fannie Phelps Adams and Celia Phelps Martin, respected educators, appear "under the hair dryers" in "Miss Juanita's Beauty Salon." So does "Miss Jeannette White/ The licensed mid-wife/ Who was getting her hair dyed."

Dorothy's words for the Wheeler Hill she knew? "Calm, dangerous, simple, mysterious." Like people, places can be contradictory.

"Eminent Domain" is such a useful phrase. In just two words it tells us that a place has been changed, cleared out, destroyed for the greater good. It's a bloodless term that ignores the messy emotions of people forced to leave their homes.

"They're furious," said Bobby Donaldson, a history professor at the university who has studied its urban-renewal practices and befriended many people who couldn't afford to stay on Wheeler Hill once it started gentrifying. "There's never been an apology or acknowledgement. If you're living in a neighborhood for generations and your parents and grandparents are all rooted in that space, and suddenly you're stripped, then you're uprooted. That's a powerful word. It was not tearing down a house. It was destroying a history."

In "Wheeler Hill" Dorothy tells us where some of her neighbors went—to Philadelphia, Trenton, and New York, but also cheaper neighborhoods in Columbia, like Greenview and Newcastle. You can trace some of Black Columbia's twentieth century through her work.

Those who stayed in Columbia gather frequently, Donaldson said. Classes from Booker T. Washington High hold joyous reunions, and many still worship at St. James AME, one of the few landmarks still present in Wheeler Hill. Standing amid a tangle of narrow, winding streets of pricey brick townhomes, vine-covered brick walls, and postage-stamp yards, St. James blends in, thanks to its red brick exterior.

What else is left? The railroad tracks, where the Norfolk Southern comes through, and a few homes that appear to be shotgun houses updated and enlarged. The concrete fountain in the enchanted-seeming Myrtle Court neighborhood still bubbles, though the "KEEP OUT" fence is gone. At the top of Pickens Street, where Dr. Ezra Wheeler's 1870 home once stood, rises a giant water tower bearing the words "CAROLINA GAMECOCKS." Fewer than twenty affordable housing units were built in Wheeler Hill; fifty were promised. Across from them is DiPrato's Delicatessen, a popular lunch/brunch place with an uptown menu. Decades ago, it was a neighborhood store famous for peanuts. "It really does feel like a lost neighborhood," says Sophie Kahler, a 2021 university graduate who spent two years researching its archives for a published academic paper and her honors thesis. "You could live here and not know about it, because there's not much here to tell you it existed."

But there is Dorothy's poetry. And Donaldson's work to save its history and document Columbia's civil rights struggles as director of USC's Center for Civil Rights History and Research. And Kahler's dramatic discovery after going through box after box of university archives to track the methodical destruction of a community of tenants who couldn't afford to control their destinies. It was a letter from Thomas F. Jones, the university's twenty-third president. Dated February 22, 1968, and addressed to members of Columbia's city council and housing authority, he wrote this: "For many years it has been the goal of the University and the City of Columbia to attempt to wipe out the entire slum area of approximately twelve blocks known as Wheeler Hill."

So there it is, a letter in black and white about the truth of Black and White. And while Dorothy wrote angry poems about racism, other colors populate her work. "If I had known/ those would be/ my happiest days/ I would have worn red/ not the modest/ white skirt and long-sleeved jacket," she writes in "Before Cancer."

I think she liked red, like Bertha Lewis's four o'clocks, and flowers in general. Daisies and azaleas, hyacinths and oleanders figure in her poems. "Still, I add red caladium, / the saffron canna" she writes in "Waiting." Beneath the title, in parentheses, is "at 52, finally, with flowers." She would have five more years to live.

Dr. Dorothy Perry Thompson loved beauty, music, dancing, friends, and family. Her denigrated community gave her all those things, shotgun houses be damned. "Walk tall, y'all," she instructs her family and ex-neighbors in her dissertation. Through her poetry, she walked tall, too.

A Ballad for Dorothy

Elizabeth Robin

in Black & White, an old photo of Gamecock Country

Don't you wonder who lived on Pickens Street? What colorful flowers
bloomed there? They don't imagine, but do you? One lively emerging
poet, scholar, professor, ran in the joyful blooming bunches playing
vacant lot pick-up games. The stew of characters that opened up
texture, the elegance in a shotgun house, a buttery biscuit, rollaway
beds, front porches, and making the middle room decent—

But Gamecock Nation, shrine of high honor and truth, announced
a goal in 1968: wipe out the entire slum area—twelve blocks—known
as Wheeler Hill. Use words like slum or blight and let's rid the scourge,
the stain, the filth and rot holding us back, has next *Carolina, forever to thee*!

Dorothy, a Wheeler Hill kid, lives the colors of poetry and jazz,
earns her doctorate at the college that barred her undergrad attendance,
that stole her neighborhood and her grandmother's view, that played
the eminent domain card, razed her high school for two athletic fields,
turned humble shotguns into suburban cul-de-sacs and keep-out gates

Kids roamed there, with Mr. Hump the plumber who took pay however,
Bertha Lewis in a perfect white house flush with prized red four o'clock
flowers, Jenkins the town taxi-man, Ma Sally's pickled jar store, Wheeler
Hill wealth dreaming at Bessie McKnight's Cafe, the cigar tree where
they snuck off to smoke, or to Copeland's, for deli meats and easy credit.

But they never crossed Wheat Street.

Life, not blight. Community surrounded St. James AME, circled close now
by hipsters who won't attend. Those teachers and grocers and drunks
staggering, the licensed midwife, the hairdresser, the neighborhood clean-up,
street noise, street quiet—all the music that climbed the hill laid out
with all the things that made the street—pushed out, wild shouts as balls fly,
pimps, hawkers, hard-working folk—replaced with silence. A tomb.

She could tell you, but you need to care. She did show you, how promised
housing evaporates, what richness lived in what you erased, how she triumphed,
wrote their stories
        But you let them, her, go out of print
        Even her stories aren't good enough for you

Shotgunning

Dorothy Perry Thompson

They said if you stood
at the front door
and shot a double barrel through,
it would go straight out the back.
I preferred to think
If Tonto bent a sure elbow
behind a keen eye
in my living room,
he'd mark one less mean kemo sabe
standing on my back step
fussin' 'bout my dog.

I rinse summer dust
from hop-scotched feet
and skin-the-cat limbs.

Under a cool, blue nightgown
strange things grow,
gangling with me
through thin cotton
through thin walls
and through night duties
at 12 years old:

Latch the front screen
and bolt the door,
five strides across
the living room floor

A middle room leap
'cross two little brothers
(Josh and Shang in their roll-away bed)

Straight to the kitchen
'tween the sink and stove
ducking Mama's things on the kitchen floor line
to the back door
to flip the light switch and look outside.

The wood bin's locked
and Gypsy's tied
fast to the tree trunk
but loose enough to move
if John Augustus comes
to bother him tonight
(Crazy old man,
Wantin' to shoot a dog—
The dog don't know not to bark after midnight.
Next time I'll tell
that old wrinkled face fart
to tie his wristwatch
to Gypsy's front paw
then pray the good Lord
will take it from there.)

Look in the warmer
top of the stove
Cuss out Shang
'cause the last biscuit's gone.

Arrow on back to the front room bed.
Pull Lil's thumb
Out of her mouth.

I will be shoot if I wanna hear
her sucking and pulling
all night long.
Dumb old finger's already flat.

"Turn out the light
And go to sleep, gal
And none o' that pokin'
Your sister tonight.

I'll put you on the porch
In just your nightgown,
then I'll lock the door.
Stop that foolin' round!"

Our Land Too

Echinacea in the Field of Daisies— Memories and Hope for Horticulture

Teresa Speight

I have always been enamored with flowers, nature, books, and writing. I was also a little bigger than my peers, a geek, and painfully shy. When puberty hit, my books and curious nature were my lifesavers. I remember hiking with my older brother in the woods near our suburban homestead in Silver Spring, Maryland. I was always noticing beautiful woodland flora and amazing reptiles and rushed home to the encyclopedia. The urgency of finding out what I had just witnessed was always the most important thing to me. There was no internet at the time. I looked at the pictures and flipped every page until I recognized what had captured my soul. I remember Podophyllum peltatum, commonly known as mayapples. It was the first woodland species I fell in love with.

Fast forward to adulthood. A life-altering event made me realize the significance of the garden, and I found it fitting to merge my favorite things. The garden reflects the journey of life in so many ways. On this new life journey, I felt the need to elevate my voice. Sharing my perspective and observations in the garden became my mission. Where others simply saw a peace rose, I saw a rose with the softness of the awakening day, with dew drops settling on the leaves like tears from heaven. The earth mourning the loss of a long night's rest yet unfurling to embrace the day. I wanted to find other African American garden writers who had similar thoughts. Seeing someone who looked like me would certainly help with imposter syndrome. This research proved to be shocking and futile. The two African American authors who repeatedly came up as I researched were Lee May and Jamaica Kincaid.

I was disappointed. I knew there had to be more. I assumed I was merely overlooking something or using the wrong search words. In the meantime, I read everything Lee May wrote and even reached out to him. The conversations we shared about perennials, shrubs, and shade gardens are etched in my heart. Lee May encouraged me to write, as there were not many African Americans active in horticulture—as writers. I began to write in earnest. When I learned of his passing, I knew I had to follow his instructions.

I started blogging, became active on all forms of social media, and attended everything I could afford to attend. Reading everything from everyone I could, I found authors I liked, and I looked for more of anything related to my journey as a garden writer. I searched for professional organizations, blogging conferences, and anything that could elevate my voice. The mission was to find other people of color who wrote about horticulture or even worked in horticulture. As I continued this journey, countless people asked me if I had heard of Jamaica Kincaid. I began to be annoyed. I knew there had to be more. It was hard to believe that just one woman represented the African American voice in horticulture.

My research continued. I left no stone unturned. I did find a few more African American authors writing about farming and vegetables. As a former founding farmer of a community-supported-agriculture farmette in Virginia, I was interested in vegetables. Who doesn't want a stuffed squash blossom or a freshly harvested carrot? What I realized, however, was that I did not want to write about them. Not because it was not important, but I wanted African Americans to notice the entire garden, not just the vegetables. Black people know vegetables. But we also need to know those pollinators that aid in the growth of vegetables. Pleasure gardens—ornamental gardens that feature no edible food items, but are grown purely for pleasure—are also a part of the African American garden story. African American garden clubs across the United States have staged flower shows where arrangements are judged for form and beauty. Cooperative extension offices across the South have hired African American women to instruct others how to keep the house and grow prolific gardens. I knew I had to help change the conversation. I knew I had to be the echinacea in the field. I'll explain what that means to me.

I joined The Association of Garden Writers (GWA), focused on writing about all things horticultural. This was a big step. I just knew this was where I would find people who would accept me and with whom I could relate. I also thought this was where I would find other African Americans who wrote about diversity in the world of gardening. Bonding with people who have the same interests can be amazing as well as enlightening.

But GWA quickly made me realize an uncomfortable truth. I was the only person of color in the room or on the bus tour. Initially, that was okay. When you are an African American in any group, there is always hope that eventually you will meet at least one other person of color. As I signed up for trips, trying to find a roommate was an eye opener, too. The simple act of sharing a seat or accommodations can be powerfully challenging. Struggling not to be dismissed or deterred, I continued to show up and participate in as many conversations as possible, but the reality that I was the association's only African American was not comforting. Perhaps this was not where I could truly share my voice, be taken seriously, and be offered opportunities like my counterparts.

Initially this almost shattered my spirit. I was asked to help the organization invite other minorities to join. But diversity was not reflected in the GWA marketing. How could I recruit minorities when representation is nonexistent? Representation speaks to the character of any organization. As I approached other minorities in horticulture about joining, that lack of representation was quite the issue. It became evident that diversity was only in the garden, outside the inner workings of the organization. GWA (now known as Garden Communicators International) has been in existence for more than seventy years, and inclusivity seemed to have never been a part of its story.

At one conference, I finally met another African American woman. It was quite a dramatic moment. We were on the floor of an event where vendors show off their new products. Most people familiar with African Americans know we can paint a picture with our hands when we talk. Arms flailing, hands on our hips, repeated hugs, and perhaps we were using our loud "family reunion" voices. Obviously, we were happily lost in the moment, until two White men came over to ask if we were okay. My heart sank in disbelief.

Although some years have passed, the shock of this encounter is still clear in my mind. One gentleman admitted he was concerned with the appearance of our situation. He thought we were arguing. My counterpart explained, as I stood in shock, eyeing the room for a place to hide. This is how African Americans express themselves when we meet someone, she told the White men. An uncomfortable laugh followed. The men said they were just checking to be sure all was good as they returned to their respective sides of the room. I just wanted to leave. After giving each other the knowing look of disgust, my newfound friend and I decided we would meet at another time—in private. This shook me to my core. I could not understand why we could not be authentic in mixed racial company. As much as I've tried to let it go, it still hurts and bothers me.

After that, I knew that I had to make a difference and speak up when I noticed something out of order. Making certain no other African American was ever confronted like that was my first goal. My second goal was to represent my culture in a way that would be authentic. Attending classes or conferences have also presented a few uncomfortable challenges. I have some Caucasian associates who are determined to embrace me for who I am, without question. For them, I am forever grateful. But there have been a few times when a seat was being "saved" for a friend, but the friend never arrives. When the event is over, eye contact is nonexistent and there is usually a hasty exit. Body language conveys discomfort. This saddens me. I have always embraced anyone who shows themselves as friendly.

Life should be looked at as a very large meadow. The diversity found in the meadow replicates life's diversity. This life meadow usually has tons of glistening white daisies. They might have different bloom types, but they are still white daisies. But then echinacea, noticeably pink, with diverse types of petals, large bristled golden/black centers, pops up amid the white meadow. This describes how I and many other African Americans feel when entering a room. We are still human, but noticeably different. It does not matter how accomplished we are, we are viewed differently. To clarify—not always, but often. Too often.

What makes an award-winning garden beautiful? In most cases, a beautiful garden has a mix of many different types of plants. Having a diverse palette allows plants to play on the strengths of some and complement others. As the plants bloom, they tie the garden together. Rarely does a landscape void of diversity win an overall positive reception.

Too often, when I think that a certain level of acceptance has occurred, a misstep occurs. These days, I am often asked to speak on farming. It appears to be the latest trend and the request is always prefaced with the question, "Do you know Soul Fire Farm in New York?" They ask if I know Leah Penniman, an African American farmer, educator, and author. While I am appreciative, I wonder when someone will ask me about an African American in ornamental horticulture.

How can the horticultural conversation be more welcoming, as well as encouraging to future horticulturist of color? I want to have a real conversation about cultivars, networking to help build the African American horticulture community and more. Over the past three years a new bold generation of African Americans in horticulture has emerged. While many pursue farming to reconnect with the earth, others explore ornamental horticulture. They are reaching more inclusive and diverse audiences. These young people dance with plants, design with plants, pose with plants, and share their experiences. I look at these young people as the echinaceas of the horticultural world. Their attire even expresses confidence and social-justice concerns. T-shirts and tote bags now proclaim phrases like "Plant Momma" and "Plant Daddy," along with pots that represent our heritage. They are part of the new norm. It is refreshing and amazing. Facebook groups such as Black Girls With Gardens, Stronger Roots, and Black Urban Gardeners, just to name a few, are on the scene with podcasts and other social-media outlets. Not only is this fun, but it also allows interactions in a comfortable setting of African Americans actively practicing the art of gardening, as well as professional horticulturists who many have never heard of. Having fun in horticulture creates a much-needed space where multiculturalism is the norm. In a world where we have been all but erased from the world of horticulture, these young people have found their way.

Plants provide a way to experience calm in a world that seems to think African Americans do not matter. The need to nurture and care for another living thing voids the negative depiction of the African-American community. As we realize how important diversity is in everything we do, horticulture comes naturally. Now the six-million-dollar question—Why does the old guard still think we simply grow vegetables?

I hear wonderful stories about the importance of encouraging urban gardens in African American and Hispanic communities. The Wangari Community Garden in Washington, D.C., is a non-profit community garden created in a food desert. This area was plagued with health issues and poverty, as well as crime. Utilizing the principles of creating a garden for the community, cared for by the community, this garden has been growing since 2012. It reflects the diversity of the community and has an orchard, as well as individual plots available for rent. This is a terrific way to introduce different and unfamiliar ethnic foods as well as to create a healthy acceptance of diversity as a way of life.

Such gardens can also help introduce horticulture as a career. We need to start conversations that introduce careers such as arboriculture, the study, understanding, and care of trees. Perhaps promote landscape design or even floriculture as careers. Include flower farming, floral design, and landscape architecture to young people who may not want traditional career paths. Creating a community cutting garden is a simple way to introduce an alternative career by simply appreciating the joy of ornamental gardening. Teaching the intersection of flora and food can expand the conversation. According to yourdictionary.com, urban farmers grow food for produce or animals in urban settings, but there should be so much more.

I have decided to change the trajectory of acceptance. I now choose the content I share with wisdom and clarity. I was once told my writing was too flowery—after all, I write about gardens, gardening, and the beauty that surrounds us. That once concerned me; no more.

African Americans are passionate people. We see things in a different light, and we often learn in a way that is completely different from the way White Americans learn. I am amazed at how many people of color excel in their field of choice, even with minimal training. When I write, it is from my heart. I am unapologetic about how I share my voice. It has taken me quite some time to be comfortable in sharing horticulture my way. I ask the questions and listen. Today, whenever I attend an event, my discomfort is minimal. I hold my head high, though I am still often the only African American in the room. I show up and represent cultural clarity and the need for diversity, as well as inclusivity.

One day, echinaceas will be a part of the broader horticultural landscape in all communities. The seeds have been planted and are growing each day.

The Hampton Plantation Dig

William Baldwin

This way and that, a trench we've dug
to find a way past fear,
some foreignness
that we have missed
and dream is buried where
turned earth inhales,
gives a sigh, and next a wail.
Left so long pine roots impale
thick crumbled bricks of chimney,
hearth and piers,
and ghosting children lose the way
back to this house of slavery days.
Or do they?
Hear those laughing feet?
And there is rain on cypress shakes
and thunder makes them stand
stock still and wait.

The Archaeology Department at University of South Carolina included this poem
in a report on the slave house dig at Hampton Plantation in Charleston County,
South Carolina.

A Place for Us In the Outdoors

Adrienne Troy Frazier

As Papa retrieved the remaining items from the campsite, I got our five-year-old grandson Roman into his car seat, pressed against camping gear packed in our SUV for a weekend trip to a wooded state park on the Edisto River west of Charleston, South Carolina.

I kissed his forehead as he peered at the photo of a White couple with two children and a dog on the side of the bag holding our collapsed tent. "Ms. Adrienne," he said, "I want to go where they are." He ran his finger around the picture of the family, playing, laughing, and smiling. I assured him, "You did go there, Roman." He quickly snapped back: "No, I want to go there where they are."

I told him again we went camping just as they did, under the trees with water nearby. But that explanation still did not satisfy Roman. Again he ran his finger over the White family faces and said: "But I don't see myself anywhere there." My chest felt heavy. I breathed deep with the realization that Roman was correct. We don't look like the family on the tent bag. I honed in on the longing in his voice as it trailed off, repeating: "I don't see me."

After I relocated to South Carolina from Chicago in 2012, I couldn't fully see myself at campgrounds, on waterways, or along hiking trails here. I came to the Lowcountry as an avid kayaker and swimmer, with the exciting anticipation that my husband, Herb Frazier, and I would explore coastal waterways. I also have a deep reverence for African history and culture, which is ever-present in

164

Lowcountry food, art, and the people, particularly Gullah Geechee people, whose culture is shaped by their enslaved West African ancestors, brought to this region during the trans-Atlantic slave trade.

I became involved with Outdoor Afro (OA), a national group with the mission of reconnecting Black people to the outdoors. As a local volunteer OA leader, I was equipped with training and resources to organize and promote our history and reconnect with the land for healing opportunities in nature. I partnered with the only Black-owned kayak shop in the Southeast, Sea Kayak Carolina, owned by Joe Campbell. Before meeting Joe, we had been on the waterways with White-owned kayak shops in the Lowcountry, but we did not feel the narratives they told were empowering. During a kayaking trip on the Broad River on Hilton Head Island, the guide admitted he was not familiar with the Port Royal Experiment, a federal government program, launched seven months after the Civil War began, to give Black people the opportunity to farm land abandoned by White planters, create their own towns, and attend school. We appreciated his honesty, but found it shocking nonetheless that a tour guide near Hilton Head Island was not aware of this important event in local Black history. Our connection with Joe made a difference as we sought to share with others the Black waterway stories. Because Black representation matters.

When we are in our kayaks or hiking, we acknowledge that Black communities have always been environmentally aware in ways not recognized by the colonizers. We also discuss the legacy of fear and lack of acceptance and safety so many of us have felt in water-related activities. Across all age groups, Black, and Brown children are five-and-a-half times more likely to drown than those of all other racial or ethnic groups. Many from our communities have a fear of water because they have never been offered the opportunity to learn how to swim. We hold candid conversations about sea level rise and the impact it will have on us all, but especially Gullah Geechee communities. Flooding is the number-one topic for Charleston and other coastal cities. It poses many risks to the environment and public safety and threatens to damage homes and businesses.

We have paddled historic waterways, places where Gullah Geechee people resisted their enslavement. Among them are the Stono River, site of the 1739

Stono Rebellion; Charleston Harbor, where Robert Smalls and his crew commandeered the Confederate boat The Planter and turned it over to the Union Navy; a creek along Sol Legare, a Black seafaring community on James Island where Black Union soldiers camped before a brutal assault on the Confederacy's Battery Wagner at nearby Morris Island; and we've kayaked the Combahee River rice fields in Beaufort County, where abolitionist Harriet Tubman led the Union Navy on raids to free enslaved people.

Those experiences were not tainted by the micro-aggressions Black people sometimes feel in the outdoors among White people. Twice I've attended the annual East Coast Paddle Sports Symposium on James Island near Charleston only to be greeted with curious or surprising stares that a Black woman had the courage, interest, or audacity to walk among mostly white outdoor enthusiasts. During our first camping trip to Table Rock State Park in upstate South Carolina, Herb and I were met with hostile glares as we hiked to the 3,124-foot summit. During an earlier visit to the state park on the Edisto River, we kayaked on the waterway past wind-whipped Confederate flags. When we paddled near White people lounging on the riverbank, a man remarked loudly: "Everybody on the water now!" It challenged our sense of safety. Like most Black people, my family can share those times when White people abruptly left the community pool shortly after we arrived.

African Americans face negative stereotypes when White people act surprised, alarmed, or threatened when they see us in roles in nature that do not fit neatly into their distorted views of us. These misconceptions are not limited to outdoor activities. They span nearly all sectors of American life, from classical music to science, finance to government, and even athletics beyond the typical sports that White people find acceptable and expect for black participation.

The day a Minneapolis policeman murdered George Floyd on May 25, 2020, a White woman in New York's Central Park dialed 911 to report she felt threatened by Christian Cooper, a Black birder, who had admonished her for not having her dog on a leash. A social-media video of the incident went viral, providing that rare proof of a micro-aggression Black people routinely face from Whites, including police, who harbor biases against people of African descent. The exchange between Cooper and the White woman in Central Park fortunately did not lead to physical harm to him, but it was a teachable moment for White America. In a May 6, 2021, online national town hall on creating safe outdoor spaces for African Americans, sponsored by the National Wildlife Federation, Cooper said the encounter with the angry dog owner "made a lot of White people … aware of what really does go on for so many of us that maybe they were not aware of before. So in that way, I can't call it unfortunate."[109] Cooper, the son of civil rights activists, visits New York City schools to encourage Black and Brown children to go among the birds, an admirable suggestion that could begin to change the narrative of Black people who love birds.

Black birdwatcher J. Drew Lanham, a conservation ornithologist and endowed faculty member at Clemson University, not only loves birds, but he's in love with birds. Lanham finds himself among the "minuscule percentage" of Black birders, "like the seldom-seen skulking sparrows so many of us seek, we are few and far between among an overwhelmingly white flock."[110] Lanham was once a rarity on the board of the National Audubon Society, the respected group that was named for John James Audubon, a Jesus-like figure among birders who was Lanham's boyhood idol. But he left Audubon in 2020 because the society's diversity and inclusion policies "diverged from my own, and I had to remove any conflict of interest in order to maintain my personal agenda of connecting conservation and culture." A frequently called-on speaker, Lanham ruffled birding-circle feathers when he proffered the question of Audubon's racial identity, a subject historians debate. Audubon, a slaveholder, traveled America in the 1800s to observe and gather birds, yielding detailed life-sized and colorful bird paintings. Audubon's French father was a slave trader and ship captain. The birder's mother was French or Haitian Creole, a term that describes mixed-race people. When Lanham shared this possible parentage blend with audiences around the country, the uncomfortable response was not what he had expected. He did so not to settle the question of Audubon's racial identity "but our own. Who are we as a culture, as a community?"[111]

---

[109] National Wildlife Federation, "National Town Hall on Creating Safe Spaces," https://www.youtube.com/watch?v=FFkpNiXVeNU (accessed July 21, 2021).

[110] J. Drew Lanham, "What Do We Do About John James Audubon?" *Audubon Magazine* (Spring 2021), https://www.audubon.org/magazine/spring-2021/what-do-we-do-about-john-james-audubon (accessed July 21, 2021).

[111] Ibid

Black people belong in the outdoors at national parks, national forests, and in the elegant gardens at former plantation sites. At the beginning of the movement to create the nation's national park system, people of African descent were on the forefront of that work. Charles Young was the third Black graduate of the military academy at West Point. He later commanded an army unit at San Francisco that was assigned to protect the newly designated national parks at Yosemite and Sequoia. Black men planted the trees, cut the firebreaks, and built the watch towers in the Francis Marion National Forest near Charleston and other national forests and parks around the country. Our enslaved ancestors also established with their bare hands the historic gardens at former plantations sites near Charleston. Our ancestors, like those Sol Legare seafarers, have a historic relationship with the waterways around Charleston. The tiny fishing and shrimp boats of the Mosquito Fleet in Charleston took our ancestors on the waterways to harvest the catch of the day and serve as a ferry service to nearby islands. The fleet is referenced in the famous Broadway musical *Porgy and Bess*.

After more than a year of being trapped in our home due to the Covid-19 pandemic, my husband and I were eager for the camping trip we had planned the previous summer. We had gathered with our friends, one the single Black mother of eleven-year-old twins, who is a museum critical-race theorist, and the other a single Black woman, an educator and founder of Brown Girls Hike. Like me, they are former OA leaders who share the concern that work must be done to ensure that Black and other people of color (BIPOC) feel safe in nature, and that the story of place is told. Now we were gathered after months of being quarantined and feeling the angst of relentless killings of Black people by police over the past year. I wondered if Roman sensed the tension and discomfort we felt, being the only Black group at the campground. We noticed uneasiness in the air. We shared nervous jokes about the possibility that the White people might be plotting to attack us. Did Roman pick up on this tension? Did he feel our fatigue throughout the day as we took turns napping as others stood guard?

I wondered if our attempt to make Roman's first campfire and tenting experience memorable was successful, or had his Papa and I failed him. We wanted to fill him with wonder and excitement, not anxiety. What do you say to a five-year-old who recognizes that Black representation matters in the outdoors, too?

Of Man and Nature

Horace Mungin

I like best
Those things that
Were here
Before man started building.

I like the open sky
That will not lie.

Not these city buildings
Scraping the sky with
Lies and lies, and lies.

(From Horace Mungin's first poetry collection, 1968, *Dope Hustler's Jazz.*)

Healing

The Root of the Problem

Damon L. Fordham

In his 1936 epic Black Empire, George S. Schuyler quipped that the average person knows mostly "what they see and what they are told." The unfortunate truth is that the historical experiences of many African Americans have produced what the late Charleston educator James Campbell, who once assisted Malcolm X in his Organization of Afro-American Unity, described in a 2008 conversation with me as "a culture of despair." Thus, many African Americans, raised on a mental diet of negativity, pessimism, and broken spirits, have passed these teachings to their children. To find a cure for the conditions of which Mr. Campbell spoke, we have to examine the cause, which has seldom been told to maintain the status quo.

Six hundred years ago, the concept of race was unknown to people in the Mediterranean, a blend of African, Asian, and European cultures. In the early 1500s, during the third voyage of Christopher Columbus to the West Indies, the explorer brought along a Spanish priest named Father Bartholomé de las Casas. Father las Casas was horrified at Columbus's enslavement and mistreatment of Native Americans. He had a solution: use Africans instead, a decision documented in his *History of the Indies*.[112]

---

[112] Brian Pierce, "Bartolomé de las Casas and Truth: Toward a Spirituality of Solidarity." *Spirituality Today* (1992), 44 (1): 4–19.

During the initial English settlement of colonial America nearly a century later, poor, White, indentured laborers were used along with enslaved African laborers. Not much friction existed between the two groups at first. James Oliver Horton and Lois E. Horton describe in Slavery and the Making of America how these two groups were initially closely allied and socialized openly and freely. However, in 1676, a white indentured servant named Nathaniel Bacon tried to start Bacon's Rebellion to unite the two groups in opposition to the government of colonial Virginia. After Bacon died of dysentery, the colonial Virginia leaders tried to prevent African and European cooperation from happening again by giving poor Whites an artificial status over the enslaved Blacks to ensure a "divide-and-conquer" strategy would maintain the dominance of Whites as the upper class.[113]

This action denied education to people of African descent. The deliberate under-education of Black people continued for centuries, into the segregation era. Woodrow Wilson explained on January 9, 1909, at a teachers' convention shortly before he was elected president: "We want one class of persons to have a liberal education, and we want another class of persons, a very much larger class of necessity in every society, to forego the privileges of a liberal education and fit themselves to perform specific difficult manual tasks."[114]

The effects of all this can be described in the following section of Supreme Court Chief Justice Earl Warren's opinion in the school-desegregation case *Brown v. Board of Education of Topeka*, on May 17, 1954:

"To separate [children] from others of similar age and qualifications solely because of their race generates a feeling of inferiority as to their status in the community that may affect their hearts and minds in a way unlikely ever to be undone." [115]

Thus, as the Rev. Dr. Martin Luther King stated in his sermon in Detroit, on June 23, 1963, "Many Negroes lost faith in themselves and considered themselves inferior." In The Autobiography of Malcolm X, Malcolm said in the chapter

---

[113] Howard Zinn, *A People's History of the United States, 1492-Present*. (New York: Harper Perennial, 1995), 41.

[114] Woodrow Wilson, "The Meaning of Liberal Education," Address to the New York City High School Teachers Association (January 9, 1909).

[115] https://www.archives.gov/education/lessons/brown-v-board#background (Accessed Aug. 7, 2021).

"Saved," "Little black children saw before they could talk that their parents considered themselves inferior." Many to this day really believe they were "cursed by being black," which creates a psychological barrier for African Americans to unite in spite of examples of Black excellence, such as the Marcus Garvey movement, the 1963 and 1995 marches on Washington, and the success of the 1955-56 Montgomery Bus Boycott. Nonetheless, many persist in believing we are "good at all things physical and nothing mental." President Barack Obama, in his speech at the Democratic National Convention on July 27, 2004, exemplified this phenomenon experienced by many scholarly Black children. Obama expressed a desire to "eradicate the slander that a black youth with a book is acting white."[116]

There are many sides to this story that have been obscured to all but the most passionate of historians. If the truth that would kill the negative mythology, which has poisoned many, had only been better known to the general public, then all sides of this story would become more widely known.

For one thing, it is not widely known that American slavery also existed in the northern United States, and part of the reason for its ending in that region some thirty-six years prior to its end in the South was due to an illiterate, formerly enslaved Black woman named Mum Bett. According to the Hortons' Slavery and the Making of America, Mum Bett was enslaved in Massachusetts in the 1770s, during the American Revolution, where she constantly heard talk about "all men are created equal" and their rights to "life, liberty, and the pursuit of happiness." She was barred from getting an education, but had enough sense to find a lawyer and sue the State of Massachusetts for her freedom, on the grounds that these words from the Declaration of Independence applied to her, too. She won, and that led to the end of slavery in Massachusetts; several other northern states followed until New York did so in 1827. To celebrate this victory, Mum Bett changed her name to reflect her new status, Elizabeth Freeman.[117]

Hardcore fans of Black history may have heard of Benjamin Banneker, the legendary scientist of Revolutionary-era America. Born free in 1731, he

---

[116] Martin Luther King, Record album "The Great March to Freedom—Rev. Martin Luther King Speaks," (1963) Motown Records 5342 ML, Haley, Alex and X, Malcolm, (1965) *The Autobiography of Malcolm X*, (New York: Ballantine Books), 209. Obama, Barack, "Speech at the Democratic Convention," (July 27, 2004).
[117] "Liberty in The Air" (2004) Episode 2 of "Slavery and the Making of America," Educational Broadcasting System. DVD.

happened to read Thomas Jefferson's book Notes on the State of Virginia, which included negative views on the intelligence of Black people. Banneker wrote a rebuttal to Jefferson that included Banneker's own almanac, and Jefferson was forced to acknowledge his error.[118]

Many know of Abraham Lincoln's Emancipation Proclamation, but not nearly as many today know of John Brown, the White man who was hanged for attempting to lead an armed slave rebellion in Virginia in 1859, or of Viola Liuzzo, a White woman who left her comfortable home in Detroit in 1965 to join Dr. King's march for voting rights on Selma, Alabama. She was killed by the Ku Klux Klan, and, among her last words was a moral which we can all learn from in this effort: "Freedom is everybody's fight."[119]

So, I hope that you will now understand there never would have been talk about Black pride had there not been so much Black shame. That many felt it necessary to call themselves Black kings and queens because so many for so long have been treated like peasants. There never would have been the cry of Black Lives Matter had Black lives not mattered to so many.

I really believe that if those of us who know this history took the time to educate the general public about these matters, we can help many find the cure for misinformation to have a better America.

But in order for that to work, people will have to want to be educated. These stories may not be in the classrooms today, and much of the internet is filled with false and misleading information that many have not had the training to detect, but we can encourage people to take advantage of the free public libraries available in almost any town and city. Ask the librarians for reputable books on these subjects. Go to trusted television networks, such as the Public Broadcasting Service, to learn from the interesting and well-researched documentaries that will add to the storehouses of knowledge and serve as weapons in the war against ignorance.

Some people in this country have worked diligently to keep some of us uneducated. Now we must work equally as effectively to educate our people so they can be lifted from what Mr. Campbell described as "a culture of despair."

---

[118] Kai Wright, ed. (2009), *The African American Experience—Black History and Culture Through Speeches, Editorials, Poems, Songs, and Stories*. (New York: Black Dog & Leventhal Publishers),109-112.

[119] http://pabridges.com/community/its-everybodys-fight-viola-liuzzo-civil-rights-martyr/ (Accessed Aug. 7, 2021).

Black and White Cowboys

Ray McManus

On TV, it's black and white: someone has to die and someone else has to
stand there and watch it, but it's never enough to stop the commercials.
What's the point of complicating cruelty when there's money to be made?

The boys judge what's good or bad by the only colors they're given.
There's a white man in a white hat. He beats the dust off his thighs,
reaches down with his index finger toward the trigger,
and takes the ground from under the other man's feet.

Color makes no difference to the dead, but the boys
see good guys and bad guys marked by contrast and brightness,
and they confuse it with what's left standing and what's left
to bleed, as scripted, as directed, as advertised. Soon they will yell
and squeal and cheer, ready to re-enact what they saw,
ready to turn on each other by the closing credits.

And we'll be relieved if they just do it outside where we can see them.

Why?

Horace Mungin

I come from a generation of warriors
Born into a time of strife
And the wretched years of American history:
The history of backdoor inequity
The history of trees that bear strange fruits
The history of Jim Crow
The history of Reconstruction
The history of slavery
The history of the Middle Passage
And, yes, the history of kings and queens
Back home.
I come from a generation of warriors
Who valued the possibilities of struggle
And the legitimacy of our existence,
A generation with an agenda, a vision
And the will to overcome the malicious
Contortions of our realities,
The generation of the movement
Of sit-ins and freedom rides
Of protest marches and civil disobedience
Of conflict and confrontations
Of small and permanent victories that changed a nation.
I come from a generation of dragon slayers.
I come from that generation of warriors
Who gave birth to a generation lost
The just do it generation
The BET generation
The Hip-Hop generation
The drive-by shooting generation.

A generation that was past the promise
Of a great and glorious future
Of greater victories until we reached a full partnership
And now we watch in horror
As they devour themselves in senseless bloodbaths
And orgies of violence and unforgivable distortions
Of what it is we passed on to them
And we like rejected suitors can only ask why?
Why? I asked an old holy man
Who is one hundred years old and lives on the Sea Island
Who learned to play chess ninety years ago
On a carved board with whittled wooden pieces
A holy man who says that this is a time of sorcerers and demons
But who is mainly referring to the fact that he now owns
A computerized chess set that beats him more often than not.
He thinks the chess set is enchanted
And was engineered by the wizards of witchcraft
He thinks the modern world is enchanted
There is too much magic the old holy man says.
Why are there guns everywhere?
.44 Magnums, Colt 45 pistols,
Berettas, Glock 17s, Ladysmiths, Uzis, Tec-9s,
AK 47s, M1s, M2s, M16s
And conflicts—like sex or a crack pipe
Comes easy.
Why are there so many guns in the hands
Of people so eager to use them?
And death—like cable TV or delivered pizza
Come hot, fast and easy
What do you want on your tombstone?
Is more than a commercial slogan.
Why? A little girl in Charleston asked her father
Is the church door locked and bolted?

To protect the typewriters and the copying machine
The gold cross on the altar and the other valuables
The father answers
Well, is God safe in there?
God is in there, God is out here too, God is everywhere
The father says feeling this isn't quite the answer
Why then is the church door locked and bolted?
The girl repeats.
The father says nothing.
This is not a question with a simple answer.
Raymond Otis lives in North Charleston
He learned about the police's gun buy-back
Program on the news
Raymond parts with his battered Beretta
To receive a valued gift certificate then
He drives Rivers Avenue to the nearest Toys R Us
And brings home to his four sons
Four like-real water Uzis
One real gun brings four toy guns into their world
To perpetuate the lore of the gun.
Too much magic in the world, the old holy man said.
This is the magic of the supreme architects
Of our society—ruling from their ivory towers
While breeding a generation of people so full
Of hopelessness and despair and alienation
They loathe themselves
A generation with empty hearts and
Boundless trouble
A generation whose hatred is so intense
No one is safe
No one
Not the mothers and fathers of their freedom nor
The architects of their calamity
And when the serpents reach into ivory towers

The social engineers will also cry out—why?
But what they will really want to know is
What can we do?
What can we all do?

Education For Us by Us
LaTisha Vaughn

My mother is a daughter of the segregated South. Raised in rural south Georgia, she chose to leave in 1967 after graduating high school because she refused to have cleaning someone's house or working in a field as her only life options. She left to ensure that my younger sister and I had a different educational experience beyond the segregated K-12 system she experienced in Glennville, Georgia. At that time, private, affluent schools seemed like the best option. My sister and I attended private, mostly all-White schools in Kansas City, Missouri, from kindergarten through twelfth grade because the Kansas City Public School District was not a choice in my mother's eyes.

I understand my mother and other Black families wanting the best education for us in a community where there were truly no best options that fully met our needs. But I often wonder whether parents thought about the social and emotional affects we faced being the only children of color in schools that were not meant for us and our Black culture. My Black friends and I were educated in an environment where we felt loneliness, not belonging, and never truly fitting in. The system did not have high expectations for us, as they did for our White counterparts. We faced biased assumptions about who we were and where we came from, as well as who our parents were and what did they do for a living. White people I encountered in school had a tainted view of me and other Black students and our culture. I did not begin to understand or correct this until my college years.

As a career educator and the product of private schools, I've long held the belief that the best education for Black children happened when it was illegal for us to sit in classrooms with White children. In other words, when we had education for us by us has never been a question. South Carolina native Mary McLeod Bethune, founder of Bethune-Cookman College in Florida, Charleston educator Septima P. Clark, and community activist Esau Jenkins on Johns Island near Charleston were among the Black pioneers across the South who found innovative ways to teach children of color when "separate but equal" schools were accepted. They taught our children in secret at various times of the day, using a curriculum that validated their identities to create a foundation of excellence that allowed them to enter the world with a sense of confidence, knowing they were prepared.[120, 121, 122]

Black and Brown children are now largely relegated to under-funded, underperforming schools staffed by people who do not look like them. Racial integration fundamentally changed the nature of Black communities and disrupted the ability of our communities to be self-affirming, according to Bell Hooks, author of *Sisters of the Yam*, an exploration into the experience of Black womanhood. "Traditionally, black folks have had to do a lot of creative thinking and reasoning to raise black children free of internalized racism in a white-supremacist society," hooks writes. "Even though there was so much pain and hardship then … there was also the joy of living in communities of resistance."

Segregated schools were self-affirming spaces where Black students and their teachers spoke the same language, were part of the same culture, while teachers held their students to high standards. Teachers consistently believed

---

[120] Grace Jordan McFadden, "Septima P. Clark and the Struggle for Human Rights," in *Women in the Civil Rights Movement: Trailblazers and Torchbearers 1941-1965*. Ed. Vicki L. Crawford, Jacqueline Anne Rouse, and Barbara Woods. (Bloomington: Indiana University Press, 1993), 85–97.
[121] Audrey McCluskey, "'We Specialize in the Wholly Impossible': Black Women School Founders," *Signs* (Winter 1997), 403–426.
[122] *Esau Jenkins Papers, 1963-2003*, Avery Research Center for African American History and Culture, https://lcdl.library.cofc.edu/content/esau-jenkins-papers-1963-2003/. Steve Estes, *Charleston in Black and White: Race and Power in the South after the Civil Rights Movement*. (Chapel Hill: University of North Carolina Press, 2015).

in the promise that education would lift their students out of America's oppressive culture. They lived in and created communities of resistance that helped students endure the atrocities of White supremacy that bombarded their psyche daily.

History has taught us that we are our own rescue. A school on the North Side of Chicago, a campus on the west side of Charleston, and another in Milwaukee, Wisconsin, are examples that for us by us can be applied today. Urban Prep Academies in Chicago is a collection of all-boys public schools that serve more than 1,500 young men and produce three hundred college-bound graduates annually. Education entrepreneur Tim King with a group of African American education, business, and civic leaders launched Urban Prep in 2002 with a mission to provide a comprehensive, high-quality, college-preparatory education to young men. Urban Prep responded to the need to create an educational environment that allows Black boys to thrive.

An innovative educational solution resides in the Charleston Development Academy. Birthed out of the concern of the Ebenezer AME Church congregation in 1999, the Rev. Charles E. Young and the church's Education Commission turned into a school planning committee that collaborated with the community to create the 4K-8 school where students have outperformed those in other elementary schools on end-of-year assessments. The school sends children to competitive high schools. Their performance data is an anomaly not because Black children are not brilliant, but because systems do not recognize or nurture that brilliance.

Milwaukee Collegiate Academy, founded by Dr. Howard Fuller, is another example of a school created for us by us that is changing the game for its community. In a neighborhood where its closest high school scored low in math proficiency, Milwaukee Collegiate Academy has a 97 percent graduation rate and a 100 percent college acceptance rate for its graduating seniors, with many attending historically Black colleges and universities (HBCUs). This school is proof that the right school leader and the right teachers have a tremendous impact on outcomes for our children.

These are just three examples of the countless schools founded and led by leaders of color that have uniquely and successfully educated Black children, helping families obtain the promise of education. With our distant and current history of successfully educating our children, I am perplexed why we debate the legitimacy of for us by us to create our own schools and receive funding to accomplish our goal?

Since the public lynching of George Floyd by Minneapolis police and the murders of Ahmaud Arbery by vigilantes in Brunswick, Georgia, and the police killing of Breonna Taylor in Louisville, Kentucky, we have seen a shift in the level of awareness of systemic racism. More now than ever, there are opportunities for Black people to obtain funding to create solutions for us by us. These opportunities include creating public charter schools that receive tax dollars to support the creation of public-private partnerships. In South Carolina a school-of-innovation law allows districts to create innovative educational models in partnership with school leaders or outside entities.[123] Several funding opportunities exist for schools to receive support for innovative programs through organizations such as the New Schools Venture Fund and Building Excellent Schools. We must take advantage of the opportunities to get funding to create solutions for our community. If we don't, who will?

In 2017 the NAACP called for a moratorium on charter schools, pointing out that the promise of shared innovation with traditional public schools never materialized. And yet the historical inequities in a majority of the traditional public schools in this country are jarring. The data is clear about traditional public-school systems as a whole, and it does not look good. Although the demographics of the United States are shifting dramatically toward a more diverse student population, in 2017-18 79 percent of the public-school teachers in the United States were White. Females comprised 76 percent of the teaching population. Only 7 percent and 9 percent of the teachers were Black and Hispanic, respectively. In Charleston County, less than 1 percent of the teachers are Black men, according to the most recent data from the South Carolina Department of Education.

An achievement gap exists between White and Black students across all subjects and grade levels. According to the National Assessment of Educational Progress test (NAEP), 52 percent of White students recently scored proficient or at grade level versus only 20 percent of Black students. In addition to the achievement performance gaps, there are also issues of over- and under-identification

---

[123] https://www.scstatehouse.gov/sess124_2021-2022/bills/3589.htm

of Black student in special education. In 2018 African American children comprised 13.8 percent of the youth population, but 17.89 percent of children with disabilities. African American students are more likely to be identified with an intellectual disability or emotional disturbance, and less likely to be identified with speech or language impairment, or autism. As a result, Black children do not receive the support they need for some disabilities while others are over-identified and possibly labeled incorrectly. Disproportionate numbers of Black children are suspended and expelled from school. African-American students are expelled at nine times the rate of White students in high school and five times the rate of White students in middle school.[124]

The public education system has never worked for Black children and their families, and we have the data to prove it. So, why do we continue to put our faith in systems that have never really served us or our children?

Until our most recent past, when we wanted to create safe educational spaces for our children, there was only the option to raise private dollars, which was a barrier for our most seasoned, promising educational leaders. Why is there a debate about whether charter schools should exist within the Black community? Are we really asking the right questions? And why do we think that after more than a century of poor performance, large bureaucratic systems suddenly are going to reform and do what is best for Black children and for Black families?

Because of my own K-12 experience I chose to attend Hampton University, an HBCU campus in Hampton, Virginia. My experience at Hampton changed me forever. Until then, I had never broadly experienced the diversity that existed in our culture. Although I grew up in a Black neighborhood, and in the Black church, my HBCU experience gave me something that I had not experienced, an extension of my positive racial identity beyond my family and church community. My professors were Black, my advisor was Black, and I experienced the richness of our culture, learning about our history from our perspective. For the first time I encountered Black intellectualism and academic rigor in a way that did not diminish me or my lived experiences. Although I

---

[124] *An Overview of Exclusionary Discipline Practices in Public Schools for the 2017-18 School Year ,* Department of Education Office of Civil Rights (Civil Rights Data Collection — CRDC) .

did not graduate from Hampton due to financial challenges, this invaluable experience changed my path in ways I am still understanding.

The tradition of HBCUs and other institutions that serve predominately Black and Brown children still exists today and are vital options for our children. In the article "The Impact of HBCUs on Diversity in STEM Fields," from the United Negro College Fund (UNCF), we learn that although HBCUs enroll about 9 percent of Black undergraduates, they produce significantly higher percentages of graduates in critical fields, such as engineering, mathematics, and biological sciences. The UNCF reports that 25 percent of all African-American graduates with degrees in science, technology, engineering, and mathematics (STEM) come from HBCUs. UNCF also points out that HBCUs graduate the highest number of Black students with earned doctorates.

We all remember the hip-hop apparel brand FUBU (For Us By Us). It's time that we apply that saying beyond what we wear and use it to make decisions to leverage our collective power. We should be the creators and implementers of the solutions for our communities. Historically, we have been creators out of necessity and urgency. I argue that the need for our community is just as urgent now as it was back then. Until we take the lead, we will continue to lag behind.

Under Their Gaze

Portia Cobb

under their gaze
post-traumatic slavery stress
is an angry sound bite
compressed to mitigate the gravity
of their amnesia & fright

under their gaze
we brighten our skin to lighten their burden
relax our curls,
code switch our diction

& apologize
for those who won't tie their tongues
to speak a new fiction

under their gaze
we become
lawn jockey stand-ins
at luncheons, picnics &
plantation social functions

where American history is lubricated to become
centric to savvy Saviors
not our captors nor
enslavers

where black bodies
deemed safe enough for orgies of white guilt
are found sprawled lifeless
beneath balconies in early morning light

      or swinging in the breeze
        —from trees

under their gaze
black death is justifiable homicide
our grief,
palpable spectacle,
      peacock beautiful,

a peculiar, curious
collectible/

The Spirit Reminds Me of Who I Am
Kennae Miller

My name is Kennae Miller (she/her), and I am made of Shirley Ann Richardson and William Hardy. I am the living descendant of Bundy Wesley Martin and Bonnie Jean Hames. I am the expression of the late Tracy C. Hardy and Kenneth Hardy Sr. My parents raised me to believe the value and weight of a name means something in this world and although my mother derived my name from my father, I decided my name means beautiful warrior. My father, an element of water, and my mother, an element of the earth, created me, an earthly child.

I have been afforded the opportunity to explore and engage with various cultures, and what resonates in my heart is each culture's ability to connect with its spiritual deity and rituals. I grew up in the Apostolic and Pentecostal denominations of Christianity, which informed my identity with Spirit being called God. Having grown up in Colorado Springs, Colorado, I engaged with I cultures like the Anasazi, Ute, Arapahoe, and Navajo and many of them identified with a higher being called the Great Spirit.

When I lived in Hawaii, it was easy to witness in daily life what it looked like to live with the spirit of Aloha and in communion with nature. In the practice of yoga there is Krishna and in meditation there is Buddha. For me, this signifies how vast spirituality is; no matter the physical location on the earth, each person, language, or culture can identify and connect with a higher being, or what I would reference as Spirit.

I would like to say I stumbled upon healing work or found spirituality through social-media platforms, but I was born into it. I recall when I was four years old and traveling through what looked like a galaxy before arriving in my body. At nine years old, I was baptized, then dedicated my life to the God of Christianity. For many children of the diaspora our first introduction (or, for some, indoctrination) to spirituality is through the church. Such an introduction often includes condemnation for bad behaviors or lusts and an invitation to salvation, but that was not my experience. Both of my parents were ministers in the church and very active, and they encouraged my siblings and me to be active, too. My parents allowed us to choose whether to be baptized. I knew the power of prayer, intercession, prayer warriors and prayer closets, the laying on of hands, and the commitment and dedication to show up for the women and children, the sick and the shut-in.

Internally there was always this unexplainable knowledge that I was supposed to make big changes in this world, and I made decisions as a child based on this knowing. This sense of knowing was deep in my soul. My mother encouraged me to always listen to that deep knowing, regardless of what others thought or said. This knowing led me to the practice of yoga in high school and from my first experience I never looked back. Initially, I joked about going to yoga so I could learn to levitate, but after experiencing my first class, guided by a strong and graceful woman in her sixties, I kept going back. At the time it did not matter to me that she was not a Black woman, or in a bigger body. I did not care about her social location because I knew I felt a deep connection and presence of the Spirit when I practiced yoga. I continued my practice for me.

Imagine in your head a busy highway like any in Atlanta or Los Angeles, six lanes in each direction, during rush hour. This highway is filled with speeding drivers, all blasting their own soundtracks. That is what it felt like daily inside my head. I thought this is what every human experienced. It was not until I practiced yoga for the first time that all of the traffic and noise ceased, and I saw myself standing in the center of the empty, quiet highway. This stillness allowed me to connect with the presence of communing with Spirit in a way I did not see or witness in the church.

During these communions, I heard Spirit provide guidance and affirmations in the most gentle ways. I heard course correction about ways I had engaged with others that had caused harm or created a space for healing. I felt increasingly free to journey through my internal dialogue. It was this same stillness that led me to attend yoga retreats in Thailand and Cambodia. While attending one retreat, the word for that day was "transformation." As I opened my Bible, I unintentionally arrived at Romans 12:

> I beseech you therefore, brethren, by the mercies of God, that ye present your bodies a living sacrifice, holy, acceptable unto God, which is your reasonable service. And be not conformed to this world: but be ye transformed by the renewing of your mind, that ye may prove what is that good, and acceptable, and perfect, will of God.

Then I heard Spirit whisper it was time for me to teach yoga. I questioned it. I doubted my capabilities to teach. But I trusted Spirit and I believed Spirit when it told me "my people need healing" and I should be a vessel.

The way I desire to show up in the world has always been as my most authentic self in service to collective healing. My yoga studio, Transformation Yoga, is an expression of that. I lead by knowing healing and liberation are much greater than me. They are inherent and where our divinity lies. Yoga and its philosophies are merely reminders of what our ancestors knew, whether it was passed down orally, stomped into sand through dance, or sent up to the heavens in prayers. Rachel Cargle, a social entrepreneur, philanthropic innovator, and public academic, observes: "This work is not new, it is just our turn." One day, the descendants of the diaspora will look to the healing that Transformation Yoga supports and will be reminded and empowered of their divine right to be healed, whole and liberated.

At Transformation Yoga we provide yoga classes, meditation, reiki as a movement of energy similar to the laying on of hands, private and group yoga therapy, and conversations and workshops on trauma and healing, specifically based on the intersection of identities. We emphasize and uplift the Black lived experience by sharing our ancestors' histories of healing arts and practices. All of the work and engagement we do comes from a transformative-justice and decolonized framework that makes liberation and healing the center.

Transformation Yoga is different from other yoga teachings because we provide information, historical context, and support for understanding how many of the deep wounds, intergenerational traumas, and conditioning that we experience stem from the colonization of the world, in particular for Black people in the United States. It is this understanding that requires us to see all individuals as complete and divine. One of the ways colonization has been indoctrinated into individuals is that many of us see ourselves as separate from the divine. We've been taught to see and seek God or Spirit outside of ourselves; and we see each person who interacts with us through this lens, allowing them to show the wholeness of who they are. This reminds us to treat others as we would treat any divine being. We are conditioned to mistrust one another; if we remove the tainted lens of colonization then we might enter into relationships of mutual respect and support.

Many people believe yoga to be nothing more than stretching and the movement or placement of your body into different postures or shapes. But yoga is an opportunity to experience an emotional, spiritual, psychological, and energetic transformation that returns the practitioner, even if only for a brief moment, back to her truest nature and divinity, before the world labeled, tainted, or conditioned them. This is important to the Black community especially because we know our liberation is bound in each other's liberation. We know that we all have what we need, but we have to be reminded of who we are so we are able to walk in it instead of what society has decided for us. It reminds me of more scripture; the following is found in Romans 12: 4-10, King James Version:

"For as we have many members in one body, and all members have not the same office: So we, being many, are one body in Christ, and every one members of another.

"Having then gifts differing according to the grace that is given to us, whether prophecy, let us prophesy according to the proportion of faith; Or ministry, let us wait on our ministering: or he that teacheth, on teaching; Or he that exhorteth, on exhortation; he that giveth, let him do it with simplicity; he that ruleth, with diligence; he that sheweth mercy, with cheerfulness.

"Let love be without dissimulation. Abhor that which is evil; cleave to that which is good. Be kindly affectioned one to another with brotherly love; in honour preferring one another;"

In one of the yogic sacred texts, the *Bhagavad Gita*, sloka 6:32 says: "I regard them to be perfect yogis who see the true equality of all living beings and respond to the joys and sorrows of others as if they were their own."

We all have layers of conditioning, most stemming from existing in a colonized culture that does not see each of us as divine and spiritual beings, thus placing demands and expectations on how we are allowed to show up and belong. It taints us. When we acknowledge and address these conditions, whether based in classism or racism, ageism or sexism, we are able to renew our minds and begin healing. One of my favorite workshops is a discussion on how we can show up in community with each other to create brave ways for healing to begin; we touch on all of the ways we are conditioned to believe in the classifications or separations of who we are.

We navigate how we are conditioned to give our power away and how we can choose to reject false narratives about being separated from our culture, ancestors, and innate wisdom. We come to realize that we have been taught to be individual versus communal, productive versus present, and untrusting of others. Wisdom is embodied within us, and because of this, healing is already within us. Resmaa Menakem, author of *My Grandmother's Hands: Racialized Trauma and the Pathway to Mending our Hearts and Bodies*, informs us that "trauma does not happen directly to one person but it happens communally, thus our healing must be done in communal ways." This is not a new thought merely based on science or cognitive thought on trauma and healing but rather the cultural and ancestral African philosophy practice of Ubuntu, "I am because we are."

Transformation Yoga then is an expression of healing and liberation. It is an invitation to engage in a communal setting to honor and uplift people, culture, spirituality, and wholeness. Transformation Yoga is self-determined people coming together to remember who we are—loving, kind, compassionate, and whole.

Transformation Yoga happens to be guided by someone deeply connected to Spirit. It is the Spirit that guides. It is the determination of Shirley Ann and the fight of Bundy, the spiritual connection of Tracy and the command of respect of Kenneth that live within me that remind me of who I am; of who my ancestors are. It is this deep remembering and returning to healing truths where the healing lies, because it is not and has never been separate from me or you.

Give Yourself Some flowers

Marcus Amaker

And in the beginning,
God gave your body
a checklist:

Keep your heart
on beat
and your lungs
dancing with oxygen,
not passive to air.

Make sure
the path of your blood
slows down
for checkpoints
and avoids
bumps
in the road.

Train your nerves
to keep a balanced pace
and stay within
the lines
of steady flow.

Push forward
without putting
too much
pressure
on movement.

Remember
to return to water
when your spirit
and its frame
are in drought.

Treat your body
like a well-rounded planet
built for all seasons,

or pretend you are
an adaptable star:

Float in the black
and stay there
if you need to,

save some light
for yourself.

In other words,
rest like the sun does:

Schedule some time
to stay out of sight
when too many people
praise warm energy.

Keep in mind
all of these things

when depression
tells you
nothing is working.

Keep in mind
all of these things

when it tells you
there is no
invisible force
connecting us,

when your veins
are stopped by blood clots,

when your bones are dry,
and the water
is too quick to boil.

Keep in mind
all of these things

when it tells you
that the soul is like the body:

Made to be broken,
open to deterioration
and doubt. Yes,

keep in mind
all of these things
and remember:

Even when it
seems like
the clock isn't ticking,

you were made perfectly
for this moment
in time.

On the Soul: The Soul of a Marginalized People

Dr. Karen Meadows

The year of perfect vision — 2020 — has ironically been the year of imperfect vision, or the year of the three uns, unpredictable, unprecedented, and unknown. I posit that Covid-19 and its ravishing effects, the global shutdown, the outcry after the death of George Floyd, and the political divide have impacted America's soul. This unprecedented year of questionable decision making, the neglect and paucity of basic biological needs, and the erraticism of people's emotional states have challenged our country's physical, emotional, and spiritual climate. The confluence of the three uns evoked feelings of anxiety, stress, fear, depression, and more. Many felt the weight of being the other, whether due to the pandemic, the politicization of the pandemic, or the weaponizing of the protests. Many experienced a heightened sense of uncertainty and vulnerability, sentiments that transcended economic class, power, and race. The soul of America was fragile and the experiences of many Americans traumatic. Therefore, if the soul of America was jeopardized, one can imagine that the soul of the marginalized was even more imperiled. When I contemplate the soul of the marginalized, I think of the souls of people of color, the souls of a collective who suffered/suffer violence and injustice, the souls of people who have been traumatized, and the souls of Black people who made substantial contributions to this country—free of charge. This notion of the soul is abstract, varied in its meanings, and multifaceted. Plato (Greek philosopher, student of Socrates) believed the soul consisted of three parts. While Yolanda Pierce, author of the "The Soul of Du Bois' Black Folk," defines the soul as "the seat of real life, vitality, or action; an animating or essential part, a moving spirit."[125] Pierce adds:

"The cultural expressions of black folks [in *The Souls of Black Folk*] that W.E.B. Du Bois describes in the spirituals, reflect a secondary, but highly significant, definition of the word "soul," namely, those emotions of community and cohesion that thrive in the often unexamined corners of black life."[126]

For the purpose of this essay, I too identify the soul of an oppressed people as the emotions of a community and the unexamined cohesion of Black life. I interpret the soul of an oppressed people as the counter-narratives of a collective group—"the 'little stories' of those individuals and groups whose knowledges and histories have been marginalized, excluded, subjugated or forgotten in the telling of official narratives."[127] The soul of an oppressed people is the part of the collective that holds the memory, that feels the pain of violence yet rises up against injustice, the core of a being that is resilient in the face of inequity and trauma, more specifically historical trauma. The soul of an oppressed people is the part that knows the strength and dreams of our ancestors, that finds a way to experience joy in spite of a profound sense of tragedy (tragicomedy) and the realm that knows the truth.

This essay uses historical and contemporary narrative accounts to imagine and ask readers to reflect on the condition of the soul of an oppressed people. These narratives exemplify how ongoing unpredictability, unprecedented-ness, and the unknown played out/plays out in the lives of three women of color. The author juxtaposes Plato's three parts of the soul against the outcomes resulting from a persistent state of the three uns. Contrary to the historical narratives often told about African Americans, this essay spotlights the strength, courage, savvy-ness, intellect, and resourcefulness of an oppressed people; a people who persevere, innovate, create, and evoke joy despite the barbaric and egregious treatment received from being deemed the other. This essay is a call to action, examination, and empathy.

---

125 Yolanda Pierce, "The Soul of Du Bois' Black Folk," *The North Star: A Journal of African American Religious History* 7: 1 (Fall 2003), 1.

126 Ibid., 3.

127 H. Giroux et al., *Counternarratives: Cultural Studies and Critical Pedagogies in Postmodern Spaces* (New York: Routledge, 1996), 4.

When we think of human behavior, not knowing when an act may occur (unpredictability), how egregious the act will be (unprecedented-ness), or what was coming and from whom (the unknown), it can often be more traumatic than the actual assault itself. Living in this state of being is conversely healthy and unhealthy; healthy in that it makes one aware of potential threats and unhealthy in that this hyper-vigilant state is strongly associated with trauma symptoms, in particular post-traumatic stress disorder (PTSD).[128]

Trayvon Martin, Dontre Hamilton, Eric Garner, Michael Brown, Tanisha Anderson, Tamir Rice, Walter Scott, Freddie Gray, Sandra Bland, Breonna Taylor, Ahmaud Arbery, George Floyd, and Elijah McClain. What do these names represent? The deaths of unarmed people of color. Unfortunately, by the time you read this essay, I suspect more deaths of unarmed Black citizens will have occurred; the list seems endless. Watching the nine minutes of torture as George Floyd pleaded, "I can't breathe," finally shifted the optics and the narrative to what has always been true—violence and injustice toward a specific group of people. The unpredictable, unprecedented, and unknown can occur in the lives of all people. However, it is the pervasive and persistent nature of these predicaments that burdens the soul. Psychologist Eduardo Duran identifies this hypothesis as "intergenerational trauma, historical trauma, and the Native American concept of soul wound. These concepts present the idea that when trauma is not dealt with in previous generations, it has to be dealt with in subsequent generations."[129]

From enslavement to lynching to Jim Crow to the killing of unarmed African-American adults and youth, it feels as if the humanity of a people is nonexistent; therefore, the soul of a people is not even a consideration. Horace Mungin in his poem, "The Lashing of Patsey of Bayou Boeuf Plantation," illuminates the violence, injustice, and the ravishing of the body and soul of a woman who merely sought a piece of soap.[130] In *Pedagogy of Survival: The*

---

[128] R. T. Carter et al., "Relationships between trauma symptoms and race-based traumatic stress," *Traumatology* 26:1, 11-18, https://doi.org/10.1037/trm0000217). (Accessed July 28, 2021).

[129] Eduardo Duran, *Healing the Soul Wound: Trauma-Informed Counseling for Communities Second Edition* (New York: Teachers College Press, 2019), 18.

[130] Horace Mungin, "The Lashing of Patsey of Bayou Boeuf Plantation, *Notes from 1619: A Poetic 400-Year Reflection*, (Charleston: Evening Post Books, 2020), 6.

Narratives of Millicent E. Brown and Josephine Boyd Bradley, I describe the plight of teenagers as they desegregated all-white high schools in the 1950s and '60s. Their experiences personify the unpredictable, unprecedented, and the unknown from a historical viewpoint. Millicent Brown, a 15-year-old who desegregated Charleston's Rivers High in 1963, was met with bomb threats, completely isolated, and ignored by students and teachers for most of her years at Rivers. She states:

> I was hospitalized. They thought I had a heart problem. I could barely walk without catching my breath. The diagnosis was that I had a nerve condition. The nerves in my chest tightened from the whole experience. I had physically responded when I wasn't saying things out loud.[131]

Similarly, Josephine Boyd Bradley desegregated Greensboro Senior High (now Grimsley High School) in 1957 at the age of 17. She also experienced isolation as well as physical and verbal harassment. When Bradley was approved to attend Greensboro Senior High, protestors killed her family's dog and burned down her father's store as efforts to deter her enrollment. Once she arrived, she was a party of one among an entire high-school population. Students used eggs and ketchup as weapons of choice. In these stories, the teens never knew when someone would assault them (unpredictable), how egregious the assault would be (unprecedented-ness), or what assault may be coming and from whom (the unknown).

Janine Davis, radio host, motivational speaker, and founder of Girl Talk Inc., presents a contemporary perspective on race and this notion of the unpredictable, unprecedented, and unknown. She explains how the recurrence of these memorable encounters burden the soul as she describes joining a protest:

> I had to give this some real thought. While I was not directly impacted, I still felt like a part of it because it was a movement and the movement was Jena Six. I, along with others, visited Louisiana to hear from and stand with the people protesting the Jena Six — six African American teenagers accused of beating a white student that sparked protests. We were going because it was so unjust. We couldn't believe this was happening in our country.

---

[131] Karen Meadows, *Pedagogy of Survival: The Narratives of Millicent E. Brown and Josephine Boyd Bradley* (New York: Peter Lang Publishing, 2016), 23-24.

On my way there I was concerned. I thought, what are we going to be met with? I'd never been to Louisiana and it's the deep, deep south. I'm thinking, we're not going to be welcomed. I felt afraid. As we were driving on this two-lane highway, it was pitch black with no civilization in sight. I thought what if we see a cross burning? My heart was beating fast, I didn't want anything to happen to us. I felt both angst and pride for pushing forward in spite of my fear.[132]

Davis defined the unpredictable as how she (an outsider) would be received. Not only from white citizens, but from Black citizens as well. This sensitive circumstance involved young adults whose lives would be inextricably changed forever. The unprecedented was the event itself, when approximately twenty thousand people descended on the small town of Jena, Louisiana. It was unknown territory. She states: "I was constantly processing how could this go wrong and what will I do if it does. I'm thinking about a way of escape and championing a cause at the same time."[133]

Although Davis recalled this one experience, she understood how the emotions and thinking that come with this state of being may unconsciously carry over into everyday life. For example, she became more aware that she surveilled the land when entering an environment and constantly deciphered interactions when in mixed company. While not always on a dark road in the Deep South, the unconscious processing of how something could go wrong and developing of an escape plan is always present.

"During the slave regime, the Southern white man owned the Negro body and soul. It was to his interest to dwarf the soul and preserve the body," wrote early twentieth-century journalist Ida B. Wells-Barnett.[134] Today there is no physical ownership of Black bodies, nonetheless, the devastation on the soul seems ever-present, intentional, and without remorse. Plato defined the soul as: reason, physical appetite, and spirit or passion.

REASON—Our divine essence that enables us to think deeply, make wise choices, and achieve a true understanding of eternal truths.

---

[132] J. Davis, personal communication, April 17, 2021.

[133] Ibid.

[134] Ida B. Wells-Barnett, *The Red Record Tabulated Statistics and Alleged Causes of Lynching in the United States* (1895), https://www.gutenberg.org/files/14977/14977-h/14977-h.htm#chap1 (Accessed July 28, 2021)

PHYSICAL APPETITE—Our basic biological needs such as hunger, thirst, and sexual desire.

SPIRIT OR PASSION—Our basic emotions such as love, anger, ambition, aggressiveness, empathy.[135]

I argue that this persistent state of the unpredictable, unprecedented, and the unknown confounds reason, undermines the basic biological need to live, and diminishes the spirit/passion of a people who have been the architects of this nation. It is difficult to repeatedly see the manipulation of reason to justify violence and injustice, a control at the root of racism. This logic makes it safe to deem the other as void of pain and negate the basic biological needs because of the melanin in their skin. How does one continue to swallow this pill? Emotions such as love, anger, ambition, aggressiveness, and empathy fluctuate constantly. Whether the owning of the Negro body, the degradation of the soul, the past pain of a whip, rape, separation of family, the soul is grieved. Regardless of the current institutionalized biases, incarceration, health and justice gaps, or the watching of a Black man plead for his life in plain sight; the pain is crippling, torturous, and devastating. It is the soul that holds the memories, that knows the truth.

Despite the egregiousness toward people deemed the other, much more needs to be written about the strength, courage, savvy-ness, intellect, and resourcefulness it takes to survive, excel, and still find some sense of joy under the weight of oppression. Millicent and Josephine persevered, stood tall, and achieved even in the face of blatant racism and hate. They exemplified courage and academic and social emotional intelligence; were discerning and acutely aware of the ways in which they navigated their hostile environment. Janine reclaimed her power even in fear by moving forward for justice and being fully aware that the unpredictable, unprecedented, and unknown were part of the journey. Oppressed people of color are the unpaid builders of this country, unacknowledged inventors, physicians without access to medicines, and survivors without a fair chance to survive.

So what will you do to change this narrative? You have a stake in the change, and I ask you to employ this essay as a call to action. Become more aware of

---

[135] "The Soul Is Immortal: Socrates and Plato," https://revelpreview.pearson.com/epubs/pearson_chaffee/OPS/xhtml/ch03_sec_02.xhtml (Accessed July 23, 2021).

racial inequities; seek out the counter-narratives, untold stories, and unsung heroes of oppressed people. Examine your own beliefs, biases, and isms and use this examination to empathize with the plight of one's otherness. Examine your soul for the path to a new future. All of our souls depend on it. Be a part of change, not an onlooker to violence and injustice—issues that have grave impacts *on the soul.*

Awaken to the Dream

Horace Mungin

I arrived to this consciousness
Screaming from the sudden
Jolt of awareness

The journey from naught
To wakefulness is startling
To scream is my only impulse

It is a scream absent judgment
Not of joy nor sorrow
It is a primordial sound

Realities gather and assemble
And forms for me an identity
And I have experiences which
Solidified my identity and
Gives me preference and other
Impulses; desires, urges, instincts
And whims

I am not alone, this perception
Of consciousness is widely shared
We are a community encountering
The same fantasy, the same delusion
The same hallucination

We name everything; we call it
The cosmos, the galaxies, the solar system
The sun, the moon, the stars
The world, our world—earth

We divide the darkness from
The light and name them Day
And Night and count the days and nights
It takes our earth to travel around the sun
We call it a year, we count the ticks
And the tocks between the occurrence
Of Day and Night and divide them into
Hours, minutes and seconds

We create time
The creation of time necessitates
The need to record what happens
During the tally of time—history
We are a community encountering
The same fantasy, the same delusion
The same hallucination, but our impulses,
Desires, urges, instincts and whims differ
Altering our realities and tolerance
A division that creates abrasions
And disunity, and conflicts and
Clans and tribes and countries and
Wars, and deaths and sufferings
And a reality no longer propelled
By the same perceptions

A routine is established
Monotony sets in to collect—
Consciousness dulls, controls
Are lost—some move ahead
A hierarchy emerges
Serfdom begins
Awareness is manipulated

Time flees

You are
Where you are

Things are
What they are

The reality
Is real
You think

Everything has a place
Order is time-honored

Disruptions and peace
Alternate in existence

To maintain the central objective
Ascension to top of the pyramid

The divisions become many
Natural, synthetic, imagined
Geographical, cultural

Race and ethnicity stand
A major a barrier

The more I look at a thing
The clearer it becomes to me
That I don't see a thing—elusive

My search is on to make sense
Of my perceptions—why am I here?
Why are we here and can't we all just
Get along?

We are all overwhelmed by
The rapid occurrence of
Change while too many
Things stay the same

I move to disengage from
The sense of community
I need to save myself from
The perceptions
We are all locked into

One day I bumped into the Tao
And read: to empty myself
Of all feelings, become without thought
Emotionless, opinion less, desire less
Detached and vacant, like dead wood

It was long and hard and often failing
To purge the years of habit and ritual
It took a concentrated practice, but
Finally I arrived, a hollowed vessel
Ready to awaken to the dream of
Reality, Now I'm able to disrobe from
The notion of birth and death
To return to my Natural self

Call and Response

Drowning Out
the Master's Narrative:
Ensuring that Black Voices Permeate
Cultural Heritage Institutions

Dr. Porchia Moore

In Black vocal traditions sound functions as a tool for visibility; for making joyful noise, collective groaning of grief and sorrow. The soundtrack of Blackness is our very own signature sound—rhythm, blues, jazz, rock, and more. It is messenger and message. Perhaps, no function of our vocal traditions is more informational and more important than the embodied way we as a collective communicate our being than the function of "call and response." Call and response is a kind of memory—a collective memory whose words, ideas, sounds, and messages we respond to in the collective body in a present moment.

In African descendant Black music tradition, the call functions as an auditory technique. A phrase is offered and is then responded to with a direct response or commentary. This is a kind of collective memory wisdom—a shared exchange of embodied knowledge. Cultural memory is defined by anthropologists and cultural sociologists as, "constructed understanding of the past that is passed from one generation to the next through text, oral traditions, monuments, rites, and other symbols."[136]

Cultural researchers, Jan and Aleida Assman, contend that there are two types of memory as it relates to culture: communicative and cultural.[137] Communicative memory is informal and centered on personal or autobiographical memories and experiences. Cultural memory is more complex and is memory that is institutionalized, an accumulation of stored objects and cultural heritage material signifying messages from the past about the past and its people. Yet, what happens to the cultural memory of Black people when our cultural heritage objects and subsequently our narratives are not equally institutionalized across libraries, archives, and most specifically museums? How can we properly participate in a call and response wisdom when our cultural heritage objects are rendered invisible or improperly interpreted in cultural heritage institutions? In this manner, our healing truths can only be revealed when we demand equity in representation from museums and cultural heritage sites.

When libraries, archives, and museums fail to equally represent Black material culture we are left with other people shaping our histories, with other people telling us who we are, with other people having the power and authority to omit our contributions and our lives from the historical record. As such, our call should be to de-center Whiteness and our response should return that Black material culture matters. In truth, the cultural landscape of America is markedly White and whitewashed. In the Southern regions of the United States, memorial sites and markers expressly venerate and celebrate a Confederate history while largely ignoring the exploitative labor that is the by-product of the horrific institution of slavery. Even as the tourism industry in the Carolinas and coastal Georgia benefit from millions of dollars in plantation tourism, the lives of the enslaved serve as a whimsical backdrop to the celebrated and glorified fortunes of white slaveholders.

This master narrative shapes our collective memory and casts Black people in fixed position in history. Museums and historic sites tell the same stories

---

[136] "National Geographic," Cultural Memory. https://www.nationalgeographic.org/encyclopedia/cultural-memory/.

[137] Richard Meckien. "ieA," Cultural Memory: The link between, past, present, and future, (June 07 2013), http://www.iea.usp.br/en/news/cultural-memory-the-link-between-past-present-and-future.

over and over again, using the same historical figures to shape a memory of a Great American South. Even as the excellent work of sites such as McLeod Plantation Historic Site or the work of Joseph McGill and his Slave Dwelling Project leads us away from old practices of cultural interpretation, these leaders remain in the minority. In an interview with Bill Moyers, Toni Morrison defines the Master narrative as the archetype of White imagination; a kind of wickedly designed language primer that constructs Black people and Blackness as always lacking and deficient against the backdrop of the White gaze[138] When unpacking the particular horrors of the lived experiences of little Pecola Breedlove, the protagonist of her most critical novel, *The Bluest Eye*, Morrison tells Moyers that the Master narrative is:

> No. It's white male life. The Master narrative is whatever ideological script that is being imposed by the people in authority on everybody else: The Master Fiction … history. It has a certain point of view. So when those little girls see that the most prized gift they can receive at Christmas time is this little white doll, that's the Master narrative speaking: this is beautiful, this is lovely, and you're not it, so what are you going to do about it? So if you surrender to that, as Pecola did (the little girl, the "I" of the story, is a bridge: [she] is resistant, feisty, doesn't trust any adults) … [Pecola] is so completely needful; she has so little and needs so much … she becomes the perfect victim—the total pathetic one. And for her, there's no way back into the community or society. For her, an abused child, she can only escape into fantasy, into madness … which is part of what … the mind is always creative … it can think that up.

It is this master fiction that has for far too long been the dominant narrative of America's museums and cultural heritage sites. This master narrative designed to be both neutral and rhetorically informative is a direct threat to Black people and to the collective cultural memory of not just American citizens but of our global communities. It is a particular kind of violence that erodes identity, contaminates cultural memory, and erases the contributions of a people and the evidence of their existence. The allegiance to this historical bent is predicated on an ingrained culture of White supremacy as

---

[138] Ileana Jimenez, "Feminist Teacher," Exposing the 'Master Narrative': Teaching Toni Morrison's *The Bluest Eye* (April 2010), https://feministteacher.com/2010/04/13/exposing-the-master-narrative-teaching-toni-morrisons-the-bluest-eye/.1`

the American historical record. Therefore, in order to liberate ourselves from the abuse of what Chimanda Adiche informs us is the danger of a single story; Black people and their accomplices must demand the de-centering of whiteness in our cultural heritage institutions.[139]

At one point in 2020, more than 1,712 Confederate monuments remained erect in the United States.[140] In spite of the urgent call for these monuments to come down in response to both the Mother Emmanuel Massacre and the violent protests in Charlottesville, Virginia, at the attempted removal of the Robert E. Lee monument and other political movements, in South Carolina alone there have been less than 1 percent of these monuments removed with 194 still in place. The good news is that latest reports from the Southern Poverty Law Center alerts that in 2020 after the murder of George Floyd, over 100 monuments were removed. To place in context, there are 2100 identified Confederate symbols and monuments and 704 of these are monuments.[141] Sadly, the Associated Press reported in January 2021 that of all the states with this jarring headline, "Confederate Statues Likely to Go Undisturbed in SC in 2021."[142]

Critical Data Regarding Museums

To contextualize why it is vital to have full participation and inclusion of Black visitors to cultural heritage institutions, it is imperative to examine the following statistical data. There are roughly 11,000 Starbucks in this country. Comparatively, there are more than 14,000 McDonald's restaurants. However, the combined number of these two establishments is well underneath the number of museums, which total well over 35, 000.[143] In 2019 museums

---

[139] Chimanda Ngozi Adichie, TED: Ideas Worth Spreading, The Danger of a Single Story (July 2009). https://www.ted.com/talks/chimamanda_ngozi_adichie_the_danger_of_a_single_story.

[140] Madison Hoff, Insider, "This Map Shows How Many Confederate Monuments and Symbols Still Stand in the US," (June 13, 2020). https://www.businessinsider.com/confederate-monuments-and-other-symbols-in-the-us-2020-6.

[141] Rachel Tresiman, NPR, "Nearly 100 Confederate Monuments Removed in 2020, Report Says More Than 700 Remain."

[142] Jeffrey Collins, AP, "Confederate Statues Likely to Go Undisturbed in SC in 2021" (January 11, 2011. https://apnews.com/article/legislature-columbia-south-carolina-local-governments-d345cb5894fa83abfaa622eed44017ca

[143] Christopher Ingraham, The Washington Post, "There Are More Museums in the US Than There are Starbucks and McDonald's Combined" (June 13, 2014). https://www.

contributed more than $50 billion to the U.S. economy with over 850 million visits to museums annually.[144] Not only is museum-going big business, it is so profitable that in 2018 alone more people visited museums (art museum, science center, historic house/site, zoo, aquarium) than the total number of attendees to professional sporting events.

Consider the full enormity of these statistics when we understand that of the total number of visits to museums less than 10 percent represent those of the "minority" of those representing BIPOC (Black Indigenous People of Color) visitors.[145] In fact, according to the Tronvig Group, a brand strategy and marketing consulting group, Black people make up thirteen percent of the United States population and account for less than three percent of the total number of visits to museums.[146] Not only do these numbers tell a grim tale, but they also reveal that the gross disconnect between Black people and museum-going adversely informs the future of Black people working in, leading, visiting, or even understanding the role and purposes of museums as key tools for narrating, documenting, and preserving our cultural contributions. In fact, less than 15 percent of all museum leadership positions in art museums represent Black staff.[147] To add insult to injury, a groundbreaking 2019 study revealed that in eighteen major American art museums White artists represent 85.4 percent of museum collections.[148] Here is a summary of the study's breakdown of the artists represented in the collections of the major American art museums: 85.4 percent White, 9.0 percent Asian, 2.8 percent

washingtonpost.com/news/wonk/wp/2014/06/13/there-are-more-museums-in-the-us-than-there-are-starbucks-and-mcdonalds-combined/.

[144] American Alliance of Museums, Museum Facts & Data, https://www.aam-us.org/programs/about-museums/museum-facts-data/.

[145] American Association of Museums, "Demographic Transformation and the Future of Museums" (2010). https://www.aam-us.org/wp-content/uploads/2017/12/Demographic-Change-and-the-Future-of-Museums.pdf.

[146] James Heaton, Tronvig, "Museums and Race" (Jan 20, 2014). https://www.tronvig-group.com/museums-and-race/.

[147] Carey Dunne, Hyperallergic, Diversity in Museum Leadership has Marginally Increased Since 2015, "New Survey Says" (January 28, 2019). https://hyperallergic.com/482077/diversity-in-museum-leadership-has-marginally-increased-since-2015-new-survey-says/

[148] Benjamin Sutton, Artsy News, "A Study Found that 85% of Artists in US Museum Collections Are White, and 87% Male" (Feb 19, 2019). https://www.artsy.net/news/artsy-editorial-study-85-artists-museum-collections-white-87-male.

Hispanic, 1.2 percent African American, and 1.5 percent other ethnicities. The four largest groups represented across all eighteen museums in terms of gender and ethnicity are: White men, 75.7 percent; White women, 10.8 percent; Asian men, 7.5 percent; and Hispanic men, 2.6 percent. All other groups are represented in proportions less than 1 percent.

Renowned museology scholar Stephen Weil argued that the new museum was about people and not objects.[149] Museum interpretation grew more to be about the stories regarding the people's objects as well as the people themselves. Specifically, the rhetoric and the research grew to be more about the hierarchy of the narrative in connection to communities. The rise of community-based museums became a movement that sought to serve communities with their specific cultural heritage information needs through innovative programming, service, and exhibitions.

Drowning Out the Master Narrative

If, as Audre Lorde informs us, the master's tools will never dismantle the master's house, then we must first consider what the master's house is comprised of.[150] Failing to properly collect, display, interpret and preserve Black material culture (tangible and intangible) is a kind of violence. It is an injustice both to Americans and to all those Black lives that contributed to the shaping of this nation. The American museum poet June Jordan argued:[151]

> Take me into the museum and show me myself, show me my people, show me soul America. If you cannot show me myself, if you cannot teach my people what they need to know—and they need to know the truth, and they need to know that nothing is more important than human life—then why shouldn't I attack the temples of America and blow them up? This is one America, and after black cities have been manipulated and after something like a n****r room has been reserved in the basement of the Metropolitan Museum for us, the people who have the power and the people who count the pennies and the people who hold the keys better start thinking it all over again."

---

[149] Stephen Weil, "From Being About Something to Being for Somebody: The Ongoing Transformation of the American Museum" *Daedalus*, Volume 128, no 3, (1999), 229-258. https://www.jstor.org/stable/20027573.
[150] Audre Lorde, *Sister Outsider: Essays and Speeches* (NY: Crossing Press, 1984).
[151] June Jordan, Museums Collaborative (MUSE), *A Museum for the People: A Report of Proceedings at the Seminar on Neighborhood Museums* (1969).

Drowning out the master's narrative must include incorporating new ways of thinking about Black material culture and thereby the contributions and legacies of Black people. We are not a monolith and neither are our stories staid blueprints as a backdrop for White America. Black people must demand more from cultural heritage institutions. These actions include:

- Demanding that museum boards are equitable across race and gender
- Demanding that museum staff and leadership are racially diverse
- Calling for social media content and references that are culturally broad and inclusive
- Calling for equitable representation in exhibitions (digital and physical)
- Calling for equity in acquisitions of material culture
- Demanding that cultural heritage institutions create and share DEAI (Diversity, Equity, Access, and Inclusion) policies easily accessible by the public
- Demanding reduced or free admission, transportation, and programming to historically under-engaged communities

It is also up to Black people to support both African American museums and historic sites. It is also critical for White-facing public institutions (those whose leadership is visibly and demonstrably run by Whites) to demonstrate prioritizing Black cultural heritage. It is imperative that all of this labor (intellectually and physically) become the priority of everyone regardless of racial identity. Cultural heritage institutions must be prioritized and girded as viable places for healing and learning. The more we increase our presence; the stronger our voices, demands, and influence. In taking an active role in repairing and restoring our missing voices and contributions in cultural heritage institutions we provide a resounding call and response that Black lives and material culture matters. The cultural landscape of places like Charleston and the surrounding Lowcountry are unequivocally Black historical legacies. We should demand that our cultural heritage institutions center their narratives accordingly.

Gil Scott Heron Revisited

Al Black

The revolution will be televised
It will be on YouTube, Twitter and Facebook
Brought to you by 10,000 smart phones

The revolution will be televised
No one will lead the charge
It will just spontaneously combust

The revolution will be televised
Bieber and Taylor will not be singing
But Kyle will still be posting selfies

The revolution will be televised
On laptops, iPads and Tablets
And when it is over, Kanye will still grab the mic

The revolution will be televised
Their lies no longer work
Because cell phone cameras don't lie

The revolution will be televised
The revolution will be televised
We are all being televised...

An Ode to Afro-Desideratum
Imam Hakim Abdu-Ali

El-Hajj Malik El-Shabazz, commonly known as Malcolm X, once said, "I am not a racist. I am against every form of racism and segregation, every form of discrimination. I believe in human beings, and that all human beings should be respected as such, regardless of their color."

Those profound words shape my overall view of respecting "hue-manity" in all of its amazing created variations because I can see the power of what the Creator Alone has masterfully designed. In so many norms, I've been drawn to reflect upon Brother Malcolm's view of respecting "hue-manity" by looking at what it means to be a part of today's consummate "hue-man" family's illustrious global ensemble.

Brother Malcolm's poignant thoughts about "hue-manity" have always captivated me, while at the same time, they have challenged me and made me question who I am as a person of color, born in Harlem and living in the U.S.A. And by being an observantly conscious soul of color, I know that the relevance of my ethnic identity in this country is an immediate in-your-face, wake-up reality warning; a warning that will always be there because America continues to be a "his-storically" racially divided and conflicted nation.

African Americans are the ebony descendants of the original Motherland of all creation. We have been fighting to gain a position to accurately describe ourselves and proclaim who we are and what our legitimate heritage is in this land that has delegated us to permanent second-class citizenry. All this confusion has occurred during four centuries of cruel racial inequalities, uncivilized miseducation, and bestial injustices galore. Afro-Americans and other oppressed ethnic folks were manipulated into trying to adapt to the comprehensive Euro-colonial American scheme of living, thinking, acting, and being.

So, for these suffering folk, it's been a very difficult role to acclimate to. It has been especially hard for those Afro-descendants of enslaved souls from the Motherland, who, oftentimes, because of the color of their skins, are branded less than "hue-man." It's been a daunting struggle to continually maintain dignity or show real respectful democratic passion for a politically corrupt and very racist nation that practices unscrupulous political double-dealing and unprincipled social prejudices toward Black folk and others.

Still, I'm buoyed by my people's legendary "our-storical" courage, strength, and spiritual tenacities, and that's why "Black Lives Matter," as a term of consequential ethnic endearment, takes on a more-than-emblematic phrase of the moment for me and other prideful, thinking members of the African diaspora. This understanding signifies an energizing and enduring constant reminder of what our Afro-ancestors experienced during slavery and beyond while living as captives in the hell holes of the U.S.A, Africa, Europe, the Caribbean, and the Middle East.

The horrific journeys through the inner sanctums of slavery's diabolical corridors still scar and linger within the mentalities of multitudes of the descendants of those enslaved Africans. To this very day, African descendants everywhere suffer in many psychologically disturbing ways. It's something that needs to be educationally identified and addressed; the unifying healing knowledge of one's true self and heritage is required to remedy the lingering scars in the collective mindsets and psyches of African, Afro-American, and other global Afro-ethnic communities.

If you're a reflective soul with a scintilla of the Motherland's ethnic ancestral consciousness and possess some serious African pride, then knowing that the collective benefits of being united while living in the midst of the enslavers' residual global racist systems shouldn't be hard to appreciate. Truly, no excuses to the contrary are allowed in escaping this conundrum when you concede that being Black in America is a very dangerous living vocation.

It must be voiced in those explicit terms because I sense there's still a lingering identity personality uncertainty within the minds of far too many of today's Africans and Afro-American descendants' psyches about how their desires to be respected and how the achievement of equality are to be accomplished—the truth hurts sometimes.

If you're an aware, thinking, ethnic soul of color, you probably inherently already know how difficult it is to live in a society, pretending to be free while existing under the semi-patriotic guise of pseudo-equality for all—which is, in actuality, a farce, because you are continually discriminated against. That's why the motto "Black Lives Matter" hits home every day. As an Afro-American I have to cultivate a lifelong craving for and a longstanding sense of being proud of who I am as a secure melanin being, because I know that Africa is the Motherland of all "hue-mankind." If Africa is the scholarly unquestioned and academically recognized Motherland of all "hue-manity," then please don't take me to task for also saying that "All of Mother Africa's Children's Lives Everywhere Matter."

The recent racial protests and civil uprisings throughout this nation and beyond are also alerting me to the undeniable fact that there has to be immediate corrective changes in racial and political facets of societies globally. You, too, may now even sense that something dramatic is happening in our nation's clandestine political think tanks and that the global universe is finally waking up to the alarming actualities that "his-storical" racism, bigotry, injustice, and pseudo-ethnic supremacies are no longer going to be tolerated. They will be confronted, dealt with, and abolished.

Many people, and Afro-Americans in particular, must still recognize the realities that the present-day idealistic, ballyhooed cries of "democracy for all" is a sham. We must think and envision a true democracy. In order to do this, we all must put forth our best efforts in terminating racism's cancers and bigotry's viruses out of the "hue-man" disposition.

Unless we do this, the democratic fantasies of justice and freedom for all is only that—a fantasy—and it's (apparently) not to be intended, in actuality and practice, for all of those who are oppressed and discriminated against. We should never forget that certain people, including Native Americans, Africans, people of African descent, women, and other oppressed ethnic folk of color, were never part of the original "his-storical" Founding Fathers' real definition of freedom for all. Many people have forgotten about all those valorous ebony souls who labored and gave their lives for us to be where we all are now in today's bald eagle's enclave called America. Do the overwhelming majority of Afro-descended folk and others of color worldwide have pride in who they really are?

For me, Black lives matter at all times and always will because if I don't care about, or love, me for who I am or how I was created, then who will? Author Ta-Nehisi Coates in his book *Between the World and Me* said it profoundly: "You are growing into consciousness, and my wish for you is that you feel no need to constrict yourself to make other folk comfortable."

Being Black and proud is more than being beautiful, if you ask me. It's who the Creator made us to be. Please think about that as an important ode, or as a significantly inherent symbol of praising or glorifying one's natural Afro-consciousness and unparalleled uniqueness with adroit spiritually intellectual honor and pride.

Those are superlative gifts to all aware and humbly prideful folk of color from the Creator alone. Yes, Black Lives Matter, and if that's clearly understandable, then who cares if racist, partisan naysayers and ignorant political xenophobic pundits question why you, me, or other conscientious prideful and created souls of color proclaim with rightful dignity to one and all that Black Lives Matter?

We must look to unite ourselves with pride, respect and dignity in order to uplift each other. I feel that we are stronger than we know ourselves to be. We're capable of doing anything and everything possible if we believe and stick together and stop hating and destroying one another. We are Black and beautiful, and we most certainly matter.

Some inauspicious folk may have trouble with me saying that because hatred of one's self can wear even the strongest of us down if you're trying to fit into a mold (or skin) that is not your own. In many instances, the truth hurts, but sometimes it has to be told to establish a respected united front.

So, I believe that to attain a unified self-empowering mechanism, all aware folk of color have to realize the importance of many factors that make anyone respected, self-sufficient, and liberated, and that is understanding the important unifying essential realms of faith, economics, and political power.

To know this is only a beginning in establishing the commemorative acknowledgement of and building for our needed spiritual survival and economic growth, as beings who know who we really are and want to be. I offer this as "An Ode to Afro-Desideratum," acknowledging that as people of color we intrinsically want and collectively need to never forget that Black Lives Matter.

Tribal Dancing

Susan Madison

For years,
I raped you like you were a back-alley whore,
silenced by shame

I disallowed your character,
though you curled
I straightened you out,
by dousing you with lye,
killing the very quality of you that made you-you

But, you refuse to give up,
you talked back,
with new growth that crouched low,
and crinkled close to the nap of your roots

with warrior tools in a freedom ceremony
I cut off the damage of other folks' beliefs,
and watched you cut up,
like a cooped-up child,
raised by old timey grandparents,
suddenly let out the house by death —
you bent where and how you wanted to
stood like defiant tulips in garden patches,
and floated in waves to meet my neck
you doubled over in crowded spaces,
curled into yourself,
and giggled when you felt the wind

You flirted at the edge of my temples
and caused ancestral eyes to shine from mine
arched my cheekbones
and gave flare to my nose

You danced a freedom dance in puzzled patterns,
unique as thumbprints
you celebrated emancipation
tens of thousands strong
each an individual
you formed an army
full of glory
tribal dancing on my head

Pathology not Privilege:
New Paths toward Racial Healing

Marnishia "Neesha" Jenkins-Tate

Some of the world's earliest philosophers were healers. Their highest goal was to elevate and enlighten the human soul. As a doctor of philosophy who has studied cross-cultural communication and social psychology as avenues toward racial healing, I believe that perhaps it is time we get back to those basics.

Early philosophers encouraged human beings, even beyond organized religion, to elevate their souls (their character or psyche) by embodying higher levels of spiritual consciousness (virtues such as kindness, wisdom, temperance, justice, and courage). Goodness was symbolized as an illuminating ascension toward love and light.

Philosophers cautioned against falling prey to the darkness of the lower levels of human consciousness (character flaws such as ignorance, wickedness, greed, immorality, and amorality). These were thought to be symbolic of turning away from love and light.

Goodness was once a self-actualizing measure of the degree of light or darkness in the human soul. But somewhere in our human history that script was flipped. Goodness became a measure of the degree of lightness or darkness in the human skin.

Lighter skin was positioned higher in social order than darker skin and an entire industry of human captivity emerged. Contrary to Spiritual

Enlightenment, the Age of Enlightenment, with its origins in Europe, sought to justify human hierarchical systems to support the seventeenth-century rise in global capitalism that required cheap and free labor to maintain its cash crops. History scholar Dr. Danielle Bainbridge explains that through the artificial social construct of race, darker skin people were justified as human sacrifices for wealth because they were designated as sub-human property, distinctly identifiable based on skin color.

With that misconception came codes of misconduct, exclusionary doctrines, cultural values, and institutions all built around justifying and solidifying this social system. It became a way to engage lighter-skin enablers to help feed the greed of a few materially wealthy souls who lived otherwise spiritually impoverished lives.

The father of Western philosophy, Socrates (470-399 B.C.), taught that care for one's soul and aspiring toward one's highest level of consciousness are the foundation of human wellness. He espoused that taking good care of the soul was how human beings differentiate themselves as a higher species. Accordingly, Socrates encouraged us to constantly examine our lives and make adjustments in our souls, striving for goodness instead of evil, toward becoming better human beings, and ultimately toward building greater societies and civilizations.

It has been my observation that too often today we lack accountability for the wellness and goodness of our souls. More frequently we witness human beings behaving as beasts while desperately wanting to believe they are best—with no sense of the need for soul-work nor any remorse for the impact their toxic behaviors may have on the greater good.

Therefore, in the spirit of the Socratic method, I propose in this essay that the current social phenomenon of heightened racism, colorism, ageism, and even gender-bias all can be usefully examined through the lens of the disease of narcissism. I propose that by leveraging what clinical psychologists have learned about the damaging effects of toxic interpersonal relationships, we might also recognize and treat similar damaging effects across group dynamics.

What can clinical psychologists teach us about Narcissism?

Clinical psychologists, such as Dr. Ramani Durvasula, tell us that narcissists and toxic abusers typically exhibit these behaviors, among others:

- A lack of empathy toward others;
- Arrogance and entitlement;
- A high need for control;
- Gaslighting, causing others to question memory, sanity, or self-worth;
- Triangulating, pitting people against each other to maintain ultimate control;
- Feeling inconvenienced by other people's pain and suffering;
- Superficial relationships based on shallow feelings;
- Anger, indignation, and rage when validation needs are not met;
- Remorse about being seen in a bad way, but no remorse about bad behavior.

Clinical psychologists also have learned that victims of narcissistic abuse tend to:
- Feel they are not good enough;
- Keep giving and forgiving, believing the narcissist will eventually change;
- Blame themselves and make excuses for being treated poorly;
- Numb themselves or self-medicate to adapt to toxic environments;
- Become magnets for other narcissists as mistreatment and a sense of unworthiness become normalized; and
- Sometimes evolve into narcissists themselves, especially if they felt either unprotected or overly protected.

Racism as Socialized Narcissism

I want to suggest that the social disease of racism must be examined as a form of socialized narcissism. Behaviors become socialized when they are tolerated, imitated, enabled, normalized, rewarded, and even institutionalized as an acceptable means of navigating society. In modern American culture in particular, with the help of traditional and social media, there is evidence that narcissistic behavior has become socialized. And racism is one of the historically permissive stages upon which narcissistic behavior can be acted out with few repercussions.

It has been my observation that nobody is killed because of his or her race, ethnicity, sex, age, or sexual orientation. People are killed and harmed because other people choose to hurt them. There is no natural cause-and-effect relationship between one's ethnicity, race, age, or gender and the infliction of death, pain, discrimination, or disdain upon a person or group.

People are attacked not because of who they are, but because of who the abusers and attackers are—humans who act from dark places in their souls, who use others as targets for their own ignorance, arrogance, amorality, fear, anger, and rage. And too often now, the perpetrators of these harmful, hateful, and heartless acts are a handful of people who embrace "Whiteness" as a license of entitlement to wreak random and orchestrated havoc on others.

How can victims of racism be survivors and thrivers?

If you identify with being a "victim," strive to understand the dynamics of narcissistic relationships that were shared earlier in this essay. Use that as a lens, a way of knowing, so that it might be useful toward understanding and healing the mindset of victimization and all the disempowering fears that come with it.

Stop self-blaming and victim-shaming yourself as though your darker face, ethnicity, age, or gender is a justifiable reason for mistreatment and hate from others. Know that yours is a beautiful human face conceived by love as an expression of God's grace—just like every other face the Creator has intentionally placed on this earth.

Recognize that when people repeatedly are allowed to behave in an ugly way that not only angers and frightens us, but also violates and offends our human spirit, it can cause anyone to start to question him or herself. Self-blame is often merely a coping mechanism used to grasp for some sense of control.

Rid yourself of self-defeating self-talk: if only I were White ... my skin color is a curse ... maybe if I act more like them ... and so forth. How dare you shrink yourself to fit inside a narrow mind? What kind of person tries to impress an oppressor? That mindset in itself is a form of self-hate and denigration. That thought process alone will make a victim justify his own abuse.

Until society stops pathologizing victims by suggesting that people are the cause of their own injuries—by virtue of their physical attributes, ethnicity, gender, or age—and start calling out the dark souls who impose physical, mental, and emotional anguish on others, this social dysfunction will only get worse.

If you feel like a victim, examine your life and empower yourself. Speak up. Speak up about micro-aggressions you experience that feel unfair or deliberately unkind at your job, in your business dealings, within your social circle, in your intimate relationships, and even within your own family. Recognize when others try to gaslight you or treat you as a scapegoat who should be blamed for provoking bad behavior in others. Distance yourself, when you can, from these enabling influences.

Speak up for others, too, wherever you see injustice. Examine yourself daily by asking: "How wide is my 'we'? Is it a 'wee-we' that can only accommodate the folks who look like me? Or is it a 'wide-we' of great scope and empathy that can embrace the notion of serving all of humanity just by doing my small part?"

Speak up with your wallet, your talents, your vote, and with the internal work you do to enlighten your soul. Speak up because you love and honor yourself as a human being. Speak up because God granted you the privilege of birth, the privilege of breath, the privilege of being a spiritual being in a body, and the privilege of being created equally.

And know that no human being should ever have the right nor the privilege to snatch any of that away from you.

How do good people enable racist behavior?

An over-attachment to one's side of the artificial social construct of "race" will disconnect any of us from the rest of humanity. It will cause us to detach from what it means to be an empathetic member of the human race whenever people don't look like we do.

An enabler might be inclined to ask: "How can I as a privileged White person help Black people and other minorities?" However, any person asking this question might fail to recognize that the tone of presumed privilege, while also self-identifying with Whiteness, is a major part of the social problem. Condescending sympathy is no substitute for accountability or empathy.

If you consciously shrink-wrap yourself in Whiteness and consider yourself to be humane, you may be expected to explain whether you are ashamed of any of the mean-spirited actions being done under the divisive banner of Whiteness. For many people of color, conscious identification with Whiteness today has come to be socially symbolic of self-identifying with bullying, violence, a desire for dominance, self-righteousness, and presumed privilege. Sometimes this identification is even steeped in religion, but it is almost never grounded in any inclination toward spiritual enlightenment.

Even a well-meaning person can become an enabler, unintentionally gas-lighting victims by making excuses for bad behavior or by remaining neutral about unfair situations. We may unwittingly excuse abusers because they look familiar, because we feel exempted from their abuse, or because we stand to benefit from their transgressions.

I once heard Gloria Steinem say that sexism breeds racism, because if you can discriminate and dominate within your own family based on gender, it becomes easier to tolerate and perpetuate the hate beyond your family that fuels racism. So, it is important to examine your life by asking yourself whether you are doing what you can where you can to bridge differences and look for commonalities that help you to see the humanity in every human being.

For example, ask yourself, if you witnessed children being abused or elderly persons being bullied, would you empathize with the abuser? Would you ignore it? Would you ask the victims: "As a privileged independent adult, what can I do to help underprivileged you?" Or would your humane instincts kick in to say: "This is wrong. Seeing this hurts me. If I don't speak up, this can happen again. My silence could enable more violence."

Too many good people have become passive enablers unwilling to sit in their own human discomfort, so they expect victimized others to remain quiet or act happy, just so they can feel okay. But how long can anybody maintain sanity while quietly repeatedly suffering at the random indiscretion of others? How long should anybody categorically endure discrimination, death, and daily discomfort? Similarly, how long can anyone call himself or herself humane while ignoring harmful unjust acts imposed on others? Certainly, the Creator had greater reasons to place each of us on this earth than to accommodate the needs of toxic human souls and their heartless greed.

Pathology not Privilege

The artificial social construct of race serves one core purpose — to sup-port racism. Race is a useful tool for triangulating groups of people based on skin color to pit them perpetually against each other. Racism is a narcissistic approach to keeping victims and enablers in rivalry with each other such that neither recognizes that the bulk of power over material resources is being channeled into the controlling hands of a hoarding few.

So let's examine this term, privilege. Recognize that if you feel victimized and you see the persons who treat you poorly as a "privileged" group of people, you are actually relegating yourself to being merely a problem of the privileged, an anomaly constantly striving to prove yourself worthy of human dignity.

Failing to call out bad behavior and its agents only feeds the ill-conceived notion of white privilege. Telling someone else or yourself that you have "white privilege" is actually an act of narcissistic validation. It suggests that diminishing, destroying, and ignoring human rights or turning a blind eye toward this behavior is a privilege.

God has granted no one any such privileges. Why continually do we?

We simply cannot keep calling hurtful, harmful things, or those turning a blind eye to those things, privileged and then expect that these same people will change. Let's face it. Nobody feels badly about being called privileged in any context of the word and few will voluntarily give up anything perceived as a privilege. In fact, generally speaking, most of us take great pride in having privileges—so on any path toward racial healing, that term privilege must be banished because it is a big part of the perception that enables the racial problem.

Racism is not a privilege. It is a dysfunctional social disease with a pathology. Individually, we must learn how to recognize the disease and protect ourselves from it, as well as take measures to heal ourselves once exposed to it. Pursuing a path of spiritual enlightenment is one way to pursue healing.

Society also has a role to play in the space of public health to protect us from the disease of racism. Through legislation and education, it must contain the spread by educating people about the disease and by minimizing toxic influences because, if left untreated or if accepted as normal, the disease of racism will continue to spread at a viral speed.

How can we start to erase racism?

The best and most sustainable reparation a society can offer any victimized group is the reassurance that past atrocities will not be repeated. Anything else is just a momentary pacifier.

We have socialized narcissism in the form of racism, so perhaps we can also socialize measures to heal the harm it is causing. Perhaps we can raise our social standards by institutionalizing expectations that normalize striving to become more enlightened human beings.

What does that mean? It means flipping the script back to philosophical basics. It means that abusers, victims, enablers, and intentional people of all hues must ultimately consciously do the soul-work required to elevate ourselves and enlighten our souls toward mending our human race.

It means the intolerance we've directed at skin color under the artificial construct of race must be internalized and applied to a construct of personal spiritual growth, striving toward more inner light and driving out inner darkness. It means we must learn how to see and elevate the light in ourselves and in others—and we must call out inner-darkness, mean-spiritedness, and evil when we see it in all its forms.

Otherwise, in a diseased society where not all lives matter, eventually no lives will matter at all—and our society will continue to build a herd immunity to human decency.

The Curse
after Genesis 9:20-29
Ed Madden

"God did this, and it is in his holy word."
– letter to *The State* newspaper, August 22, 2017,
arguing that God created slavery

We heard it growing up, a story about
a boat, a rainbow, and Noah getting drunk,
Old Testament riddle rendered racist fable.
A father curses his son to be a servant
of servants, even among his brothers, now other
to them—Ham, a man whose name they used
to say meant burnt though it doesn't. A man
who'd never learned a foreign tongue cites Hebrew
to instruct us on the way it was (or is) meant
to be, bully pulpit bigot exegesis for brothers
willing to walk backwards, to look the other
way to not see that it's not a story about
fathers or honor or enslavement but the shame
of what we do, what we have done to one another.

Changing the Narrative
One Dwelling at a Time

Joseph McGill

Since launching the Slave Dwelling Project a decade ago, I've spent nights in more than 150 cabins and larger structures, many built by enslaved people, in twenty-five states and the District of Columbia, to change the American slavery narrative one dwelling at a time. I've bedded down in likely and unlikely places, in the Deep South, the western and New England states, and the upper Midwest. After all, slavery existed across a third of the United States. I've traveled to rural and suburban landscapes, college campuses, private homes and the homes of U.S. presidents, national and state parks, barns, churches, and the modest residences of northern merchants. There's no place in this country that has not been touched by slavery, one of this country's most immoral acts, just as the entire country has been shaped by the ingenuity and tenacity of enslaved people.

I began this work in the spring of 2010 with the mission to call for the preservation of slave cabins. At that time, my program was called the Slave Cabin Project. As I learned that enslaved people did not live only in slave cabins, my work became the Slave Dwelling Project. Initially, I slept alone. But eventually others joined me, creating the opportunity around a night-time campfire for candid and sometimes emotional conversations on race. Unexpectedly, I am helping some White people address their misconceptions about racial issues.

The more I traveled, the more I realized my high-school education distorted my view of slavery. I call it junk history. My teachers in Williamsburg County, South Carolina, repeated the "happy slave" narrative from textbooks written by authors like Mary Simms Oliphant, who produced an incomplete version of South Carolina's history that was used in South Carolina classrooms for decades. Oliphant was among those Southerners who sympathized with the defeated South as part of a broader plan to blame the Civil War on the North, while casting their "lost cause" as just and noble.

That junk history, combined with continuing media narratives portraying Africans and Native Americans as savages, angered me. History shows, however, that enslaved Africans in America came from great civilizations before they were packed tightly in sea-going vessels for the largest forced migration in human history.

These repeated misconceptions of the ancestors radicalized me. While I was a program officer with the National Trust for Historic Preservation I was still guarded, but I became increasingly outspoken against the false idea of the great White-male colonizers. Many Americans see this country as great, but they fail to admit the crimes committed to achieve that greatness. In the process of proclaiming greatness, some paint others as inferior. As I spoke against this narrative, I felt empowered, knowing I was building trust among Americans nationwide.

The junk history I received in high school also gave me a limited and slanted view of the Civil War. As a park ranger at Fort Sumter National Monument I was accustomed to handling difficult questions. But one query knocked me back. At nearby Fort Moultrie, another National Park Service property, Confederate reenactors camped and presented living-history demonstrations. Some wore gray Confederate uniforms. Others wore Union blue. I was invited to join them. Knowing the real Confederate forces waged war to keep people who looked like me enslaved, I declined. I also suspected that the reenactors felt they needed my Black face to validate their actions. I resented what they were doing. However, I realized that they were honoring their ancestors and heritage. I could respect that. Then I saw their sincerity. They were honoring soldiers. My respect grew, but became more complicated.

Declining their offer got me thinking about forming a group of Black Civil War reenactors. After I saw the movie Glory, about the Massachusetts Fifty-fourth unit, I realized Charleston did not have a Black reenactment group to tell the story of Black Union soldiers. Atlanta, Boston, and Washington, D.C., had Black reenactors; why not Charleston, where the war started? Restaurateur and Civil War relic-hunter Robert Bohrn encouraged me to organize such a group. His advice meshed with my desire to do so. About a year after the movie was released, I joined several others in starting the Fifty-fourth Massachusetts Volunteer Infantry, Company I. The idea took hold immediately, attracting prominent members of Charleston's Black community, including the city's first Black police chief, a funeral-home director, the owner of a Gullah art gallery, and the director of the African-American research center at the College of Charleston. We didn't play war games when we donned woolen blue uniforms and slung reproduction-model rifles over our shoulders. We were living historians portraying brave Black Union troops who fought to end slavery.

Confederate reenactors trained us on military tactics and weapons safety, enabling us to gain our certifications as reenactors. We could have traveled to Atlanta to train with Black reenactors, but that would have delayed our plans. Ironically, the Confederate reenactors needed us as much as we needed them. They benefited from having us around for reenactments, because then they had an enemy to shoot at.

I began this essay noting that slavery was one of this country's most immoral acts. The other was the theft of land from North America's people—Native Americans. Manifest Destiny was the nineteenth-century philosophy that America would inevitably expand across the continent. When America acquired from France more than five million acres through the Louisiana Purchase it nearly doubled the size of the country and eventually opened space for fifteen new states. Purging Native Americans was the next step before the push westward and another example of an American sin.

In an essay I wrote for *Slavery's Descendants: Shared Legacies of Race & Reconciliation*, I tell how I came to know a group called Coming to the Table[152]

---

[152] Dionne Ford and Jill Strauss, eds., *Slavery's Descendants: Shared Legacies of Race & Reconciliation* (New Brunswick, Camden, and Newark, N.J.: Rutgers University Press, 2019), 188-192.

Soon after I began sleeping in slave cabins and publishing blog posts, several news outlets, including National Public Radio (NPR), reported on my work. That early coverage led to a 2012 invitation from Coming to the Table to join them for the Coming to the Table National Gathering in Richmond, Virginia. There I discovered a group that had similar goals to my own.

While I am interested in the buildings that once housed the enslaved, Coming to the Table's focus is on the descendants of people who both enslaved and were enslaved. The mission of both organizations, however, is to uncover history and to affect systemic and institutional changes that more accurately and equitably tell our nation's story.

A few months after my initial contact with the group, three Coming to the Table members joined me for a sleepover at the Bush Holley House in Greenwich, Connecticut. The relationship led to a Slave Dwelling Project partnership with Coming to the Table, one of only two partnerships I have with a national organization. (The other is with the National Park Service's Network to Freedom.)

Coming to the Table has especially assisted the Slave Dwelling Project when—despite archaeological and genealogical research that establishes ties between a particular family and an extant slave dwelling—the ensuing interactions between the descendants and the property owners proves challenging. With CTIT's continuing assistance, I hope more relationships can be established between the descendants of both the enslaved and enslavers through my work with and research of extant slave dwellings.

The Slave Dwelling Project thrives because of the vast portfolio of sites with which I work. Many of the owners of those sites are still content with feeding their visitors a sugarcoated and watered-down version of history. Unfortunately, some visitors are comfortable remaining in the dark about the true history of these sites, which presents another challenge all its own.

I'm in my fifties now and mostly retired from Civil War reenacting; however, I continue to don the uniform of the Massachusetts Fifty-fourth while conducting living-history programs connected to the Slave Dwelling Project. It is important to commemorate the two hundred thousand African American men who served the United States during the war, especially now that Civil War reenactments are decreasing—in part, because of the problematic symbolism of the Confederate flag. After nine members of Emanuel AME Church in Charleston, South Carolina, were murdered on June 17, 2015, by a white supremacist, the upcoming largest reenactment was canceled. Because the killer's propaganda was peppered with the Confederate flag, locations reexamined their relationship with it and many removed it. Nonetheless, reenactments—Union or Confederate—are a great educational opportunity.

In the face of this downward trend, and now that the Covid-19 pandemic is nearing an end, I hope the Slave Dwelling Project will continue to open further educational opportunities for in-person meetings around campfires and in classrooms. Through genealogical and archival research, descendants of the enslaved can discover and establish their ties to these extant properties. Our enslaved ancestors built these antebellum buildings. They cut down the trees to provide the frameworks, made the bricks to create the walls, and provided the labor to give the structures life. Unfortunately, African Americans do not own any of these buildings that I know of, so we must develop creative ways to access these historic structures—if not through sleepovers, then through special tours, interviews, and research—even if such access is temporary. Through our efforts, it is my ultimate hope that every extant slave dwelling in this country will be restored, interpreted, maintained, and sustained so we can embrace our history and sit around the campfire for those hard conversations about race relations.

Rice Kingdom

Yvette R. Murray

Eight grains of rice remain
on a gold trimmed plate
after Sunday dinner

Far away from the swamp
away from the mud
a hoe rusts on the back porch

Gravy drops dark like blood
onto a bright white tablecloth
next to pan bread crumbs

Cypress tree centerpiece
casting Gullah Geechee shadows
since 1685.

Silverware dancing slowly
in the drawers of a buffet
crammed full

with fruit
from a Pullman Porter's
tree. Almost

every inch covered
with Normal School
diplomas. Plastic

front room full
of faces and kin:
Legacy. Built.

Growing up Racist
in the Jim Crow South

Steve Bailey

C all this my confession, if you want. I call it the truth.

I was maybe 14 when Dick Jones, Mount Pleasant's charismatic young recreation director, who would go on to become mayor, started the town's first youth basketball league. This was huge for those of us who spent almost every day after school playing pick-up games at the Old Village basketball courts in the early 1960s.

Jones was nothing short of a god to us. Not long out of The Citadel, he had been a basketball and baseball star for the Bulldogs and had played minor-league baseball before an injury turned a promising prospect into a small-town playground director. He used to delight in showing us film of the night he covered a kid named Oscar Robertson. (The Big O scored sixty on him.)

I had been among the noisiest and most persistent of the kids lobbying for a basketball league. So I was over the moon when I got to Moultrie High School's gym that Saturday morning to sign up. But when I went inside, I was paralyzed by what I saw: There were my friends, for sure, but there were other kids, too: Black kids.

I had never considered such a heresy. I asked my hero, Dick Jones: How could this be? He said that is the way it is now. I told him I couldn't possibly play with them. I ran out of the gym in tears, never to return.

It's a mistake to deny your past even if you are not proud of it today. Growing up a racist in the Jim Crow South, things were simple: There were White schools and colored schools. Separate bathrooms and separate water fountains—all clearly marked—were common. So was the "N" word, and I used it, too.

It was June 11, 1963, and we were already out of school for the summer. Together, my younger brother Michael, our Black "maid" Lilly, and I were transfixed, watching the TV (black and white, of course) as Gov. George Wallace stood in the schoolhouse door, blocking Vivian Malone and James Hood from entering the University of Alabama. We didn't say a word, but Lilly, maybe 20, and I (12 then) knew we were on different sides that momentous day.

In that summer of protests in Charleston, South Carolina, across the river from Mount Pleasant, more than a thousand Black people went to jail in what came to be known as the Charleston Movement. When Lilly showed up on the local evening news outside a sit-in on King Street, my parents fired her the next day. This was the life I grew up in during the '50s and '60s.

When I was ten, there was no bigger day for white Charleston in 1961 than April 12, the centennial celebration of the firing on Fort Sumter. In Mount Pleasant, Alhambra Hall was decorated and awash in people who had come to watch the reenactment of the bombardment of the Union forces and the start of the War Between the States (never "Civil War"). When the Star of the West tried to resupply the Yankees at Fort Sumter and was turned back by Rebel cannon fire, we all cheered wildly. There was never a question that day about whose side we were on.

Mount Pleasant was a very different place then, compared to today. There were five thousand locals, about 60 percent White and 40 percent Black. (Today, Mount Pleasant is the state's fourth-largest municipality with a population of 85,000—95 percent White.) White kids stayed with White kids and Black kids with Black kids. That's just the way it was for the most part.

But there were exceptions. At the minor-league baseball games at College Park near Hampton Park in Charleston, White people sat in the seats around the infield, Black people in the bleachers in the outfield. The guy selling peanuts and Crackerjacks had a key to unlock the gates between the two segregated sections. By the fourth inning or so, the kids were bored, and we dropped down through the old wooden bleachers to the ground. There the kids, Black and White, played our own game, using a broomstick and crushed snow cone cups for a ball. We had fun.

And then there was my friend Wayne Brown. Wayne, a teenager, was the only employee at my dad's struggling printing-and-office-supply shop on East Bay Street in Charleston and one of his Saturday jobs was to entertain me when I tagged along. One day we drove to lunch at the Piggy Park drive-in, but my dad parked across the street and left us in the car while he went over to order.

"Dad, Dad, why aren't we going to the drive-in like usual?," I wanted to know. Wayne, who was Black, knew they wouldn't serve him. But I would serve him. I knew Wayne, personally. He was my friend.

My high school, Moultrie, was integrated in 1964, when seven brave Black kids transferred from Laing. Among them was Otto German, who became a high school and college basketball star and went on to have a long, distinguished career at the College of Charleston. Integration happened without incident, though many affluent White families moved their kids to fancy private schools like Porter-Gaud and Ashley Hall. My family never considered such a thing; we could barely pay the mortgage.

In my senior year, I got my first real job as an office boy at the old *News and Courier*. I worked the weekend after Martin Luther King Jr. was murdered, and we were locked down in the building, fearful that Black people in the neighborhood would extract vengeance on the newspaper, a symbol of white supremacy in those days.

Things were changing in the country—and for me, too, though I didn't know it yet.

****

It was 1968, Vietnam was on fire, Martin Luther King and Bobby Kennedy were murdered, the Democratic Convention in Chicago was a war zone, and the Beatles' "Hey Jude" was No. 1 on the charts. It was the first time I had been out from under my parents' roof, and it was a great time to be in college (and not Vietnam).

I made new friends, many of them from the North (though all White). I grew my hair long. I smoked a lot of dope. And I started reading. *The*

Autobiography of Malcolm X was the most important book I had ever read. I devoured Richard Wright, James Baldwin, and more. I knocked on doors for Tom Broadwater, a young Black lawyer in Columbia, South Carolina, who ran a third-party campaign for governor in 1970.

The summer after my freshman year I got a job back home measuring houses for the county tax assessor's office. One week we were assigned to work an appalling slum area somewhere deep in North Charleston. I had never seen anything like it: People lived in shacks with no plumping. They used a pot for a toilet and dumped it out back. The roads, such as they were, were unpaved. The place stank.

I knocked on a door to get permission to measure the house. A young boy, maybe five, saw me at the door and immediately fled back into the house.

"Mama, Mama, there's a cracker at the door," he screamed in fear.

Fifty years later, I remember being overwhelmed with grief that day. How could this be Charleston, my hometown, not some slum in a third world country? I wept in the street. If there was a single moment of reckoning for me, that was it.

After college, I went to work for *The State* newspaper in Columbia, the start of a half-century in journalism. I have worked in Boston and London as an editor, reporter, and columnist, but the single best reporting job I ever had was my two years in Rock Hill, South Carolina. I was 23, and the newspaper gave me an office, a car, and the northern half of the state to cover. I worked non-stop, writing about everything from cops to textiles to race.

It was in the tiny town of York that I had one of my most satisfying moments as a journalist, and it had nothing to do with anything I wrote. I was there to cover the growing racial tensions—the particulars of which elude me decades later. The Ku Klux Klan showed up to burn a cross. They seemed like pathetic clowns to me.

There was a rumor, though, that they would be back that night to torch a Black church. I talked to the pastor and other Black leaders, and we decided these cowards in sheets would be less likely to threaten the church if there was a big-city (Columbia!) journalist there. So I spent the night in the back of the church, playing cards and listening to the stories these good York people had to tell. I went home the next morning feeling good about myself; they stayed to defend their community.

****

Today, at 71, I remain a work in progress when it comes to race. In that way, I don't think I'm very different from a lot of other White people.

America, indeed, has come a long way—yet we have a long way to go. Identifying the problems has been easier than identifying the solutions. The gulf between Blacks and Whites is wide: in wealth, health, education, and what to do about it. Trying to talk about race is painful and dangerous.

Yet, I remain an optimist.

After forty-five years away from Charleston, I am back home, where my heart has always been. I was born in a tenement on East Bay, and now live a mile and a half away on the Eastside, a neighborhood where race is always front and center. Impoverished Blacks and middle-class Whites live side-by-side, and it is not always easy. Sometimes it is very hard for both sides.

When I first returned to Charleston, I lived South of Broad, and race, day to day, was no issue at all. Why should it be? We were all White professionals, successful. The only Black people we interacted with in the neighborhood every day worked for us, often keeping the grand old homes from falling down.

Three floods later, we moved to the Eastside. Life is more complicated. My house was built before the Civil War by one of Charleston's wealthiest freed Black men for six enslaved people he owned. Over the years, the two-family house was home to Germans and Irish and then generations of Blacks after Whites fled to the suburbs in the '50s and '60s. Now I am happy to call it home.

Unlike South of Broad, race is ever present in the Eastside—one neighborhood, two communities. The income disparities between Blacks and White are stark. We frequently see things differently: Whites, for instance, welcome the cops. Blacks often would rather be left alone, not surprising given the history. Blacks see Whites as gentrifiers; Whites see themselves as neighbors, and good ones at that. I understand well that many of my Black neighbors would tell this story another way.

But the Eastside is where I want to be. I like my neighbors, Black and White. The Eastside and neighborhoods like it have a chance to show the way forward. It's not easy and won't be easy; it would be naive to say otherwise. But if we're going to learn to live together—to learn from one another—we need to live together, not apart.

Accept this as more than a confession. It's an apology, too. I am sincerely sorry for the times in my life when I have been the problem. I very much hope to be part of the solution.

This must be fixed. We have no other choice.

Centennial

Gary Jackson

*... put our best foot forward or the Civil War will be commemorated
from a Northern point of view.*
–E. Milby Burton, director of the Charleston Museum, circa 1951

The parade begins. The old flag is raised
above the State Capitol, above every theater
and high school. Young women strut
for Miss Confederate as the canons fire
on Fort Sumter. Men play pretend
in their grays and blues as the spectators
cheer and crowd hamburger stalls.
Strom Thurmond reenacts the vote to secede
live on SCETV. That's history:
The Francis Marion Hotel refusing to admit
Madaline Williams from the Centennial
Commission Board. The men call it
providence—a sign things are off
to a fine start. Nothing less than Kennedy
can persuade a change in venue
to the desegregated Charleston Naval Yard
prompting Southern delegates to secede
from the commission and host their own
meeting somewhere else. That's history
repeating itself, that's Charleston,
that's The Citadel awarding
the Star of the West every year—
named after the ship fired upon
by Citadel cadets, triggering The Civil
War. That's pride, that's Charleston's
centennial stamp featuring a soldier

hunched forward ready to fire his cannon,
palmetto fronds falling in the background,
falling downtown, covering unmarked
graves and well-manicured plantations
where you can take a hayride, pick straw
berries, see the acrobatic dog show, get
married, wave to the cheering crowd,
pelted with rice, christened in white.

Truth's Clear Far-off Light
Josephine Humphreys

In Anderson, South Carolina, there's a Confederate memorial on Main Street in the middle of town, a tall column topped with the statue of a South Carolina soldier who looks vaguely like a diminutive Mark Twain. His name is not on the monument, but he isn't an unknown soldier. He's my dad's paternal grandfather, Major William Wirt Humphreys. He died in 1893, so my father, who bore his name, never knew him, and when I was growing up, the major was barely mentioned. I knew his name, I knew he was the son and grandson of Presbyterian preachers, and that's all. Last year I learned that there was a movement in Anderson to take down the monument, so I went about trying to learn a bit more about the man.

I started imagining that he might, after more than a century of looking down from on high, want to have himself removed.

What grounds could I possibly have for thinking such a thing? After all, the inscription on his monument says,

> The world shall yet decide
> In Truth's clear far-off light
> that the soldiers who wore the Gray and died
> with Lee, were in the right.

I don't know who wrote that, but it might well have been one of the Anderson ladies who spearheaded the memorial project in the first place. In any case, the words stuck in my memory. First of all, it's not going to happen. The soldiers who wore the Gray will not be proved right. But truth's light may indeed show us something else about them.

In June of 1861, at the age of 24, William Wirt Humphreys volunteered for military service and helped organize the Fourth South Carolina Infantry, Company B, Palmetto Riflemen, and was elected first lieutenant. The war was young; nobody thought it would last long. Six weeks later he found himself promoted to captain and leading the Palmetto Riflemen into battle at First Manassas, stationed near the Stone Bridge. The battle began at 9 a.m. and lasted all day, with a total casualty count of 4,793 dead or wounded. At some point afterwards, rumors began to circulate that the captain had left the field and deserted his men in the middle of the fighting.

But what had actually happened, according to written accounts of witnesses, was that after hours of battle (I believe it included bayonet combat), Captain Humphreys suddenly stopped fighting. Covered in the blood of fallen soldiers, he looked around at the carnage. Then he walked into the woods, to the bank of a creek, and sat there with his head in his hands. After about twenty minutes he rose and rejoined the battle, fighting the rest of the afternoon without stopping. He would go on to fight at Williamsburg, Seven Pines, Gaines' Mill, and Frayser's Farm, where he was shot in the chest. When he recovered, he was promoted to major in the reorganized company, now called the Palmetto Sharpshooters, and served in the campaigns of Suffolk and Knoxville, the battles of Will's Valley, Wilderness, Spotsylvania, Second Cold Harbor, Bermuda Hundred, Fort Harrison, and the Siege of Petersburg. After the war, he went home to Anderson, married Josephine McCully, edited a newspaper, practiced law, became a judge, president of the Savannah Valley Railroad, and mayor of Anderson. But whenever I think of him, I see not the statue, not the businessman and judge, not the mayor ... but the young soldier sitting by the creek with his head in his hands.

Was it a moment of truth for him? I want to think so.

I want to think he'd been suddenly struck, and paralyzed (if only for a time), by the pure horror of what he'd seen and done and now knew, not only in that specific bloody battle but in the larger horror, the whole world of southern slavery and racial injustice. Did he have second thoughts there by the creek, or later at home in Anderson, or in his old age, looking back over the years?

Did he ever change his mind? I want to believe that the light dawned.

But now—now, writing this—I suspect all of that may have been wishful thinking on my part. I'm a fiction writer. Given a few known facts, I may tend to construct around them a story that serves my purposes, and in this case I really want to exonerate my ancestor. But other facts arose that make that story doubtful. For a while Humphreys was a newspaper editor, and he wrote a number of editorials supporting slavery and secession. I haven't seen any writings that indicate a change of mind.

****

I am 76 years old now. I own a burial plot in Magnolia Cemetery, next to the grave of another ancestor, my father's maternal great-grandfather, George Alfred Trenholm, a member of Jefferson Davis's cabinet. His tiny gravestone, about nine inches high, bears only the initials "G.A.T.," a memorial quite different from a life-size statue on the town square, and yet the story of this ancestor, as I interpret it, echoes that of Major Humphreys in some ways. Like Humphreys, Trenholm was a widely admired, even beloved man; like Humphreys, he supported slavery. And around him, as with Humphreys, I was able to construct a story, a framework that would enable me to posit a good heart underneath his Confederate skin. I hold onto two things he is quoted as saying, the first from prison after the war, in answer to a question from his daughter, who wanted to know what would be her relationship to their former slaves, now that slavery was ended. "We must be to them," he wrote, "what we have always professed to be—their closest friends." And the second was an answer to a newspaper reporter who asked how he felt about the end of slavery: "I am glad to be rid of it," he said.

In a history study group I was once accused of "failing to honor" my Confederate ancestors. Well … yes, that is true. I don't honor them. But I don't regard that as a failure, and I don't think they would be disappointed in me. I hope the best of them knew they would not be honored; they had made terrible mistakes, perhaps unknowingly, unaware of the magnitude of the implications, or knowingly but without the courage to try to correct the error. A man who was a double-legacy of Presbyterian preachers surely must have had a sharp sense of right and wrong, of charity and sin. When I think about him, and of my other predecessors, I remember something the North Carolina novelist

250

Kaye Gibbons once told me: "In the South, we have had to learn ways to love those whose ideas we hate." And I do believe that is a possible, if mysterious, kind of southern love.

And I believe that some of those Confederate ancestors, a few anyway, may indeed have undergone, eventually, a kind of transformation, an encounter with Truth's clear far-off light. My father, the descendant of both of these men, experienced that kind of revelation. It came very late in life, after many decades as a conservative defender of the values he grew up with—segregation, states' rights, anti-unionism, anti-feminism. In his old age he became more reflective, reconsidering his positions. In 2008, at the age of 92, he voted for Barack Obama. In 2010, when he moved in with us, he had a recurring dream in which a Black man came asking for his help. Dad said later to me, in desperation, "It won't be enough to just give him $100. He needs a job. He needs a decent chance." And once, late at night not long before he died, he told his hospice helper, Ellie, that he realized he'd been wrong about many, many things. She grabbed a pen and wrote down what he said. Among other things, he regretted having opposed labor unions during his professional life. "I've come to realize that every man—and every woman, Ellie—deserves a living wage."

Finally, I hope for the light of truth to fall not only on the old ones who are now gone, but also on those of us still living, including me. What do we stand for, and with whom? Will our descendants see us clearly, as we really are? For that matter, will we understand and see our own selves? I think of one more memory, from a past not so distant as these I've mentioned. My grown son was talking about how we (the family) had benefited from slavery, and I protested. I said, "But at the war's end, all the wealth was gone. Nothing was left. We were dirt poor."

"We benefited," he said. "We had education, we had connections and advantages beyond money. We had hope."

I hope we can spread hope wide.

I hope we can also remember these brilliant words from the late actor Chadwick Boseman, who has been suggested as a replacement for Major Humphreys atop the column in Anderson, where he once lived. He spoke at a film awards ceremony in 2019, addressing his fellow cast members:

"We all know what it's like to be told that there is not a place for you to be featured, yet you are young, gifted and Black. We know what it's like to be told there's not a screen for you to be featured on, a stage for you to be featured on. We know what it's like to be the tail and not the head. We know what it's like to be beneath and not above. That is what we went to work with every day because we knew ... that we had something special that we wanted to give the world. That we could be full human beings in the roles that we were playing. That we could create a world that exemplified a world that we wanted to see."

Let us create that world.

One River, One Boat

Marjory Wentworth

I know there's something better down the road.
—Elizabeth Alexander

Because our history is a knot
we try to unravel, while others
try to tighten it, we tire easily
and fray the cords that bind us.

The cord is a slow-moving river,
spiraling across the land
in a succession of S's,
splintering near the sea.

Picture us all, crowded onto a boat
at the last bend in the river:
watch children stepping off the school bus,
parents late for work, grandparents

fishing for favorite memories,
teachers tapping their desks
with red pens, firemen suiting up
to save us, nurses making rounds,

baristas grinding coffee beans,
dockworkers unloading apartment size
containers of computers and toys
from factories across the sea.

Every morning a different veteran
stands at the base of the bridge
holding a cardboard sign
with misspelled words and an empty cup.

In fields at daybreak, rows of migrant
farm workers standing on ladders, break open
iced peach blossoms; their breath rising
and resting above the frozen fields like clouds.

A jonboat drifts down the river.
Inside, a small boy lies on his back;
hand laced behind his head, he watches
stars fade from the sky and dreams.

Consider the prophet John, calling us
from the edge of the wilderness to name
the harm that has been done, to make it
plain, and enter the river and rise.

It is not about asking for forgiveness.
It is not about bowing our heads in shame;
because it all begins and ends here:
while workers unearth trenches

at Gadsden's Wharf, where 100,000
Africans were imprisoned within brick walls
awaiting auction, death, or worse.
Where the dead were thrown into the water,

and the river clogged with corpses
has kept centuries of silence.
It is time to gather at the edge of the sea,
and toss wreaths into this watery grave.

And it is time to praise the judge
who cleared George Stinney's name,
seventy years after the fact,
we honor him; we pray.

Here, where the Confederate flag
flew beside the Statehouse, haunted
by our past, conflicted about the future;
at the heart of it, we are at war with ourselves

huddled together on this boat
handed down to us—stuck
at the last bend of a wide river
splintering near the sea.

In memory of Walter Scott and Muhiyyidin d'Baha

Marjory Wenworth wrote "One River, One Boat" with plans to deliver it in January 2015 during the second inauguration of Republican South Carolina Governor Nikki Haley. State officials said the two-minute poem was cut for time, but others suspect the poem was tossed because it mentions slavery. The poem was subsequently published in *Illuminations 31*, Summer 2016.

Return to Africa

For the Love of Black Children

Kim Nesta Archung

I am reading *We Be Lovin' Black Children*.[153] As I read, I find myself reflecting on the work I have done across the globe, and particularly across the African diaspora over the past forty plus years. I think of the many people of African descent I have worked with from early childhood through adulthood whose lives have been shaped by educational systems that were not constructed to provide safe, loving, nor thriving places where they can live and grow.

As Gloria Swindler Boutte and her colleagues point out, people of African descent must constantly battle living in "a world in which White supremacy flourishes."[154] I find myself having deep emotional responses to this text and want to use it as inspiration and reference for this essay.

I have lived in South Carolina for the past fifteen years, and it is here where I have seen most profoundly the ways Black children[155] are hurt daily in deep and long-lasting ways by educational institutions built on white supremacist values and foundations. I began my tenure here teaching at the university

---

[153] Gloria Swindler Boutte, Joyce Elaine King, George Lee Johnson Jr., and LaGarrett J. King, eds., *We Be Lovin' Black Children: Learning To Be Literate about the African Diaspora* (Gorham, ME: Myers Education Press, 2021).
[154] Ibid., 15.
[155] Throughout this essay the terms Black, Brown, People/Children/Teachers of Color are used interchangeably to indicate People of African Descent.

level. I taught undergraduate and graduate students at schools of education in historically Black colleges and universities (HBCUs) where undergraduate students studied early childhood, elementary, and secondary education and graduate students at all three of these levels worked toward becoming masters of their craft.

While I had some incredibly bright and talented students, I also had a majority of students, both at the undergraduate and graduate levels, who had very poor reading and writing skills. In fact, I taught a number of undergraduate students who literally could not read or write at a third-grade level. This gave me my initial bird's eye view of what South Carolina's school systems were doing to and not for Black students. A few years later I did substitute teaching in Head Start and public early-childhood through middle-school classrooms, filled with mostly Black and Brown children. Most recently I have worked across South Carolina to support the state's early childhood system and early childhood providers where I have had even closer views of the damage being done to young Black children.

What the authors illustrate in *We Be Lovin' Black Children* as damage being done to Black children can be described as cultural violence.[156] Cultural violence includes physical, symbolic, linguistic, curricular/instructional, and systemic expressions of anti-Blackness.[157] According to Boutte, cultural violence is often disguised and difficult to see and can easily be described as being passive-aggressive. This passive aggressiveness is most often part of policies that reinforce systems of oppression that continuously promote inequities at the earliest levels and beyond, leaving Black children behind before they have had a healthy start.

I think of the four-year-old Black boy I observed in South Carolina who had an incredible vocabulary and could clearly describe his feelings but was expelled from his childcare center for jumping off the furniture. I think of the number of early childhood classrooms I've assessed and observed filled with little Black babies where there is little developmentally appropriate curriculum and instruction taking place and basics in health and safety are not met.

---

[156] Nsombi Okera, "Virginia's role in Americanizing the Ideology of African inferiority," *National Social Science Journal* 52:1 (2019), 63-75.

[157] *We Be Lovin' Black Children: Learning to Be Literate About the African Diaspora.* Edited by Gloria Swindler Boutte, Joyce Elaine King, George Lee Johnson, Jr. & LaGarrett J. King, 2021.

I often enter these spaces feeling that I would not put my child there but knowing that many Black families have few if any alternatives. I compare these places to the predominantly White centers in more affluent communities where the opposite is true. Unfortunately, the forces of white supremacy and institutionalized racism have impacted systems of education and care, beginning at the earliest stages.

Educational communities world-wide have long recognized the importance of laying a strong foundation for healthy social, emotional, and intellectual development beginning at the earliest stages of life. Early childhood education has gained traction on the world stage over the past twenty or so years because of this information. Widely conceived understandings of how quality early childhood education influences the life trajectories of young children into their adulthood has propelled global initiatives from organizations like the United Nations Children's Fund (UNICEF), Save the Children, and other local and international non-governmental and non-profit organizations that focus on communities with the highest rates of poverty and inequity.

Consequently, African diasporic communities across the globe have typically been focal points for programming and reform. However, these programmatic models tend to reflect and replicate the same values and systemic structures that created the situations of inequity in the first place. While statistical reports may indicate slight gains in educational outcomes for Black and Brown children where such reforms have occurred, Black children are still confronted in schools daily with experiences of symbolic violence (negative stereotypes), systemic violence (overcrowded conditions), physical violence, and curricular and instructional violence (absence of African and African-American history), each of which leaves its own psychological and traumatic repercussions on the healthy social, emotional, and intellectual development of Black and Brown children. Very few models of quality early childhood education and care that implement culturally resonant perspectives and approaches have been used widely.

We need to reach back and pull forth those aspects of African heritage, culture, and practice that can refute the negative experiences and outcomes for Black people. In the Akan culture of present-day Ivory Coast and Ghana, the Adinkra symbol Sankofa means "to go back and fetch." Sankofa illustrates the importance of reaching back to knowledge gained in the past in order to bring it into the present so that we can make positive progress. This is a concept we as people of African descent must practice, particularly where the education and rearing of our children and youth are concerned. In order to actualize Sankofa, particularly in the realm of educational practices, which I believe touch and influence all aspects of our lives, I want to draw attention to models of education from across the African Diaspora that provide frameworks for providing safe, nurturing spaces filled with love, where Black children and students can thrive and reach their highest potentials. I want to highlight using culturally resonant approaches across the educational spectrum, from early childhood to higher education. I want to call attention to the Black teaching tradition.[158]

I cut my teeth as an educator in spaces where the Black teaching tradition was the norm. When I was nineteen years old I co-founded Paige Academy, a community-based independent school in Roxbury, Massachusetts, a predominantly Black community. Paige Academy, which offered a community-based nursery and elementary school, continues to provide an example of Sankofa in action. The school is based on the Nguzo Saba, the seven principles of Kwanzaa. Kwanzaa is an African American celebration based on principles and practices that Maulana Ron Karenga honed in 1966 from his travels across the African continent. The Nguzo Saba provides a framework for how African people should define, uplift, and function in a community-wide network. The principles of unity, self-determination, collective work and responsibility, cooperative economics, purpose, creativity, and faith undergird how children are educated at Paige. This provided me with the foundation through which I developed my own teaching practices in the Black teaching tradition.

The legacies of the Black teaching tradition refute the negative outcomes experienced by so many Black children and youth and promote the protection of Black people while ensuring our achievement and success in a world that would otherwise lead toward our demise. Akosua Lesesne's 2020 definition of the Black teaching tradition is comprised of "characteristics, roles, and embodiments [that] transformative Black teachers have been collectively innovating for

---

[158] Akosua Lesesne, "A sistah circle of seven: Black women's self-perceptions of their Teach for America (TFA) experiences in the U.S. Mid-Atlantic region" (dissertation, University of Pennsylvania, 2020).

over a century in governing teaching practices"[159] In my experiences working in various contexts across the African diaspora, I have found the elements of the Black teaching tradition alive and well in spaces where Black and Brown teachers lead the charge in the educational experiences of their students.

In the southern United States and South Africa, I conducted comparative postdoctoral research on Black teachers. I wanted to fully understand how their life histories and professional development influenced their practices of culturally responsive pedagogy. In each instance, whether in all-Black, mixed racial, or predominantly White settings, the Black teachers in my study saw their roles as advocates with high expectations, who believed in and cared deeply for all of their students, and most particularly their Black pupils and other students of color. In Belize, I provided professional development to teachers of color who taught in early childhood settings with very little material resources and little more than high-school diplomas. Yet, these teachers traveled up to two hours after teaching all day to participate in week-long workshops I facilitated. Their love for the Black and Brown babies they taught and their commitment to their own professionalism embodied the qualities of the Black teaching tradition.

Regardless of the resources available to all of these teachers each element of the Black teaching tradition remained a part of their repertoire and praxis[160] with respect to their characteristics (high expectations, professional expertise, and the drive to increase their professionalism), their roles (advocate, bridge, community member/extended family), and embodiments (answering, believing, caring, overcoming through healing and spiritual practices). Loving Black children, loving Black people, and loving Black community are at the forefront in the minds and hearts of Black teachers who embody the Black teaching tradition.

I cannot emphasize enough how important it is for people of African descent to reclaim our destinies and the destinies of our children. We cannot wait to be saved by initiatives, programs, or the good will of well-meaning people to save us from white supremacist systems of oppression. They were not designed for us to survive in, let alone thrive. Our salvation must come from within. We have examples of success; we have a rich history of healing, creative, nurturing

---

[159] Ibid., 43.

[160] Praxis refers to the nexus between a teacher's thoughts and actions; it is the intersection between beliefs and practice and how a teacher establishes classroom practices and customs.

practices. We must simply have the courage to reach back, to practice Sankofa, to find ways of freeing ourselves from the vestiges of what is far too often seen as the best example to follow because it is White.

I am reminded of Margaret Walker's poem, "For My People," particularly the last two stanzas, which have always left me with a sense of hope and inspiration as I have dedicated my life to the love of Black children,

For my people standing staring trying to fashion a better way
from confusion, from hypocrisy and misunderstanding,
trying to fashion a world that will hold all the people,
all the faces, all the adams and eves and their countless
generations;
Let a new earth rise. Let another world be born. Let a
bloody peace be written in the sky. Let a second
generation full of courage issue forth; let a people
loving freedom come to growth. Let a beauty full of
healing and a strength of final clenching be the pulsing
in our spirits and our blood. Let the martial songs
be written, let the dirges disappear. Let a race of men [and women]
now rise and take control.[161]

---

[161] Margaret Walker, "For My People," from *This Is My Century: New and Collected Poems* (Athens: University of Georgia Press, 1989), Copyright ©1989 by Margaret Walker. Used with permission of the University of Georgia Press. https://poets.org/poem/my-people.

A Little Black Boy

Horace Mungin

I'm just a little black boy
I like video games, hip hop music
Candy, chips and dips, Air Jordans
Laughing out loud, walking free
I be
Trying to reach black adulthood in
America

I'm just a little black boy
Born cheated, to a mistreated history
Prey for the system, oh, how they fear me,
Snuff out my potentials, success not near me
Stop and Frisk me, bait and switch me,
Disenfranchised me, prison pipeline me
All to stop me, when they see me
Trying to reach black adulthood in
America

I'm just a little black boy
Told to take heed to the talk
Black boys get from black mothers on how
What I say to white policemen should
Be measured in servile drabness always
Keeping my hands where they see them
Empty

Then pray that this is not the vacant eyed one
So horrendous my mere color produces a gun
To his fearful eyes—pray that he is not that one
In three that I may live another day
Trying to reach black adulthood in
America.

"The Mystery Of Return"

Maya Angelou's Sojourn in Kwame Nkrumah's Ghana

Bernard E. Powers Jr.

The broad sweep of African-American history chronicles two stories. The first is about the struggle of a people to achieve their rights and fulfillment in the country of their birth. The second, embedded in the first, charts how those people define their relationship to Africa. So, to be African American is to experience a uniquely hyphenated form of Americanism in which sometimes the two components, African and American, compete for primacy. Are we fundamentally American or African has been a perennial question among Black intellectuals and leaders; the answers have varied over time with changing conditions in America and Africa.[162]

African-American writers have evocatively illustrated this complex identity. Historian W. E. B. Du Bois's 1903 *The Souls of Black Folk* posits that racism

---

[162] Martin Kilson and Adelaide Hill eds., *Apropos of Africa: Afro-American Leaders and the Romance of Africa* (Garden City: Anchor Books, 1971). During the American Civil War, interest in Africa was comparatively low because the conflict brought prospects for emancipation and racial justice in America. By contrast, World War I and its immediate aftermath heightened racial conflict, which in part fueled the Africa-oriented Garvey Movement. See Floyd J. Miller, *The Search for a Black Nationality: Black Colonization and Emigration 1787-1863* (Urbana: University of Illinois, 1975), 250, 262-63, and Cameron McWhirter, *Red Summer: The Summer of 1919 and the Awakening of Black America* (New York: Henry Holt, 2011), 26, 67.

inflicts a "double-consciousness" on African Americans. It was "a peculiar sensation" that caused one to feel "his two-ness, an American, a Negro; two souls, two thoughts, two unreconciled strivings; two warring ideals in one dark body." For Du Bois, this "strife" was the history of African people in America.[163] Poet Countee Cullen's famous 1920s work "Heritage" rhetorically asked: "What is Africa to me: One three centuries removed." He concluded that while separation from Africa and adoption of western civilization attenuated African culture among Black Americans, it continued in atavistic and inchoate forms.[164]

Between the late 1950s and early 1960s, even as the civil rights movement in America gained momentum, African American interest in Africa rose to unprecedented levels, as newly independent Black nations burst onto the international stage. Ghana was the first sub-Saharan nation to emerge, on March 6, 1957; coverage in the Black press was intense and African-American expectations for it and the continent soared. Two months before independence arrived, the *Pittsburgh Courier* contended, "history will not only reverse itself, but millions of people throughout the world will pause to wonder if what they have been taught is true and decide that they must change their ideas about Africa to fit reality."[165]

President Dwight Eisenhower's administration embraced Kwame Nkrumah as an exceptional leader and a friend to the West and sent a delegation to the independence ceremony. Prominent African American and other leaders from the diaspora also attended at Nkrumah's personal invitation. Many

---

[163] W. E. B. DuBois, *The Souls of Black Folk* (New York: Fawcett, 1961), 16-17.

[164] In "Heritage" Cullen uses the drumbeat and jungle as metaphors to describe someone under Africa's suppressed yet still formidable spell. That section of the poem reads thusly:

So I lie, who find no peace
Night or day, no slight release
From the unremittant beat
Made by cruel padded feet
Walking through my body's street.
Up and down they go, and back,
Treading out a jungle track.

"Heritage" by Countee Cullen, https://www.poetryfoundation.org/poems/42619/heritage-56d2213a97c6cby, accessed May 11, 2021.

[165] Roger A. Davidson Jr., "A Question of Freedom: African Americans and Ghanaian Independence," *Negro History Bulletin* 60 (July-September, 1997): 8, 10.

believed that Ghanaian independence would quicken nationalist movements throughout the continent and also positively affect the American civil rights movement. As evidence of the latter, the *Amsterdam News* reported a meeting in Ghana between Vice President Richard Nixon and Rev. Martin Luther King Jr. where King requested bolder administration support for racial change in the South.[166]

The year 1960 was known as the Year of Africa because an unprecedented seventeen African countries emerged from colonialism. Africa's success proved somewhat of a mixed blessing for Black Americans because it showed how little they had achieved for their efforts. Dr. King confided these frustrations in his "Letter From the Birmingham Jail" where he lamented, "The nations of Asia and Africa are moving with jetlike [sic] speed toward the goal of political independence, and we still creep at horse and buggy pace toward the gaining of a cup of coffee at a lunch counter." The prospects that Ghana excited compared to America's deeply entrenched racism led a small yet significant number of African Americans to seek their futures there.[167]

Maya Angelou, the writer and performing artist, had already worked as a journalist in Cairo for two years before deciding to relocate in 1962. Her plan to assist her son's matriculation at the University of Ghana and to move on to Liberia changed after his injury in a car accident required her to stay in Ghana. Angelou took an office job at the university and quickly joined an eclectic group of African American ex-pats. Its informal leader was Julian Mayfield, the journalist, novelist, and activist; the group included other intellectuals, professionals, and tradesmen. Their motives for coming were varied but they were united by the unique experience they were sharing. For most, she wrote later, this was the first place they lived where their color was considered "correct and normal."[168] Angelou called her group "revolutionist returnees" because they were highly political, "impassioned and ... dedicated to Africa, and

---

[166] Ibid., 7-10.
[167] https://www.africanexponent.com/post/8498-in-1960-seventeen-sub-saharan-african-countries-attained-independence, accessed May 12, 2021; James M. Washington, ed., *A Testament of Hope: The Essential Writings of Martin Luther King, Jr.* (San Francisco: Harper and Row, 1986), 292; Davidson, "A Question," 10-11.
[168] Angelou, *All God's Children Need Traveling Shoes* (1986; Vintage Books, 1991), 3-4, 8-9, 17.

Africans at home and abroad." During gatherings, they lambasted American racism and imperialism, praised Nkrumah's speeches and deeds, and pledged to sacrifice for Ghana. They felt valued because a president had invited them to work for this nation, a citadel of black freedom.[169]

The new Ghana was also a monument to black competence. When Maya Angelou visited the seat of government in Accra and witnessed African professionals passing through the buildings, she said those scenes "made me tremble with an awe I had never known. Their authority on the marble steps again proved that Whites had been wrong all along. … We are capable of controlling our cities, our selves and our lives with elegance and success." This seemed to be the home that generations had prayed for, and where "no one would wage war against us again." Once fully accepted, these ex-pats expected to open the doors for successive generations to "enter through the hallowed portals and come home at last."[170]

Finding "home" in Ghana was far from routine, though, in part because African Americans and Africans shared less in common than many returnees expected. Emigres assumed that the right to "return" was theirs as descendants of enslaved Africans and many expected to be welcomed home as long-lost brothers and sisters. Angelou said, "At least we wanted someone to embrace us and maybe congratulate us because we had survived. If they felt the urge, they could thank us for having returned." However, their presence had little impact on Ghanaians who generally ignored them.[171] Not only that, but at this time most Ghanaians knew nothing about the details of the Atlantic slave trade or enslavement in America. To appreciate this we only have to remember that in the United States Alex Haley's book *Roots: The Saga of an American Family*, published in 1976, was the first modern book on slavery with mass appeal. A television series followed the next year, but in Ghana it

---

[169] Ibid., 18, 23, 77-78
[170] Ibid., 16, 20, 23.
[171] Ibid., 19, 21-22.

was not broadcast until 2006! Maya Angelou captured the mixture of disappointment and dejection some returnees felt when they realized their story was not known. Less than a century after American "slavery was abolished, some descendants of those early slaves … returned, weighted with a heavy hope, to a continent which they could not remember, to a home which had shamefully little memory of them."[172]

Maya Angelou overcame such disappointments because she was captured by the Ghanaian culture and people. The gait of the women reminded her of her own grandmother's graceful carriage. The laughter reminded her of home and she loved the musical sounds of Ghanaian place names and the melody of the languages she heard on the street. Angelou worked hard to learn the Fante language and one African observer remarked that this was the sign she would make a good Ghanaian. In fact, when her hair was plaited, she was pleased that her appearance resembled that of any other Ghanaian woman.[173] Once, when driving through the interior, she had to rely upon residents of a small town to house her overnight. She spoke to them in Fante but her speech pattern convinced residents that she was a Bambara from Liberia. Angelou acquiesced because she "didn't want to remember that I was an American. For the first time since my arrival, I was very nearly home. Not a Ghanaian, but at least accepted as an African." When residents came by to bring food for her, Maya remembered how people down South showed similar hospitality to traveling strangers. In this moment she "felt the distance narrow between … [her] past and present."[174]

Ultimately though, Maya Angelou doubted whether diasporic people "could really return to Africa" because they "wore skeletons of old despair like necklaces, heralding our arrival, and we were branded with cynicism." That cynicism dissolved when Angelou visited the coastal town of Keta, which had been once decimated by horrifying slave raids. Stories from there reported parents so desperate that they killed their own children rather than let them

---

[172] https://www.history.com/news/remembering-roots, accessed May 12, 2021; Michelle D. Commander, "Ghana at Fifty: Moving Toward Kwame Nkrumah's Pan-African Dream," *American Quarterly* 59 (June, 2007): 431, 440; Angelou, All God's Children, 20.

[173] Angelou, *All God's Children*, 16, 20-21, 96, 38.

[174] Ibid., 98-105.

be captured. When market women saw Maya Angelou and heard her speak, they were convinced she descended from people kidnapped long ago. Angelou recalled as she was introduced around the market as an American Negro, startled, incredulous women mourned "for the lost people, their ancestors and mine." Her tears were alloyed with joy, though, because a people with a "pillaged past" had seen their ancestors in her face and heard them through her voice. She also rejoiced as the embodied strength of those who survived unspeakable cruelty in the diaspora. Although she hadn't found "home," she began to demystify the meaning of "return" while finding her roots and a new appreciation of her identity.[175]

---

[175] Ibid., 76

On Human Rights

Horace Mungin

American politicians, the American media and that freed privilege
segment of the
American people always want American
Leaders and diplomats to press the other
Countries of the world about their Human
Rights record; their treatments of their citizens.
America lectures:

Don't slaughter them in Cambodia
Don't imprison them in Russia
Don't starve them in North Korea
Don't poison-gas them in Syria
Don't famine them in Mali
Don't force marry them in Saudi Arabia
Don't suicide bomb them in Iraq
Don't create refugees in Somalia

America will travel the world pointing
A finger of superiority at these Human Rights
Violations in other countries while it turns a
Blind eye to the plight of black and brown
People within its own borders where these
Don't do also apply

Don't prison pipe-line them around the country
Don't poison water them in Flint
Don't disenfranchise them in the South
Don't execute them unarmed around the country
Don't redline them around the country
Don't miss-educate them around the country
Don't restrict medical care from them around the country
Don't gentrify them in the cities

America must turn its attention inward
To learn that its Human Rights record is
Dismal from its very creation
And the other countries of the world owe
It to America to tell it so
My God America, have you no shame?

Afterword

From January 6, 2021, to Juneteenth—
Is America "Finding its Roots"
or Desiccating Them?

Gloria Holmes

Like many Americans, I've become entranced by the extraordinary stories that Henry Louis Gates has unearthed about a wide variety of Americans using ancestral research by genealogical and DNA sleuths. These stories caused me to look inward and backward and reflect on my being, my essence, my raison d'etre. His guests, Black, White, Asian, Hispanic, Mestizo, white-skinned, brown-skinned, tan-tinged, chocolaty, all learned things they did not know about their roots. They learned that ancestral roots don't simply grow and spread horizontally or vertically; they get tangled, ingrown, and intersect so what we thought we knew and understood about ourselves gets uprooted and blurred.

Gates's guests learned they are descended from kings, scoundrels and murderers, peace-makers, pacifists and warmongers; heroes, felons, and cowards;the enslaved and the enslavers. They've discovered extraordinary strength and cowardice in their forebears, responding with shock, awe, pride, sadness, shame and inexpressible pain or joy; sometimes all of them simultaneously.

One guest discovered that on one side of her family she had an ancestor who was a Spanish conquistador who tortured and mutilated Mexican people from whom she was descended on the other side of her family. Tearfully, she accepted she had to ingest this painful reality whole because it was true.

Another guest interrupted the taping and went away for a few weeks to process the enormity of what he had learned about how slavery stained his past. This new knowledge pierced and deeply challenged his worldview. It was an extraordinary thing to witness in real time; humans being human; vulnerable and stripped of pretense and the socially constructed protective gear they wear to shield themselves from other humans.

This morning, I began to think, not just about the narrow significance of one individual's search for her or his ancestral roots but about America's tortured search for its roots in the context of the withering racial and cultural crisis that threatens to suffocate us in 2021.

I was trying to make sense of America's death match with itself as it grapples with the systemic racism and structural and institutional discrimination that is deeply and inextricably rooted in the American way of how things were done in the past, and are being done today throughout our economic and socio-political strata. Unfortunately, some Americans are wedded to a dangerous single story of America as mythically heroic in the past as well as in the present, and are trying to decouple hateful aspects of America's past and present, like separating the cars of a locomotive train.

Searching for roots is seductive and scary, especially for a country. It's bound to be an emotion-shredding process that is alternately embraced, shunned, and devalued.

Yet, despite the predictably deep chasms of denial, searching for and acknowledging our roots, it is something we must do because January 6, 2021, weakened and exposed America to the reality and the myth.

We all know that if those had been Black bodies storming the Capitol no one would have mistaken them for tourists. Americans would have witnessed a soul-searing racialized American carnage.

This is not hyperbole.

Acknowledging our roots is something we must do to save ourselves. The increasing racial tension is destabilizing, like shifting tectonic plates; it has exposed America's chronic psychic disequilibrium, a side effect of its troubling racial history. This pathology is evidenced by the concurrent designation of

Juneteenth, as a national holiday while nationwide governors are enacting restrictive laws that make it illegal to teach students to think critically about the atrocity of human bondage and how it putrefies American values.

The contradiction of two impulses is staggeringly illogical.

America is torn between what it believes, what it is, and what it hopes to become. Sadly, America is wallowing in a twisted form of cognitive dissonance as it engages in a pathetic tragicomedy of peekaboo with itself.

If we take an unadulterated look at America's roots, we will find things that are good, and we will find things that are bad.

America's democratic ideology is exceptional; a city set on a hill, a light for the world, as Puritan leader John Winthrop said. Inspired by Jesus's Sermon on the Mount, Winthrop inferred that the founding of America had divine sanction, and that American exceptionalism is rooted in the country's DNA.

But, America is also rooted in a shameless propagation and defense of its original sin, slavery, and it kept this unique cauldron of evil molten for centuries.

Not only did America revel in and profit from its original sin for centuries, it allowed the vestiges of slavery to morph into new forms of human oppression behind the facade of formal and informal policies and practices like Jim Crow, sharecropping, fugitive slave laws, lynching, segregation, redlining, school-to-prison pipelines, oppression masquerading as policing, gerrymandering, and voter suppression masquerading as safeguards for democracy.

Thinking about this reminded me of a two-part article I wrote several years ago, "Rethinking History: Whose 'Story' is it Anyway?"

In 2016, I asked is history merely a commodity? Can you simply shop for a version of it that you like? Can it be bought like a pound of meat? Can anyone simply trim off the fat and the gristle of history, wrap it up in a neat little bundle then store it away?

I went on to say, Americans have to ... own our history; it's our DNA. It is what it is. In the end, we can't change it or alter it any more than you can unscramble an egg. Our history is baked. Different voices, realities and perspectives are not easy to manage or contain, but then, America's story was never neat and tidy. You can't stuff the ugly parts of the story into a Pandora-like box and expect the demons to vanish.

Demons usually don't just go away; they need to be exorcised and exposed to the disinfecting sunlight of truth, not because of a sick voyeurism that relishes human depravity, but because even when it's painful and shameful we have to grapple with the harsh racist roots of the past to understand the strange fruit they are producing in 2021.

In *Playing in the Dark*, Toni Morrison addressed America's racial dilemma, arguing the heart of America has been, and is, corrupted by "racial disingenuousness and moral frailty." And yet, even though racism is like an ever-present third rail, Americans have always recoiled from the thought of being called a racist country, despite living in what Morrison called a "wholly racialized world."

Ironically, despite living in a wholly racialized world, many Americans have made an industry of denying it. They deny that racism has meaning in the context of culture or that it infects or inflects our thinking about and behavior toward people and cultures that are different from the perceived norm or that racism is systemic and structural, influencing all levels of government. And yet, it is counterintuitive to think we can live in a wholly racialized world without the existence of racism in it.

However, living in a wholly racialized world is only part of America's race problem. America's chronic moral frailty further complicates its racial issues.

Political theorist, Y.N. Kly argues that moral frailty subverted America's fundamental ideals and values from the beginning of the American experiment. According to Kly, American colonists attempted to reconcile the ideal of human freedom, with unwritten and unspoken anti-ideals which included their right to enslave Africans, dispossess Native Americans, promote their own self-interests at the expense of human rights, and profit from human devastation. Despite this troubling dichotomy, a belief in American exceptionalism endured because America's official morality as articulated in the Constitution, the Declaration of independence and the Pledge of Allegiance, unambiguously supports equal justice and human rights.

And yet, in America, racism and discrimination are unofficially endorsed. Officially they are illegal, and officially regarded as un-American. This official morality is a construct anthropomorphized in the self-righteous face Americans show the world.

However, there is another American face and it's ugly, frightening and dangerous. We saw that face on January 6, scaling the Capitol's walls, destroying property, defecating in the halls, crushing police and threatening to hang the vice president. And, we've seen that face on some police officers.

In a sense, that face exposes America's alter ego.

When James Baldwin wrote "We are trapped in our history, and our history is trapped in us!" he reminded us that we can never escape history, even when publishers collude to whitewash history books or we try to hide our moral frailty under a cloak of self-righteousness.

Everything about 2021 tells us we are trapped in our history, and our history is trapped in us. Everything about 2021 tells us we are at a pivotal moment but we're not in poet Robert Frost's quiet place contemplating "two roads diverging in a yellow wood." Instead, we are rushing toward a dangerous precipice, dragging our fragile democracy behind us. This is perhaps a place of no return.

Everything about 2021 tells us Americans are in turbulent waters and, like it or not, we are in the same boat together; breathing the same air, a modern iteration of Plato's ship of fools "wandering between the two poles of generation and decay."

Our democracy is at stake, and American exceptionalism is being smothered.

Yes, we are in the same boat; Black, white, Asian, Hispanic, Mestizo, Indigenous, white-skinned, brown-skinned, tan-tinged, chocolaty. We're scoundrels and peace-makers, pacifists and warmongers, heroes, felons, and cowards. We're greedy and generous, humane and cruel. We're gay, straight, cis, transgender and neutral. Some of us are racists; some of us are not. Some of our forebears were racists, and some were not, but they laid the groundwork for racist structures that have petrified from the unrelenting pressure of human suffering.

These are our roots. The wounds from racism in the past remain open and that bloodstain corrupts the present. Dwelling in denial is self-mutilating because in America race matters. It has always mattered in profound life-altering ways. To ignore that disturbing symbiotic relationship between democracy and slavery, justice and injustice, equality and inequality is disingenuous. To do so further erodes America's moral center.

The question is, can we, will we, allow the past to inform the present and future in reconstructive ways, or will we continue to wander between the two poles of generation and decay?

Ukweli Contributors

Essayists

Imam Hakim Abdul-Ali is a native of Harlem, New York, with familial and residential ties to the Lowcountry. A graduate of Howard University in the 1960s, he received a religious scholarship to study at Al-Azhar University in Cairo, Egypt. He has studied Arabic at New York University, and he received a Certificate in African Studies from the University of Ghana at Legon in conjunction with the American Studies Program at Fordham University. He is a nationally recognized speaker and lecturer and collector of African and Afro-American memorabilia and artifacts. He has been involved in the fields of social work, education, personnel administration, and journalism. For thirty-five years, he wrote a weekly column as a cultural critic for the *Charleston Chronicle*. He currently serves as the resident imam at the U.S. Naval Consolidated Brig in North Charleston, South Carolina.

Dr. Kim Nesta Archung received her Ph.D. in educational studies from Emory University in Atlanta, Georgia. She is a co-founder of Paige Academy, an African-centered nursery and elementary school in Boston, and currently serves as the senior vice president of global student affairs for the African Diaspora Consortium (ADC), and as a program officer for South Carolina First Steps. Dr. Archung's professional life has included working on education development projects and issues of educational equity across the African Diaspora. She is specifically interested in educational equity, social justice, and culturally responsive multicultural curriculum, instruction, and teacher development beginning in early childhood.

Steve Bailey has spent a lifetime as a journalist. After working as an editor and reporter for South Carolina newspapers, he was at the *Boston Globe* for thirty years, where he was the business editor and wrote a column. He spent seven years in London as a finance editor with Bloomberg News. He's a regular contributor to the *The Post and Courier*'s op-ed page.

Al Black is a Hoosier in the land of cotton. He writes poetry and hosts workshops and arts events in the midlands of South Carolina. He is author of two books of poetry, *I Only Left for Tea* (2014 Muddy Ford Press), *Man with Two Shadows* (2018 Muddy Ford Press); co-editor *Hand in Hand: Poets Respond to Race* (2017 Muddy Ford Press); co-founded the Poets Respond to Race Initiative, and co-hosts "Chewing the Gristle," a poetry chat Youtube series. He was the 2017 Jasper Literary Artist of the Year.

Dr. Millicent E. Brown is co-founder and project director of an oral history initiative to identify the "first children," like herself, to desegregate previously all-white schools. She has held a variety of history and museum-related faculty positions and serves as consultant for numerous museums, historic sites, and social justice programs in North and South Carolina.

Dr. Vicki Callahan is a professor at the University of Southern California's School of Cinematic Arts in the Divisions of Media Arts + Practice and Cinema and Media Studies. Her research and teaching are focused on the integration of theory and practice with attention to issues in film and media history, feminist studies, digital culture, media strategies for social change, and public scholarship.

Dr. Karen Chandler, associate professor in the Arts Management Program at the College of Charleston, has taught in its undergraduate and graduate programs since 1999. She has also served as director of both programs during her tenure including its recent Graduate Certificate program in Arts and Cultural Management. She is co-founder/principal of the Charleston Jazz Initiative (CJI) that documents South Carolina musicians who contributed to jazz history in America and Europe. With a National Endowment for the Arts grant, she served as executive producer of LEGENDS (2011), a CD of songs by musicians the initiative is studying. Among her publications are "Bin Yah (Been Here): Africanisms and Jazz Influences in Gullah Culture" in *Jazz @ 100: An Alternative to a Story of Heroes* (Frankfurt: Wolke Verlag) and articles in *The Journal of Arts Management, Law and Society*. In 2012, she was awarded the South Carolina Governor's Award in the Humanities for her leadership and research with the Charleston Jazz Initiative.

Sara Makeba Daise aka **Geechee Gal Griot** (she/her/hers) is a Black, fifth-generation Gullah Geechee woman, Afrofuturist, space and time-traveller, dimension-hopper, gatekeeper, griot, cultural history interpreter, writer, singer, and healer from Beaufort, S.C. She received a bachelor's degree in communication and a minor in African American Studies from the College of Charleston. She received a master's degree in public history from Union Institute & University. Her creative thesis: "Come on in The Room: Afrofuturism as a Path to Black Women's Retroactive Healing," was a 2018 recipient of the Brian Webb Award for Outstanding MA Thesis in History and Culture from Union Institute & University.

Damon Fordham teaches U.S. and African American History at Charleston Southern University and The Citadel. He leads a walking tour called "The Lost Stories of Black Charleston." He is the author of *True Stories of Black South Carolina*, *Voices of Black South Carolina*, and the novel *Mr. Potts and Me*. He has a YouTube channel called "The American Storyteller."

Adrienne Troy Frazier is co-founder of the Berkeley Early Education and Care Collective, a birthing and healing justice network designed to support the early childhood community. She is also executive director of Berkeley County First Steps. In 2020 the YWCA of Greater Charleston presented Adrienne with its What Women Bring Educator of the Year Award. She is a former Lowcountry leader for Outdoor Afro, a national organization that empowers African Americans to reclaim the outdoors. She was named Outdoor Afro's 2017 National Leader of the Year.

Herb Frazier is special projects editor at the *Charleston City Paper*, a weekly newspaper in his hometown. He's an author and the former marketing director at Magnolia Plantation and Gardens in Charleston. He has edited and reported for five daily newspapers in the South. When he was on the staff of *The Post and Courier* in Charleston he was named the S.C. Press Association's 1990 Journalist of the Year. He is a former Michigan Journalism Fellow at the University of Michigan. He has led journalism workshops in Africa and South America for a federal agency and a

Washington, D.C.-based journalism foundation. He is a member of the Gullah Geechee Cultural Heritage Corridor Commission.

Shawn Halifax is the new executive director at the National Trust for Historic Preservation's Woodlawn/Pope-Leighey Historic Site in Alexandria, Va. He moved to Charleston in 1998 as the African American interpretation coordinator at Middleton Place. He later joined Charleston County Parks to initiate their public history program at Caw Caw Interpretive Center, a site of the Stono Rebellion. In 2010 he became public programs and Casemate Museum director at Old Point Comfort and Fort Monroe, sites of the 1619 arrival and 1861 Contraband decision. In 2013 he returned to Charleston to lead ground-breaking work at McLeod Plantation Historic Site, whose primary purpose is to interpret the lives and culture of enslaved people, their descendants, and the legacies of slavery.

Jonathan Haupt is the executive director of the nonprofit Pat Conroy Literary Center, the former director of the University of South Carolina Press, and coeditor of *Our Prince of Scribes: Writers Remember Pat Conroy*, published by the University of Georgia Press and winner of seventeen book awards.

Heather L. Hodges is the director of external relations at the Historic New Orleans Collection, a museum, research center, and publisher dedicated to preserving the history and culture of New Orleans and the Gulf South. She was the executive director of the Gullah Geechee Cultural Heritage Corridor from 2017-2020. She is a member of the the board of trustees of the American Folklife Center of the Library of Congress and the advisory board of the Joyner Institute for Gullah Geechee and African Diaspora Studies at Coastal Carolina University.

Stephen G. Hoffius is a freelance writer and editor in Charleston. Among his books are *Upheaval in Charleston: Earthquake and Murder on the Eve of Jim Crow*, with Susan Millar Williams, and *Landscape of Slavery: The Plantation in American Art*, which he edited with Angela D. Mack.

Dr. Gloria Holmes is a professor emerita at the School of Education at Quinnipiac University in Hamden, Connecticut, where she served as both chair and director of the Master of Arts in Teaching Program. Presently, she is an adjunct professor at the University of South Carolina in the Department of Education. Committed to promoting cultural literacy in schools and communities, she has also worked as a diversity trainer for the Anti-Defamation League and the Connecticut State Department of Education, and she has conducted anti-bias workshops for community organizations and public school teachers and school leaders in Connecticut and South Carolina.

Josephine Humphreys, a Charleston native, is a graduate of Duke University, where she studied writing with Reynolds Price. She is the author of four novels: *Dreams of Sleep*, winner of the Ernest Hemingway Award for best first novel of 1984; *Rich in Love*, made into a film starring Albert Finney; *The Fireman's Fair*, named a Notable Book of the Year by the *New York Times*; and *Nowhere Else on Earth*, a historical novel about the Lumbee Indian outlaw Henry Lowry, winner of the Southern Book Award. Her work has been published in seven foreign languages.

The Rev. DeMett E. Jenkins is the Lilly Director of Education and Engagement for Faith-based Communities at the International African American Museum in Charleston. She is the granddaughter of civil rights icon Esau Jenkins and his wife, Janie Jenkins, a community engager.

Dr. Marnishia Jenkins-Tate, author and native Charlestonian, lives in Washington, D.C. Granddaughter of civil and human rights icon Esau Jenkins, she earned a Ph.D. degree from Howard University with studies in cross-cultural communication and social psychology.

The Rev. Patricia Bligen Jones is an ordained minister of Word and Sacrament in the Presbyterian Church, (USA). She serves as pastor at Hebron Zion Presbyterian Church (USA) on Johns Island, S.C. She is a former writer for *The Post and Courier*, and she is the creator and host of the podcast, "She Speaks Too." She is a native of Edisto Island, South Carolina, and a 1989 graduate of Morris College in Sumter, S.C. She earned a Master in Divinity from Erskine Theological Seminary. She and her husband have been married for 30 years, and are the parents of two adult children.

Joseph McGill Jr. is the founder of the Slave Dwelling Project. He has traveled to more than 150 locations in the twenty-five states, including the District of Columbia, to call attention to how the preservation of slave cabins and structures where enslaved people lived can change the narrative of the Black experience. McGill is also a history consultant at Magnolia Plantation and Gardens in Charleston. His forthcoming book, *Sleeping with the Ancestors: Slave Dwellings Matter*, co-written with Herb Frazier, is scheduled to be released in 2022 by Hachette Books.

Dr. Karen Meadows, is a high school counselor in Guilford County Schools and an adjunct professor at the University of North Carolina at Charlotte. She serves on the School of Education Board at the University of North Carolina at Greensboro, is the co-chair for the Conference Committee and former board member for the North Carolina School Counselor Association. She is the author of *Pedagogy of Survival: The Narratives of Millicent E. Brown and Josephine Boyd Bradley*, and an educational presenter/trainer.

Born in Frankfurt am Main, Germany, **Kennae Miller** (she/her) is founder of Transformation Yoga in Charleston. She is the descendant of grandparents from Cherokee (Gaffney and Blacksburg, South Carolina), Lumbee (Gresham, South Carolina), and Kusso land (Charleston). She has practiced yoga since high school. She is passionate about assisting others in reconnecting with the origins of who they are and the limitations that have been created for them on their journey toward liberation.

Born in Hollywood, South Carolina., **Horace Mungin** moved with his family to New York City in 1946, where he attended public schools and majored in English at Fordham University. He served three years in the U.S. Army and was a member of the 82nd Airborne Division. In 1989, Horace and his wife, Gussie, also from South Carolina, moved to Ridgeville near Charleston. He started writing poetry in the mid-sixties, during the genesis of the Black Arts

Movement. In 2017, the National Museum for African American History and Culture included a video of *Black Forum Magazine*, which Horace founded in 1970. His magazine is a permanent part of the museum's statement of the Black Arts Movement. Horace Mungin (August 5, 1941 – September 25, 2021)

Dr. Porchia Moore is department head and assistant professor of Museum Studies at the University of Florida. She also serves as affiliate faculty for the University of Florida's new Center for Arts, Migration, and Entrepreneurship. She is a critical race scholar who interrogates the role and function of race in museums and the cultural heritage sector. Her curatorial vision is to be a storycatcher and abolitionist. She is the co-creator of The Visitors of Color Project. She speaks nationally and internationally on issues of race, equity, and inclusion. She has partnered with museums across the nation on education, training, and workshops on race and anti-racism in museums. You can follow her on Twitter @PorchiaMuseM.

Yvette R. Murray has been published in *Emrys Journal, The Petigru Review, Catfish Stew, A Gathering Together, Call and Response Journal,* and *Genesis Science Fiction* magazines. She is a 2021 Best New Poet selection, a 2020 Watering Hole Fellow, and a 2019 Pushcart Prize nominee. Presently, she is writing her first collection of poetry, more science fiction short stories, and a children's book series. Find her on Twitter @MissYvettewrites.

Adam Parker earned degrees in music, then spent a decade in the business world before going back to school for a graduate degree in journalism from Columbia University. At *The Charleston Post and Courier*, he has worked as a copy editor, general assignment writer, metro and arts editor, and restaurant critic. He has worked on several beats over the years, including crime and breaking news, religion and culture, education, city and state government and, most recently, race and history. A long-time student of the civil rights movement and race in America, he has written extensively about the African-American experience. He is the author of the biography *Outside Agitator: The Civil Rights Struggle of Cleveland Sellers Jr.*, published by Hub City Press.

Dr. Bernard E. Powers is professor emeritus of history at the College of Charleston and founding director of its Center for the Study of Slavery in Charleston. His book *Black Charlestonians: A Social History 1822-1885* won a Choice Outstanding Academic Book Award. He co-authored *We Are Charleston: Tragedy and Triumph at Mother Emanuel* and edited *101 African Americans Who Shaped South Carolina*. Powers' film credits include *The African Americans: Many Rivers to Cross* and *Emanuel*. The Association for the Study of African American Life and History has recognized Powers' lifetime commitment to "research, writing, and activism in the field of African American life and history" with the Carter Godwin Woodson Scholars Medallion.

Aïda Rogers is a writer, editor, and instructor at the South Carolina Honors College, University of South Carolina. She is the editor of *State of the Heart: South Carolina Writers on the Places They Love*, an anthology series published by the USC Press. Her articles have won national and regional awards, and in 2018, her work on *My Tour through the Asylum: A Southern Integrationist's Memoir* (USC Press), received an IPPY Award silver medal. She writes her "Everything and Nothing" column from an old home in Columbia and a new porch in McClellanville, where she lives with her husband, Wally, and their two rascally Boykins.

Margaret Seidler is a retired nationally recognized organization development (OD) consultant, master trainer, and author. She was born and raised in Charleston. In the aftermath of the 2015 Mother Emanuel massacre, she and former city police chief Greg Mullen created and led the Charleston Illumination Project, a year-long effort designed to give all parts of the local community a voice in shaping effective citizen/police actions and relationships. Over 1,000 residents engaged in strengthening relationships between the community and police. Today, it serves as a model for addressing those racial tensions.

Teresa Speight is a native Washingtonian, author, former head gardener for the City of Fredericksburg, Va., garden writer, podcaster, visionary, and estate garden coach. She is the former Region II director of GardenComm, International and president of the Jabali Amani, an African American virtual garden club. As a true steward of the land, Teri shares her passion on her website, Cottage in the Court.

Dr. Jennie L. Stephens received a bachelor's degree in Business Administration from the College of Charleston and a master's degree in Public Administration from the University of Charleston/University of South Carolina. She earned a doctorate degree in Organizational Leadership from Regent University in Virginia Beach, Va. Jennie has served as chief leader of the Center for Heirs' Property Preservation since its inception in 2005.

Kieran "Kerry" Taylor is an associate professor of history and director of the Charleston Oral History Program at The Citadel. A native of Lombard, Illinois, he worked as a labor and education reporter at The Post-Tribune in Gary, Indiana, and editor at the Martin Luther King, Jr. Papers Project at Stanford University before receiving his Ph.D. in history from the University of North Carolina at Chapel Hill in 2007. He is the author of *Charleston and the Great Depression: A Documentary History, 1929-1941*. He co-edited Volume Four and Volume Five of *The Papers of Martin Luther King, Jr.* and *American Labor and the Cold War*. Since 2018, he has served as Tri-Chair of the South Carolina Poor People's Campaign: National Call for Moral Revival. He is a proud occupant of a New Deal-constructed office at The Citadel and equally proud to live in government-subsidized housing on the Charleston peninsula.

As a school principal for twenty-five years, **LaTisha Vaughn** has coached and strengthened educational systems in the midwest, southwest, and on the east coast through LaTisha Nicole Consulting (formerly Vaughn-Brandon Consulting). She is co-founder of E3: Educate, Empower, Elevate LLC, an organization that focuses on equitable outcomes for Black and Brown children and families. As the chief operating officer of the Tri-County Cradle to Career Collaborative in Charleston, she oversees the organization's strategies to ensure equity and authentic engagement in supporting ambitious goals for all children in Berkeley, Charleston, and Dorchester counties.

Ernest L. Wiggins is professor emeritus of journalism and mass communications at the University of South Carolina. He retired from teaching in 2020 after nearly thirty years in the classroom, having taught professional practices of journalism, news media and community engagement, public opinion and persuasion, and mass media criticism, among other courses. His research focused on the representation of marginalized communities by the media, primarily news agencies. A native of Washington, D.C., Wiggins was a reporter and editor at the *Columbia Record* and *The State* newspapers before joining the faculty at USC, where he earned both his bachelor's and master's degrees.

Treva Williams is lead organizer of the Charleston Area Justice Ministry, a network of faith-based congregations working together to address community problems. She came to Charleston to lead CAJM before the organization had a name. She is married to Garin Williams, and they have two grown children, Shayd and Finean.

Poets

Marcus Amaker was named Charleston's first Poet Laureate in 2016. He's also the graphic designer of a Grammy-winning album and a national music journal. His poetry has been recognized by the Kennedy Center, the Washington National Opera, the Portland Opera, the *Chicago Tribune, Washington Post, People's World,* PBS News Hour, NPR and other organizations. In 2019, he won a Governor's Award for the Arts in South Carolina, and was named artist-in-residence of the Gaillard Center in Charleston. He has recorded three albums with Grammy Award-winning drummer and producer Quentin E. Baxter, and thirty-four albums as an electronic musician. His ninth book is *Black Music Is,* from Free Verse Press.

William P. Baldwin is a lifelong resident of the Carolina Lowcountry. He is an award-winning novelist, poet, biographer, and historian. He graduated from Clemson University with a bachelor's degree in history and a master's degree in English. He ran a shrimp boat for nine years, then built houses, but the principal occupation of his life has been writing.

James M. Brailsford III, a direct descendant of General William Moultrie, is a native of Orangeburg, South Carolina. He majored in English and studied poetry under Professor John Robert Doyle Jr. at The Citadel. After earning a J.D. degree from the University of South Carolina School of Law, he spent four years in the U.S. Army Judge Advocate Generals Corps, and then he practiced law for thirty years in Columbia. In 2002, he and his wife, Marian, moved to Charleston County where he served on the board of directors of the Edisto Island Historic Preservation Society, as director and president of the Edisto Island Community Association, and as director and chairman of the Edisto Island Preservation Alliance. He has been an active member of the Poetry Society of South Carolina and the Edisto Art Guild.

Portia E. Cobb is a professor of Film, Video & New Genres at the University of Wisconsin-Milwaukee as an interdisciplinary artist working in documentary, photography, and poetry. She draws inspiration from personal and collective history and memory to create work concerned with the politics of identity, place, dislocation, and forced forgetting. Her short documentary videos center on her family's Gullah Geechee heritage, and have been screened globally. Recent poems appear in *Through this Door: Wisconsin in Poems* (2020); and *Where I Want to Live: Poems for Fair & Affordable Housing* (2018). She is currently working on her first poetry and photographic collection.

Tim Conroy is a poet and former educator. His work has appeared in journals, magazines, and compilations, including *Fall Lines, Blue Mountain Review, Jasper, Marked by the Water, Sheltered, Twelve Mile Review, The Post and Courier, Greenville Business Magazine,* and *Our Prince of Scribes: Writers Remember Pat Conroy.* In 2017, Muddy Ford Press published Tim's first book of poetry, *Theologies of Terrain,* edited by Columbia, South Carolina, poet laureate Ed Madden. A founding board member of the Pat Conroy Literary Center established in his brother's honor. He and his wife Terrye live in Dunedin, Florida.

Originally from South Carolina, **Savannah J. Frierson** is a graduate of Harvard College with a joint concentration in African and African American Studies and English. She received the Dorothy Hicks Lee Prize for Most Outstanding Thesis relating to African or African American Literature for her novella *Reconstructing Jada Channing.* She is also a *USA Today* best-selling and award-winning author of romance and women's fiction, as well as a freelance editor, formatter, and consultant for publishers and authors alike, including Macmillan, Hachette, and Simon and Schuster. Currently, she is the office manager at the College of Charleston's Avery Research Center for African American History and Culture.

Born and raised in Topeka, Kansas, **Gary Jackson** is the author of *origin story* (University of New Mexico, 2021) and *Missing You, Metropolis* (Graywolf, 2010), which received the 2009 Cave Canem Poetry Prize. He's also co-editor of *The Future of Black: Afrofuturism, Black Comics, and Superhero Poetry* (Blair, 2021). His poems have appeared in numerous journals including *Callaloo*, *The Sun*, *Los Angeles Review of Books*, and *Copper Nickel*. He teaches in the MFA program as an associate professor at the College of Charleston.

Ray McManus is the author of three books of poetry: *Punch.* (Hub City Press, 2014), *Red Dirt Jesus* (Marick Press, 2011), and *Driving Through the Country Before You Are Born* (USC Press, 2006). He is the co-editor for the anthology *Found Anew* (USC Press 2015). McManus is a professor of English at the University of South Carolina Sumter, and he serves as the Writer in Residence at the Columbia Museum of Art.

Ed Madden is a professor of English and former director of the Women's & Gender Studies Program at the University of South Carolina. He is the author of four books of poetry, most recently *Ark*, a memoir in verse about his father's last months in home hospice care. In 2015, he was named the inaugural poet laureate for the City of Columbia. In 2019 he was named a Poet Laureate Fellow of the Academy of American Poets and a visiting artist fellow at the Instituto Sacatar in Bahia, Brazil.

Susan Madison is a poet, essayist, and short story writer who merges visual artistry with literature. Her work explores culture, history, and consciousness. The author of two chapbooks: *if i can't sing the blues*, and *Gullah Paths*, Madison has been published in local and national publications, including *Chicken Soup for the Soul*. A native of Chicago, Madison studied fiction and poetry at Columbia College of Liberal Arts in Chicago. She lives on St. Helena Island, South Carolina.

Elizabeth Robin is a retired high school teacher. She has two collections of poetry through Finishing Line Press: *Where Green Meets Blue* (2018) and *Silk Purses and Lemonade* (2017); a third, *To My Dreamcatcher*, will be released in June 2022. A poet of witness and discovery, She relates both true and fictional stories about her Lowcountry present and world-traveling past. The 2021 winner of the South Carolina Writing Association's Carrie McCray Nickens Fellowship, she emcees a monthly open mic and partners with arts groups to bring literary programs to Hilton Head Island, South Carolina.

Ronda Taylor is a poet and storyteller based in Charleston. She has a master's degree in writing and a bachelor's degree in English with a minor in creative writing from Coastal Carolina University in Conway, South Carolina. Ronda performs poetry, leads workshops and speaks at events. She is the visionary for FLYbara, an organization that equips and empowers a diverse community of creatives by organizing events and workshops.

Marjory Wentworth is the *New York Times* bestselling author of *Out of Wonder, Poems Celebrating Poets* (with Kwame Alexander and Chris Colderley). She is the co-writer of *We Are Charleston, Tragedy and Triumph at Mother Emanuel*, with Herb Frazier and Dr. Bernard Powers and *Taking a Stand, The Evolution of Human Rights*, with Juan E. Mendez. She is co-editor with Kwame Dawes of *Seeking, Poetry and Prose Inspired by the Art of Jonathan Green*, and the author of the prizewinning children's story *Shackles*, as well as four collections of poetry. Wentworth served as the Poet Laureate of South Carolina from 2003-2020. She teaches courses in writing, social justice and banned books at The College of Charleston.

Artist

Hampton R. Olfus Jr. creates art using acrylics, ink, pencil, watercolor, and mixed media; the pieces are detailed and introspective. Born in Washington, D.C., he frequently visited the free museums and art galleries located on the National Mall. His artistic knowledge was acquired in the classroom and from visiting the studios of local artists and attending local art exhibits. He has exhibited his art nationally and internationally, receiving awards and reviews from the press. He has participated in various positions for numerous art groups and art organizations within the private and public sectors. Art is an integral part of his life by way of expression, vision, education, and communication. It reflects his formal training and personal studies. Olfus said, "Let art be art, fresh and new, no egos or selfish wants just the artist's pure spirit."

Index